Nick Vandome

iPhone for Seniors

7th edition

covers all iPhones with iOS 14

In easy steps is an imprint of In Easy Steps Limited
16 Hamilton Terrace · Holly Walk · Leamington Spa
Warwickshire · United Kingdom · CV32 4LY
www.ineasysteps.com

Seventh Edition

In Easy Steps Limited supports The Forest Stewardship Council (FSC), the leading international forest certification organization. All our titles that are printed on Greenpeace approved FSC certified paper carry the FSC logo.

MIX
Paper from
responsible sources
FSC® C020837

Printed and bound in the United Kingdom

ISBN 978-1-84078-908-9

Contents

1 Your New iPhone

The iPhone is a sleek, stylish smartphone that is ideal for anyone, of any age. This chapter introduces the four models of the latest version – the iPhone 12 – and takes you through the buttons and controls used to navigate around. It also shows how to set it up, ready for use.

Hands on with the iPhone

The iPhone is one of the great success stories of the digital age. It is one of the world's leading smartphones: a touchscreen phone that can be used for not only making calls and sending text messages, but also for online access and a huge range of tasks through the use of apps. Essentially, the iPhone is a powerful, compact computer that can be used for everything you need in your mobile life.

The latest range of iPhones includes the iPhone 12, the iPhone 12 mini, the iPhone 12 Pro and the iPhone 12 Pro Max. All models use the iOS 14 operating system and the A14 Bionic chip processor.

iPhone 12

This is the standard iPhone and its specifications include:

- **Screen**: The iPhone 12 has a **6.1 inch** (measured diagonally) Super Retina XDR display screen.
- **Storage**: This determines how much content you can store on your iPhone. For the iPhone 12, the storage capacity options are: 64GB, 128GB or 256GB.
- **Camera**: A dual-lens 12-megapixel (MP) camera for taking photos, and a front-facing 12MP TrueDepth camera for selfies, videos, and for use with Face ID.
- **Face ID**: Unlock the iPhone by looking at the screen.
- **Battery power**: The iPhone 12 provides up to 65 hours of wireless audio playback, 17 hours' video playback, 11 hours' video streaming, and fast charging capability.
- **Input/Output**: There is a Lightning Connector port (for charging, headphones, and connecting to a computer); a built-in speaker; and a built-in microphone.
- **Water-resistant**: Water-resistant up to six meters for up to 30 minutes. Also splash- and dust-resistant.
- **Sensors**: The sensors are: accelerometer, barometer, ambient light sensor, proximity sensor, and gyroscope.

The New icon pictured above indicates a new or enhanced feature introduced with the iPhone 12, 12 mini, 12 Pro, 12 Pro Max, or the latest version of its operating system, iOS 14.

One of the main new features of all of the iPhone 12 models is that they can be used with 5G networks for mobile data and communication. Check with your service provider whether 5G is available in your area. All iPhone 12 models can also access 4G and 3G networks.

All iPhone models have connectivity for fast 802.11ax Wi-Fi, and Bluetooth 5.0.

iPhone 12 mini

This is a smaller version of the standard iPhone 12. Its specifications include:

- **Screen**: The iPhone 12 mini has a **5.4 inch** (measured diagonally) Super Retina XDR display screen.
- **Storage**: This determines how much content you can store on your iPhone. For the iPhone 12 mini, the storage capacity options are: 64GB, 128GB or 256GB.
- **Camera**: A dual-lens 12-megapixel (MP) camera for taking photos, and a front-facing 12MP TrueDepth camera for selfies, videos, and for use with Face ID.
- **Face ID**: Unlock the iPhone by looking at the screen.
- **Battery power**: The iPhone 12 mini provides up to 50 hours of wireless audio playback, 15 hours' video playback, 10 hours' video streaming, and fast charging capability.
- **Input/Output**: There is a Lightning Connector port (for charging, headphones, and connecting to a computer); a built-in speaker; and a built-in microphone.
- **Water-resistant**: Water-resistant up to six meters for up to 30 minutes. Also splash- and dust-resistant.
- **Sensors**: The sensors are: accelerometer, barometer, ambient light sensor, proximity sensor, and gyroscope.

The iPhone 12 models do not come with a power adapter or EarPods/earphones. The rationale behind this is that a lot of people already have them from previous models of iPhones, and by not including them, Apple is helping to protect the environment by reducing the number of accessories. However, if you do not have a compatible iPhone power adapter you will need to buy one before you can charge your iPhone. A USB-C to Lightning cable is included with the iPhone, and this can be connected to a compatible power adapter if you have one.

...cont'd

The amount of storage you need may change once you have bought your iPhone. If possible, buy a version with as much storage as your budget allows, as you cannot add more later.

All of the iPhone 12 models are made with Ceramic Shield glass for the display, which makes them four times more durable than previous iPhones, if they are dropped.

None of the latest range of iPhones has a separate headphone jack: this is accommodated using the Lightning Connector port.

iPhone 12 Pro

This is the second iPhone with "Pro" in its designation. Its specifications include:

- **Screen**: The iPhone 12 Pro has a **6.1 inch** (measured diagonally) Super Retina XDR display screen.
- **Storage**: This determines how much content you can store on your iPhone. For the iPhone 12 Pro, the storage capacity options are: 128GB, 256GB or 512GB.

- **Camera**: A triple-lens 12MP camera for taking photos, and a front-facing 12MP TrueDepth camera for taking selfies, videos, and for use with Face ID.
- **Face ID**: Unlock the iPhone by looking at the screen.
- **Battery power**: The iPhone 12 Pro provides up to 65 hours of wireless audio playback, 17 hours' video playback, 11 hours' video streaming, and fast charging capability.
- **Input/Output**: There is a Lightning Connector port (for charging, headphones, and connecting to a computer); a built-in speaker; and a built-in microphone.
- **Water-resistant**: Water-resistant up to six meters for up to 30 minutes. Also splash- and dust-resistant.
- **Sensors**: The sensors are: accelerometer, barometer, ambient light sensor, proximity sensor, and gyroscope.

iPhone 12 Pro Max

This is a larger version of the iPhone 12 Pro, and has the same camera system and the longest display screen of any iPhone to date. Its specifications include:

- **Screen**: The iPhone 12 Pro Max has a **6.7 inch** (measured diagonally) Super Retina XDR display screen.
- **Storage**: This determines how much content you can store on your iPhone. For the iPhone 12 Pro Max, the storage capacity options are: 128GB, 256GB or 512GB.
- **Camera**: A triple-lens 12MP camera for taking photos, and a front-facing 12MP TrueDepth camera for taking selfies, videos, and for use with Face ID.
- **Face ID**: Unlock the iPhone by looking at the screen.
- **Battery power**: The iPhone 12 Pro Max provides up to 80 hours of wireless audio playback, 20 hours' video playback, 12 hours' video streaming, and fast charging capability.
- **Input/Output**: There is a Lightning Connector port (for charging, headphones, and connecting to a computer); a built-in speaker; and a built-in microphone.
- **Water-resistant**: Water-resistant up to six meters for up to 30 minutes. Also splash- and dust-resistant.
- **Sensors**: The sensors are: accelerometer, barometer, ambient light sensor, proximity sensor, and gyroscope.

The phone services for the iPhone are provided by companies that enable access to their mobile networks, which you will be able to use for phone calls, texts, and mobile data for access to the internet. Companies provide different packages: you can buy the iPhone for a reduced sum and then pay a monthly contract, typically for 12 or 24 months. Despite the fact that the initial outlay for the iPhone will be cheaper, this works out more expensive over the period of the contract. Another option is to buy the iPhone (make sure it is unlocked so that you can use any SIM card) and use a SIM-only offer. This way, you can buy a package that suits you for calls, texts and mobile data. Look for offers that have unlimited data for internet access.

iPhone Nuts and Bolts

On/Off (Side) button

The button for turning the iPhone On and Off (and putting it into Sleep mode) is located on the top right-hand side of the body (looking at the screen). As with other buttons on the body, it is slightly raised to make it easier to locate just by touch.

Volume controls

Volume is controlled using two separate buttons on the left-hand side of the body. They do not have symbols on them but they are used to increase and decrease the volume.

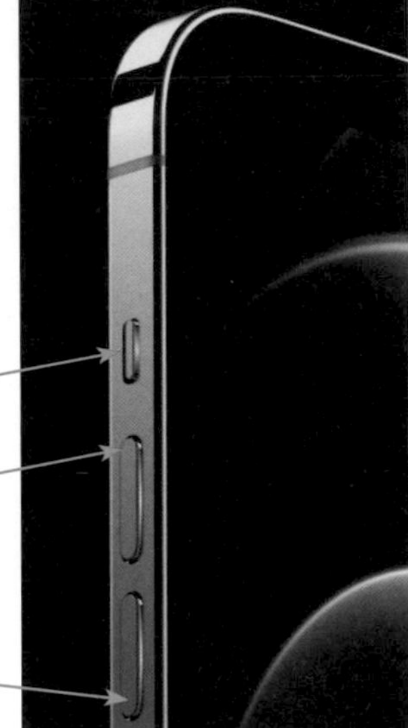

Ringer/silent (use this to turn the ringer On or Off for when a call or a notification is received)

Volume Up

Volume Down

Top notch

All iPhones have a notch at the top of the screen that accommodates the TrueDepth camera, sensors for use with Face ID, built-in stereo speakers, and a built-in microphone.

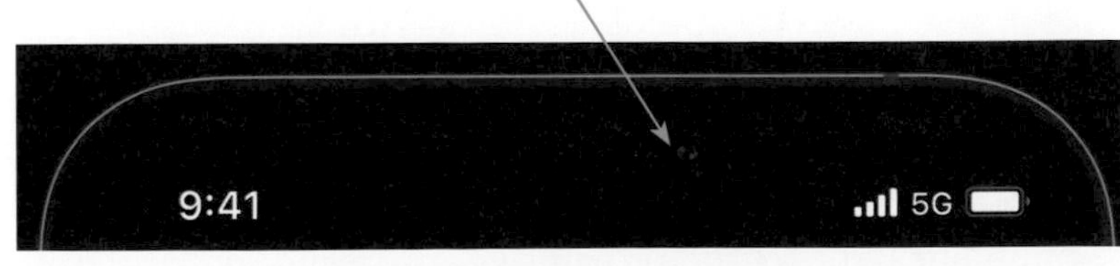

Don't forget

For more details on turning on the iPhone, see page 16.

Buy a glass screen protector to help preserve your iPhone's screen. This will help prevent marks and scratches, and can also save the screen if it is broken: the protector breaks rather than the iPhone's screen itself.

To make phone calls with your iPhone you need to have an active SIM card inserted, and a suitable service provider for cellular (mobile) calls and data.

Lightning Connector, speakers and microphone

These are located at the bottom of the iPhone.

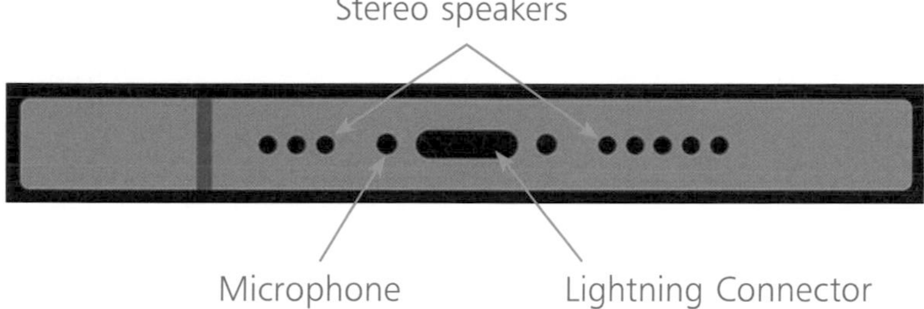

Back view of the iPhone

This contains the main camera, the LED flash, and the rear microphone.

iPhone 12 and 12 mini

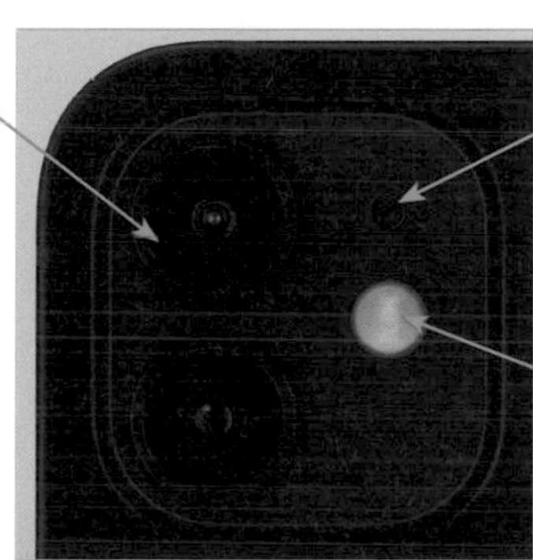

iPhone 12 Pro and 12 Pro Max

The camera on the iPhone 12 Pro and 12 Pro Max has three lenses for the main camera: one ultra wide-angle, one wide-angle and one telephoto. They combine to take each shot. This produces the highest quality photos yet on an iPhone, with a range of options such as Ultra Wide. See page 112 for more details.

The main camera on all iPhone 12 models is a high-quality 12-megapixel camera. It can capture excellent photos and also 4K (ultra high-definition) and high-definition (HD) video. The front-facing TrueDepth camera has a 12-megapixel resolution and can be used for taking "selfies": the modern craze of taking a photo of yourself and then posting it online on a social media site such as Facebook. It is also used for the Face ID functionality for unlocking the iPhone (see page 24), and for FaceTime video calls (see pages 132-133).

Inserting the SIM

The SIM card for the iPhone will be provided by your mobile carrier; i.e. the company that provides your cellular phone and data services. Without this, you would still be able to communicate with your iPhone, but only via Wi-Fi and compatible services. A SIM card gives you access to a mobile network too. Some iPhones come with the SIM pre-installed, but you can also insert one yourself. To do this:

1. Use a SIM tool to access the SIM tray on the side of the iPhone

2. Press the tool firmly into the hole on the SIM slot so that the SIM tray pops out and starts to appear. Pull the SIM tray fully out

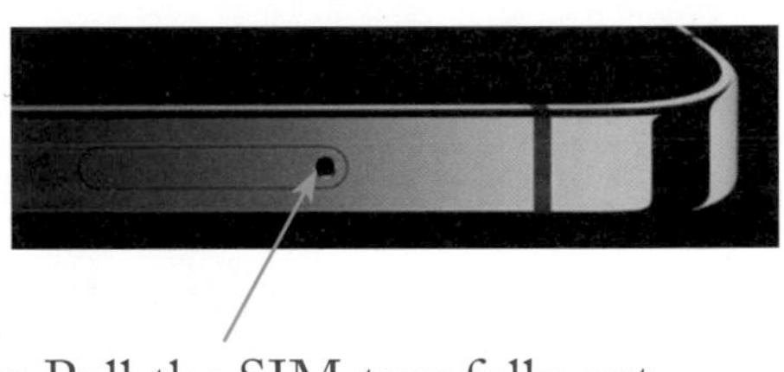

3. Place the SIM card with the metal contacts face downwards (shown facing upwards in the image). Place the SIM tray in position so that the diagonal cut is in the same position as the cut on the SIM card

4. Place the SIM card into the SIM tray. It should fit flush, resting on a narrow ridge underneath it, with the diagonal cut on the card matching the cut in the SIM tray

5. Place your thumb over the bottom of the SIM tray, covering the SIM card, and place the tray into the SIM slot. Push the tray firmly into the slot until it clicks into place

Beware

The SIM tool is not included with the iPhone 12 models. If you do not have a SIM tool from a previous iPhone, a stretched out paper clip can be used instead.

The SIM tray can only be inserted in one way. If it appears to encounter resistance, do not force it; take it out and try again.

All of the iPhone 12 models have dual-SIM capability, which means you can use two separate numbers with the same iPhone.

MagSafe Accessories

The iPhone 12 models use MagSafe technology to connect a range of accessories, including a wireless charging base station for charging the iPhone. The MagSafe technology includes a designated magnetic area on the back of the iPhone that can be used to attach MagSafe accessories.

MagSafe wireless charger

The MagSafe wireless charger connects to the MagSafe area on the back on the iPhone, for fast wireless charging. The MagSafe charger can be laid flat and the iPhone placed directly onto it. Although there are no wires required to connect the iPhone to the MagSafe charger, the charger has to be connected to a mains electricity supply via an adapter (sold separately), which connects to the MagSafe charger using the charger's USB-C connector.

MagSafe cases

MagSafe cases can be snapped to the iPhone to give it increased protection if it is dropped. The cases come in a range of colors.

MagSafe wallets

MagSafe wallets can be added individually, or snapped onto the back of a MagSafe case, so that you will always have your credit and bank cards with your iPhone.

The MagSafe accessories are stackable, which means that they can clip together as one unit. For instance, you can add a MagSafe cover and then a MagSafe wallet, and still use the MagSafe charger for wireless charging (the wallet is protected so that credit or bank cards will not be harmed by the MagSafe technology).

There is a wide range of standard accessories for the iPhone. These include cases in a range of colors and materials. These cases give some protection to the body of your iPhone.

iPhone Gestures

For older iPhones that have a physical Home button and run iOS 14, some of the functionality on these three pages is achieved with the Home button. These instances will be noted throughout the book.

If your iPhone ever freezes, or if something is not working properly, it can be rebooted by pressing the Volume Up button, then the Volume Down button, then pressing and holding the On/Off button.

The color of the bar at the bottom of the screen, for returning to the Home screen, is dependent on the background color of the app being used. If it has a light background, the bar will be a dark color; if it has a dark background, the bar will be a light color.

None of the iPhone 12 models have a Home button and, as with the previous range of iPhones, the actions that were previously accessed by pressing the Home button are performed by gestures on the screen and actions using the On/Off and Volume buttons. Gestures for the iPhone include the following (also including some general iPhone actions):

Turning on

Press and hold on the On/Off button for a few seconds. Keep it pressed until the Apple icon appears. This will display the Lock screen (see page 23 for details on using the Lock screen).

Unlocking the iPhone

This is done by using Face ID. Once this has been set up (see pages 24-25), raise the phone so that the camera can view your face, and simultaneously swipe up from the bottom of the screen to view the last viewed screen.

Returning to the Home screen

Swipe up from the bar at the bottom of the screen. This can be done from any app.

For iPhones with a Home button, press the Home button to return to the Home screen from any app.

Accessing the Control Center

To access the Control Center of useful widgets, swipe down from the top right-hand corner of the screen. (On older models of iPhone, this was achieved by swiping up from the bottom of the screen, which now returns you to the Home screen.)

Swipe up and down with one finger to move up or down web pages, photos, maps or documents. The content moves in the opposite direction of the swipe; i.e. if you swipe up, the page will move down, and vice versa. Swipe outwards with thumb and forefinger to zoom in on a web page, photo, map or document. This enables you to zoom in on an item to a greater degree than double-tapping with one finger. Pinch together with thumb and forefinger to zoom back out on a web page, photo, map or document.

Accessing the Notification Center

The Notification Center is accessed by swiping down from the top left-hand corner, or the top middle of the screen.

Accessing Siri

Press and hold the On/Off button until Siri appears. Alternatively, use the "Hey Siri" function (see pages 52-55).

Accessing the App Switcher

Swipe up from the bottom of the screen and pause in the middle of the screen to view open and recently-used apps.

...cont'd

For iPhones with a Home button, double-tap (rather than double-press) on the Home button to activate the **Reachability** function. To activate **Apple Pay**, press on the Home button with the finger that was used to set up Touch ID.

Reachability

To use Reachability, which moves the items on the screen to the bottom half to make them easier to access with one hand, swipe down from the bottom of the screen (see page 56 for more details).

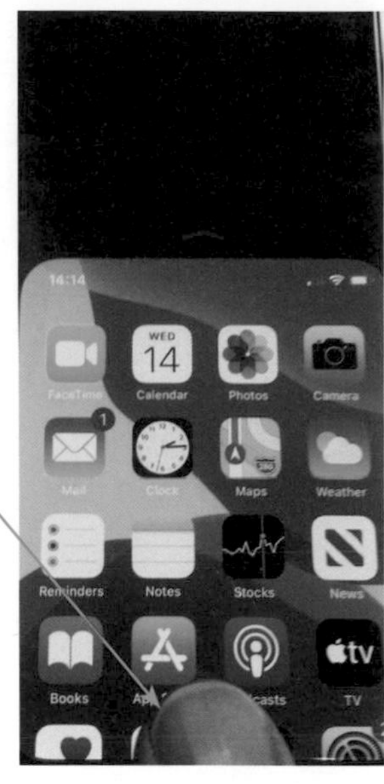

Screenshots are saved to the **Photos** app. They can be viewed from the **Photos** button on the bottom toolbar and also from the **Screenshots** album in the **Albums** section.

Taking a screenshot

To capture an image of what is currently on the screen, quickly press and release the On/Off button and the Volume Up button simultaneously. For older iPhones that have a physical Home button and run iOS 14, a screenshot can be captured by pressing the On/Off button and the Home button simultaneously.

Paying with Apple Pay

To use Apple Pay to pay for items with your iPhone, double-click the On/Off button, and authorize with Face ID. See pages 66-67 for details about setting up Apple Pay.

For older iPhones that have a physical Home button and run iOS 14, press and hold the On/Off button and access the **slide to power off** button.

Turning off

Press and hold the On/Off button and either of the Volume buttons until the Power Off screen appears. Swipe the **slide to power off** button to the right to turn off the iPhone.

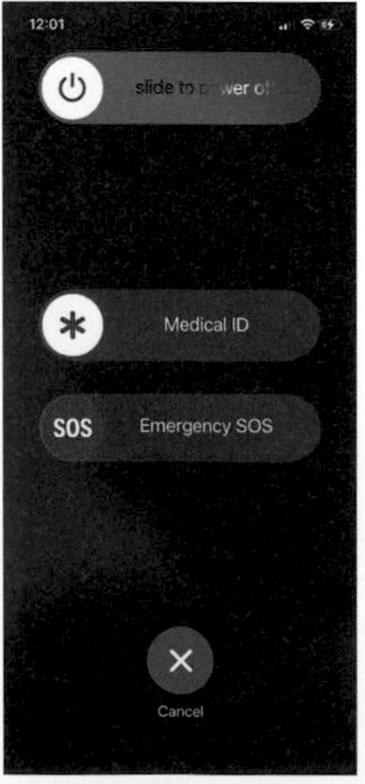

Getting Set Up

When you first turn on your iPhone there will be a series of setup screens. These include the following options:

- **Language** and **Country**. Select a language and country.
- **Quick Start**. This can be used to transfer settings from another compatible iOS device, such as an iPad.
- **Wi-Fi network**. Connect to the internet, using either your own home network or a public Wi-Fi hotspot.
- **Data & Privacy**. This is used to identify features that ask for your personal information.
- **Face ID**. Use this to create a Face ID for unlocking your iPhone by looking at it.
- **Create a Passcode**. This can be used to create a numerical passcode for unlocking your iPhone.
- **Apps & Data**. This can be used to set up an iPhone from an iCloud backup, or as a new iPhone.
- **Apple ID and iCloud**. This can be used to use an existing iCloud account or create a new one.
- **Express Settings**. This contains options for specifying how apps manage your data.
- **Keep your iPhone Up to Date**. This can be used to install updates to the operating system (iOS) automatically.
- **Siri**. This is used to set up Siri, the digital voice assistant.
- **Screen Time**. This can be used to set limits for using apps on the iPhone and for creating a usage report.
- **App Analytics**. This can allow details from the iPhone and its apps to be sent to Apple and developers.
- **True Tone Display**. This automatically ensures that the screen adapts to the current lighting conditions.
- **Appearance**. This can be used to select Dark or Light mode for the overall appearance on the iPhone.

Most of the options available during the setup process can also be accessed within the **Settings** app (see pages 20-21).

For more information about using iCloud, see Chapter 3.

iPhone Settings

The Cellular (Mobile) Data settings contain the **Data Roaming** option (**Settings** > **Cellular** > **Cellular Data Options**): if you are traveling abroad you may want to turn this **Off** to avoid undue charges when connected to the internet.

The Display & Brightness setting has an option for Dark Mode, which inverts the screen color. To use Dark Mode, tap **On** the **Dark** button. To specify when Dark Mode is activated, drag the **Automatic** button to On, or tap once on the **Options** button to specify a time for Dark Mode.

The Settings app controls settings for the way the iPhone and its apps operate:

- **Apple ID, iCloud, iTunes & App Store**. Contains settings for these items.
- **Airplane Mode**. This can be used to disable network connectivity while on an airplane.
- **Wi-Fi**. This enables you to select a wireless network.
- **Bluetooth**. Turn this On to connect Bluetooth devices.
- **Cellular (Mobile) Data**. These are the settings that will be used with your cellular (mobile) service provider.
- **Personal Hotspot**. This can be used to share your internet connection.
- **Notifications**. This determines how the Notification Center operates (see pages 28-29).
- **Sounds & Haptics**. This has options for setting sounds for alerts and actions such as tapping on the keyboard.
- **Do Not Disturb**. Use this to specify times when you do not want to receive audio alerts, phone calls, and video calls.
- **Screen Time**. Options for reporting on and limiting iPhone usage.
- **General**. This contains a range of common settings.
- **Control Center**. This determines how the Control Center operates (see pages 48-51).
- **Display & Brightness**. This can be used to set the screen brightness, text size, and bold text.
- **Home Screen**. This determines how apps are shown in on the Home screen and in the App Library.
- **Accessibility**. This can be used for users with visual or motor issues.

- **Wallpaper**. This can be used to select a wallpaper.
- **Siri & Search**. Options for the digital voice assistant.
- **Face ID & Passcode**. This has options for adding a passcode or fingerprint ID for unlocking the iPhone.
- **Emergency SOS**. This can be used to set an Auto Call to an emergency number.
- **Battery**. This can be used to view battery usage by apps.
- **Privacy**. This can be used to activate Location Services so that your location can be used by specific apps.
- **App Store**. This can be used to specify downloading options for the App Store.
- **Wallet & Apple Pay**. This can be used to add credit or debit cards for use with Apple Pay (see pages 66-67).
- **Passwords**. This contains options for managing website passwords.
- **Mail**, **Contacts**, **Calendars**. These are three separate settings that have options for how these apps operate.

iPhone app settings

Most of the built-in iPhone apps have their own settings that determine how the apps operate. These include: Notes, Reminders, Voice Memos, Phone, Messages, FaceTime, Maps, Compass, Measure, Safari, News, Stocks, Health, Shortcuts, Music, TV, Photos, Camera, Books, and Podcasts. Tap on one of these tabs to view the settings for that app. (Apps that are downloaded from the App Store also have their individual settings in this location in the Settings app.)

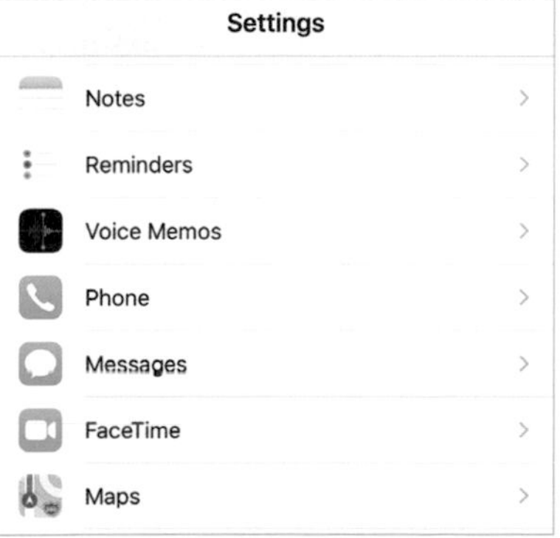

If a Settings option has an On/Off button next to it, this can be changed by swiping the button to either the left or right. Green indicates that the option is **On**. Select **Settings** > **Accessibility** > **Display & Text Size** > **On/Off Labels** to show or hide icons on each button.

Tap on a link to see additional options:

Tap once here to move back to the previous page for the selected setting:

About iOS 14

iOS 14 is the latest operating system for the iPhone.

You will need an Apple ID for all Apple online services. This is free – to register go to **https://appleid.apple.com**

Tap on **Create Your Apple ID**. You will be prompted to enter your email address and a password. Then, follow the on-screen instructions. Tap on **Create Apple ID** when ready.

To check the version of the iOS, look in **Settings** > **General** > **Software Update**.

iOS 14 is the latest version of the operating system for Apple's iPhone range including all of the latest iPhone 12 models.

iOS 14 further enhances the user experience for which the mobile operating system is renowned. This includes:

- **Today View panel**. The Today View panel, which can be accessed from the Home screen by swiping to the right from the left-hand edge of the screen, has been redesigned so that the widgets within it can be edited and also displayed at different sizes. Apps can also be included within a Smart Stack, which can display several different apps within a single widget.
- **Widgets on the Home screen**. Widgets from the Today View panel can be added to the iPhone's Home screen with iOS 14. These can then be used alongside the existing apps on the Home screen.

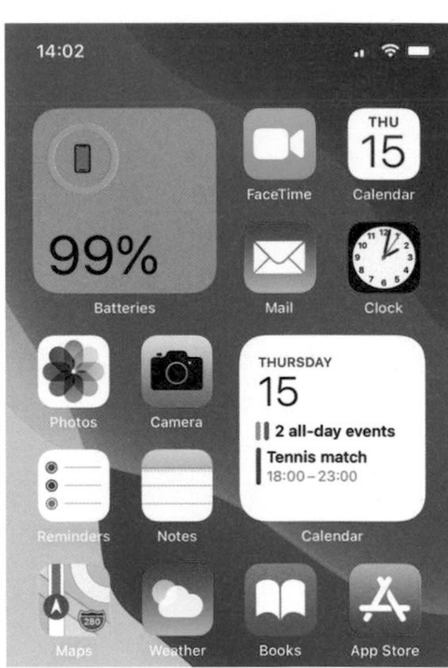

- **App Library**. The App Library is a new feature that can be used to access all of the apps on your iPhone, without the need to move between numerous Home screens to find them.
- **Compact Calls**. When you receive a phone call or a FaceTime call on your iPhone, it is displayed in a banner at the top of the screen, rather than taking up the whole display.
- **Updated apps**. A number of iPhone apps have been updated in iOS 14, including, Maps, Messages, Notes, Safari and Home.

Using the Lock Screen

To save power, it is possible to set your iPhone screen to auto-lock. This is the equivalent of the Sleep option on a traditional computer. To do this:

1. Tap once on the **Settings** app

2. Tap once on the **Display & Brightness** tab

3. Tap once on the **Auto-Lock** option

Auto-Lock Never >

4. Tap once on the time of non-use after which you wish the screen to be locked

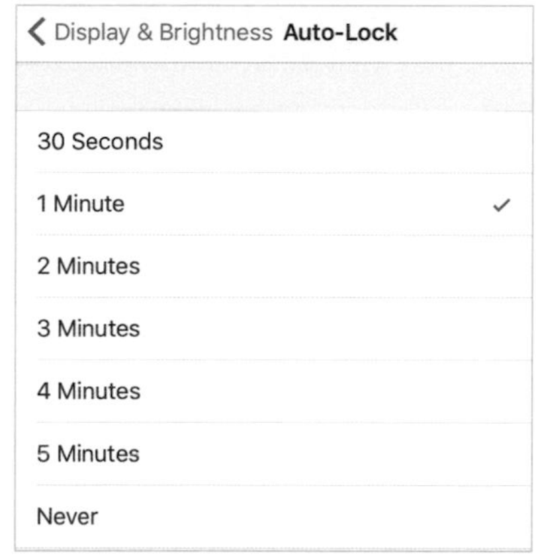

5. Once the screen is locked, look at the screen and swipe up from the bottom of the Lock screen to unlock the screen

The screen can also be locked by pressing once on the **On/Off** button on the right-hand side of the iPhone's body.

Don't forget

For older iPhones that have a physical Home button and run iOS 14, the iPhone is unlocked by pressing the Home button once if Touch ID has been set up (**Settings** > **Touch ID and Passcode**).

Swipe from right to left on the Lock screen to access the camera.

Face ID and Passcode

With the removal of the Home button on the latest range of iPhones, the means of unlocking the phone is done through the use of Face ID. If this cannot be used for any reason, a passcode can be entered instead. To set up Face ID:

1. Select **Settings** > **Face ID & Passcode**

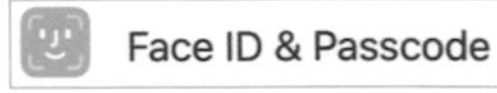

2. Tap once on the **Set Up Face ID** button

Set Up Face ID

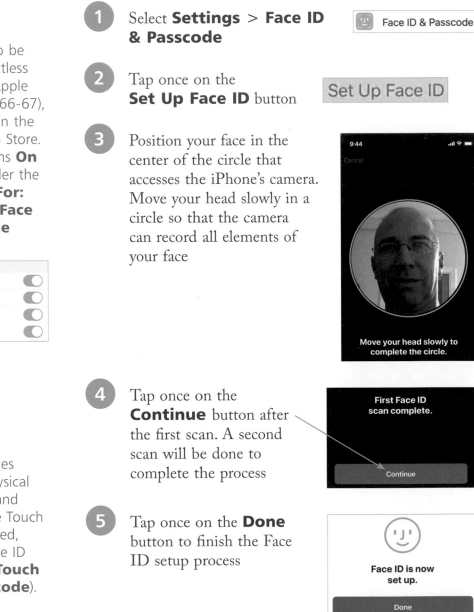

3. Position your face in the center of the circle that accesses the iPhone's camera. Move your head slowly in a circle so that the camera can record all elements of your face

4. Tap once on the **Continue** button after the first scan. A second scan will be done to complete the process

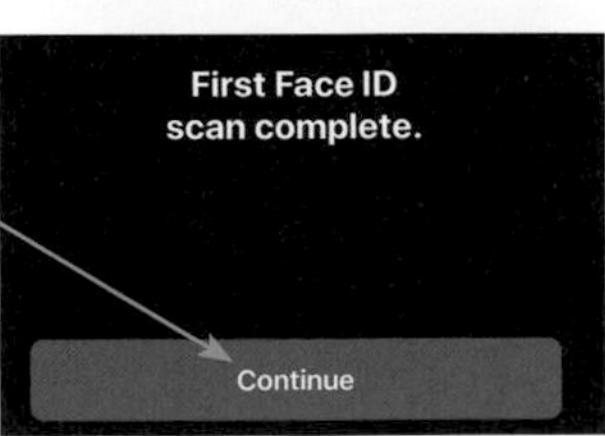

5. Tap once on the **Done** button to finish the Face ID setup process

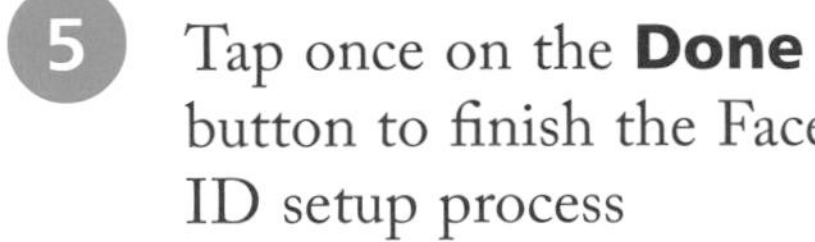

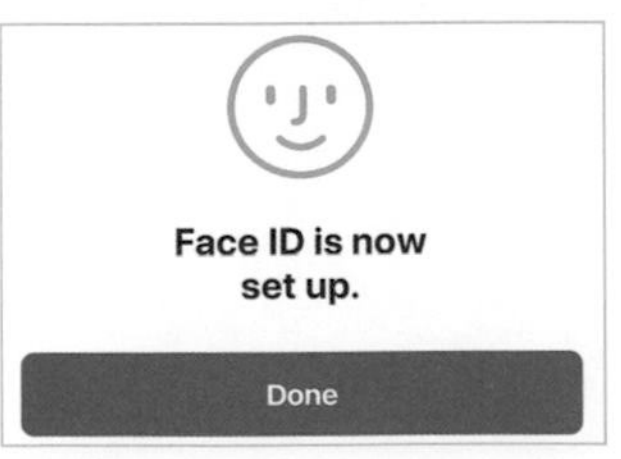

Face ID can also be used for contactless purchases for Apple Pay (see pages 66-67), and purchases in the iTunes and App Store. Drag the buttons **On** as required under the **Use Face ID For:** heading in the **Face ID & Passcode** settings.

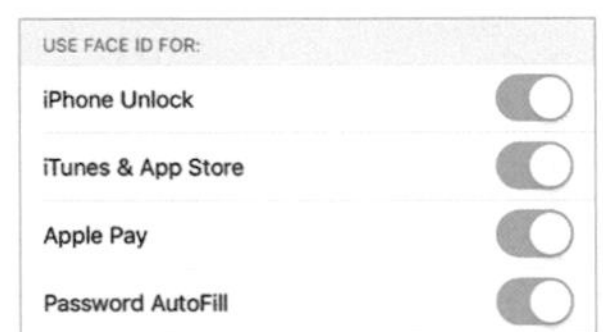

For older iPhones that have a physical Home button and run iOS 14, the Touch ID feature is used, rather than Face ID (**Settings** > **Touch ID and Passcode**).

Adding a passcode

If Face ID cannot be used to unlock the iPhone, a numerical passcode can be used instead. This has to be set up at the same time as creating a Face ID. To do this:

1. Select **Settings** > **Face ID & Passcode**

Face ID & Passcode

2. Tap once on the **Turn Passcode On** button

Settings | Passcode Lock
Turn Passcode On
Change Passcode
Require Passcode | Immediately

3. Enter a six-digit passcode. This can be used to unlock your iPhone from the Lock screen

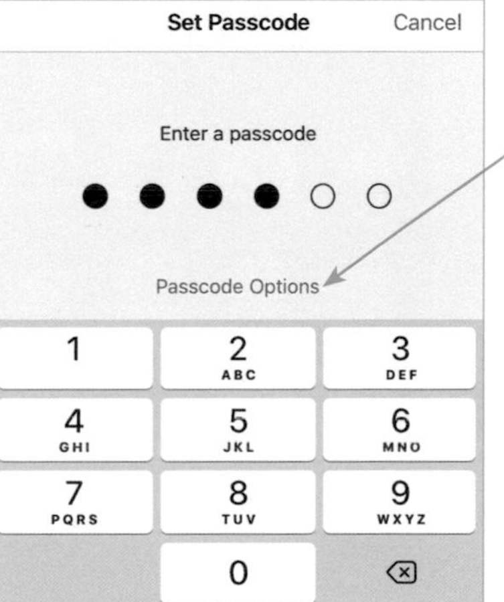

4. Once a passcode has been created, tap once on the **Require Passcode** button in Step 2 to specify a time period until the passcode is required on the Lock screen. The best option is **Immediately**, otherwise someone else could access your iPhone

Require Passcode | Immediately

If you use a passcode to lock your iPhone, write it down but store it in a location away from the iPhone.

Tap once on the **Passcode Options** link in Step 3 to access other options for creating a passcode. These include a **Custom Alphanumeric Code**, a **Custom Numeric Code**, and a **4-Digit Code**. The 4-Digit Code is the least secure, and the Alphanumeric Code is the most secure, as it can use a combination of numbers, letters and symbols.

Opening and Closing Apps

One of the first things you will want to do with your iPhone is explore the apps on the Home screen. The good news is that all apps on your iPhone can be opened with the minimum of fuss and effort:

The Home screen is the one that you see when you turn on your iPhone.

1. Tap once on an icon on the Home screen to open the app

2. The app opens at its own Home screen

3. Swipe up from the bottom of the screen to return to the iPhone Home screen

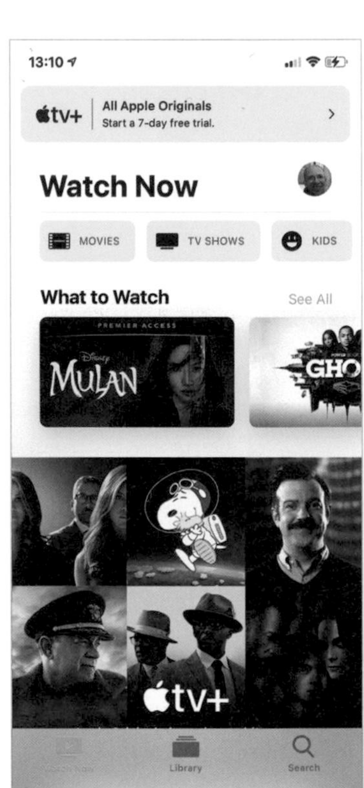

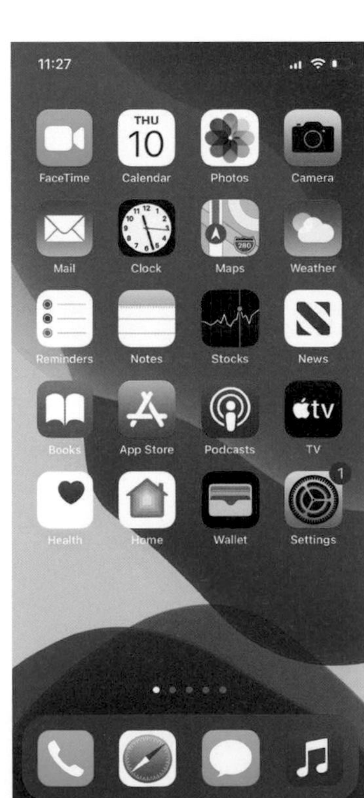

You can open as many apps as you like from the Home screen, without needing to close any. However, apps can be closed from the App Switcher (see next page).

Closing apps

Apps remain open in the background when they are not being used. This uses very little power and they can be left in this state of hibernation until they are needed again. However, apps can also be closed using the App Switcher:

1. Swipe up from the bottom of the screen and pause in the middle of the screen to access the App Switcher. From the App Switcher window, swipe left and right between open apps, and tap on one to make it the active app

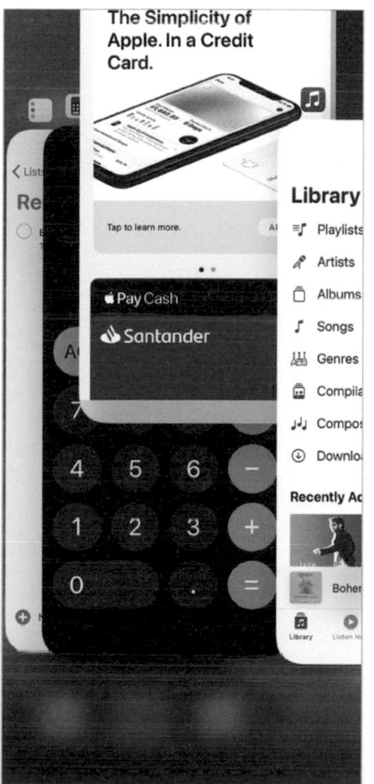

2. Swipe an app to the top of the window in the App Switcher to close it

When you switch from one app to another, the first one stays open in the background. You can go back to it by accessing it from the App Switcher window or the Home screen.

When an app is closed in the App Switcher window, the other apps move along to fill in the space from the closed app.

Swipe up from the bottom of the screen, or tap once on a free area of the App Switcher window, to return to the Home screen.

Notifications

Notifications can be used with iOS 14 so that you never miss an important message or update. Notifications can be viewed in the Notification Center and also on the Lock screen. To set up and use Notifications:

Hot tip

The Notification Center can be accessed by dragging down from the top left-hand corner or the middle of the screen, in any app.

1 Tap once on the **Settings** app

2 Tap once on the **Notifications** tab

3 Under **Notification Style**, tap once on an item to select the notification settings for a specific app

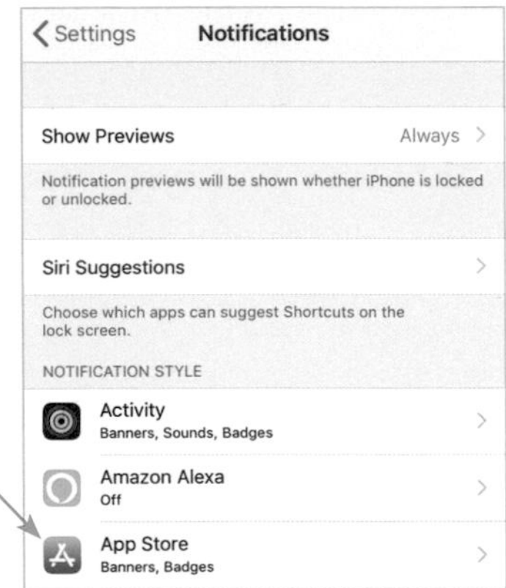

Turn the **Lock Screen** option **On** in Step 4 to enable notifications for the selected app to be displayed even when the iPhone is locked.

4 Drag the **Allow Notifications** button **On** to display notifications from this app in the Notification Center

5 Tap here to select the style for how the notification appears

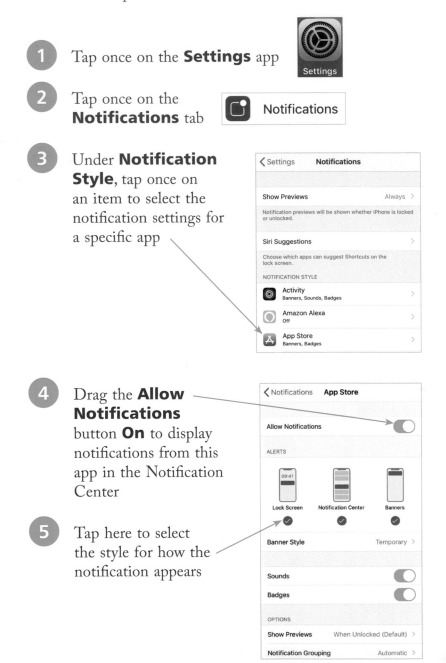

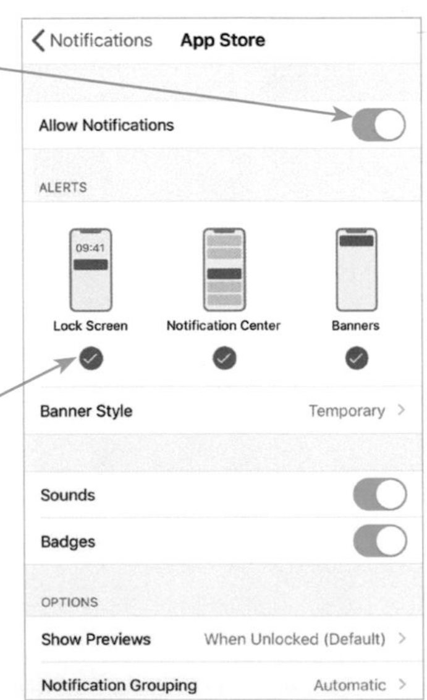

Text messages can be replied to directly from the Lock screen, without unlocking the iPhone. To do this, press on the message on the Lock screen and compose a reply as normal.

6. Swipe down from the top left or middle of the iPhone screen, from the Home screen or any app, to view your notifications in the Notification Center

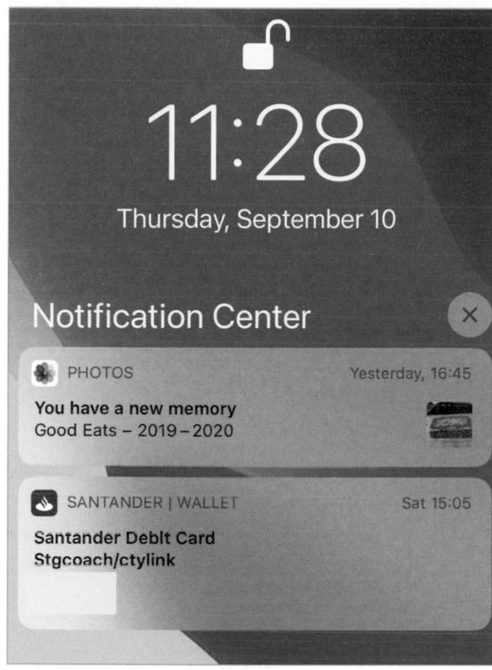

7. On the Home screen, swipe from left to right to view the Today View panel, where apps with date-specific information, such as the Calendar, Weather and Reminders apps, can be displayed

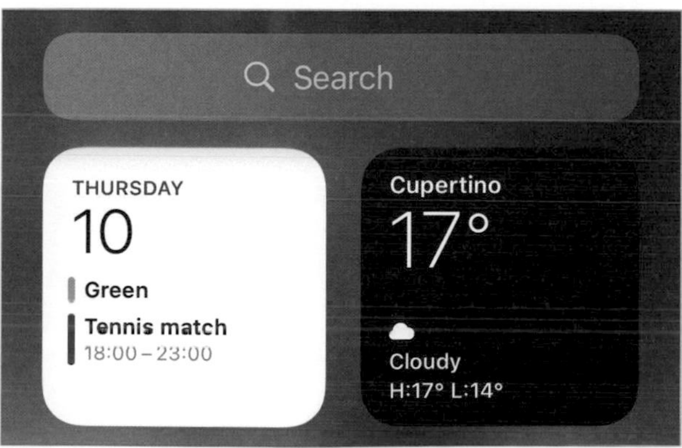

The Today View panel in Step 7 (second image) can be viewed from the Home screen by swiping from left to right. For more information about using the Today View panel, see pages 38-39.

At the bottom of the window in Step 5 on the previous page there is a **Notification Grouping** option. Set this to **Automatic**, so that all similar notifications are grouped together.

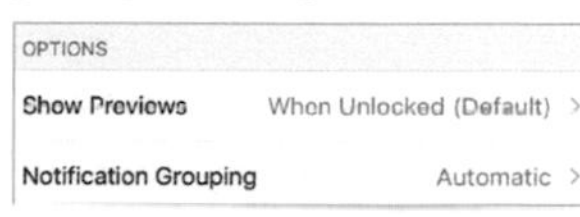

Updating Software

The operating system that powers the iPhone is known as iOS. This is a mobile computing operating system, and the latest version is iOS 14. Periodically, there are updates to the iOS to fix bugs and add new features. These can be downloaded to your iPhone once they are released:

Hot tip

It is always worth updating the iOS to keep up-to-date with fixes. Also, app developers update their products to use the latest iOS features.

1. Tap once on the **Settings** app

Settings

2. Tap once on the **General** tab (a red tag indicates that an update is available)

3. Tap once on the **Software Update** option

Software Update
1

4. If there is an update available it will be displayed here, with details of what is contained within it

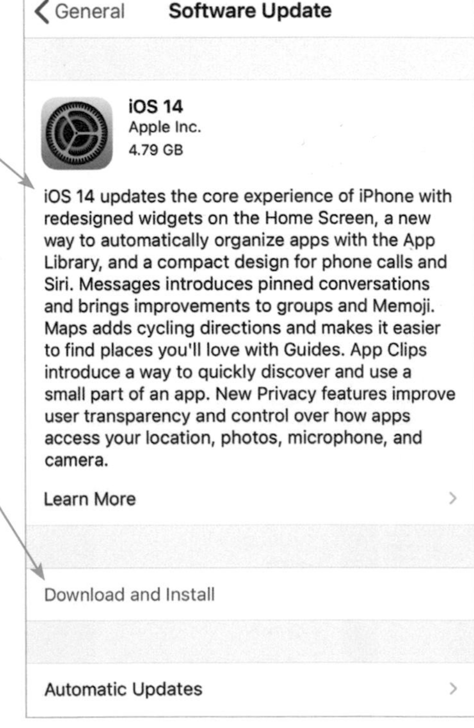
General
Software Update
iOS 14
Apple Inc.
4.79 GB
iOS 14 updates the core experience of iPhone with redesigned widgets on the Home Screen, a new way to automatically organize apps with the App Library, and a compact design for phone calls and Siri. Messages introduces pinned conversations and brings improvements to groups and Memoji. Maps adds cycling directions and makes it easier to find places you'll love with Guides. App Clips introduce a way to quickly discover and use a small part of an app. New Privacy features improve user transparency and control over how apps access your location, photos, microphone, and camera.
Learn More
Download and Install
Automatic Updates

5. Tap once on the **Download and Install** button to start the downloading process. The iOS update will then be done automatically

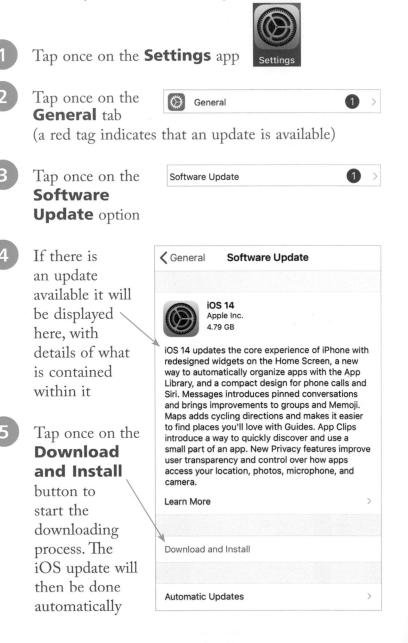

Hot tip

Software Update can be set so iOS updates are performed automatically overnight, when the iPhone is charging and connected to Wi-Fi. Tap on the **Automatic Updates** button in Step 4 and drag the **Download iOS Updates** and **Install iOS Updates** buttons **On**.

Back
Automatic Updates
AUTOMATICALLY:
Download iOS Updates
iPhone will automatically download updates over Wi-Fi.
Install iOS Updates
Automatically install software updates overnight after they have been downloaded. You will receive a notification before updates are installed. Your iPhone must be charging and connected to Wi-Fi to complete the update.

2 Starting to use your iPhone

This chapter covers the functions on the iPhone that you need to use it confidently and make the most of its features. From opening and closing apps, using the App Library and Home screens for accessing apps, using Screen Time to monitor your iPhone usage, and using Apple Pay, it explains the iPhone environment so you can quickly get up and running with it.

Home Screens

The first thing that you see when your iPhone is turned on is the Home screen. This is where the iPhone's apps are displayed. By default, there is one Home screen, containing the built-in apps. However, as more apps are added, additional Home screens are created to display them:

1 The Home screen displays the default apps

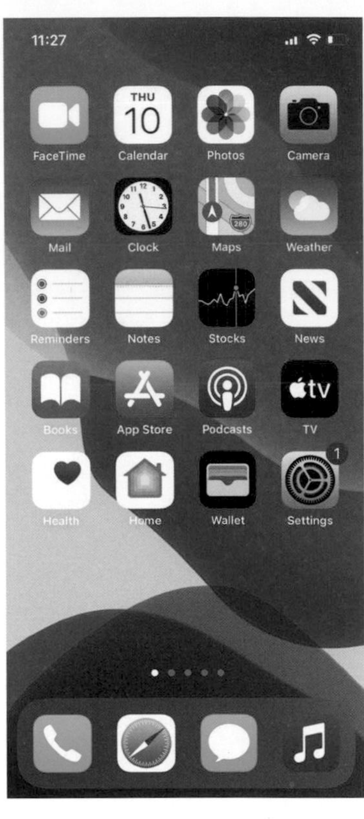

2 As more apps are added, additional Home screens are created to accommodate them. Swipe left and right to move between the available Home screens

The functionality of the Home screen has been updated in iOS 14, with the inclusion of the App Library.

Swipe to the end of the Home screens to access the App Library (see next page).

On the first Home screen, swipe to the right, from the left-hand side of the screen, to access the Today Panel widgets (see pages 38-39).

Apps on a Home screen can be opened by tapping on them once.

App Library

In previous versions of iOS, numerous Home screens could be added, and folders created to contain apps of similar categories. This can still be done in iOS 14, but there is also an option for consolidating the number of Home screens, through the use of the App Library. This can be used to display a page with all of the apps on your iPhone, without the need for numerous different Home screens. To access the App Library:

The App Library is a new feature in iOS 14.

1. Swipe from right to left until you reach the final Home screen (this is indicated by the small dots at the bottom of the Home screen)

2. Swipe from right to left to access the App Library

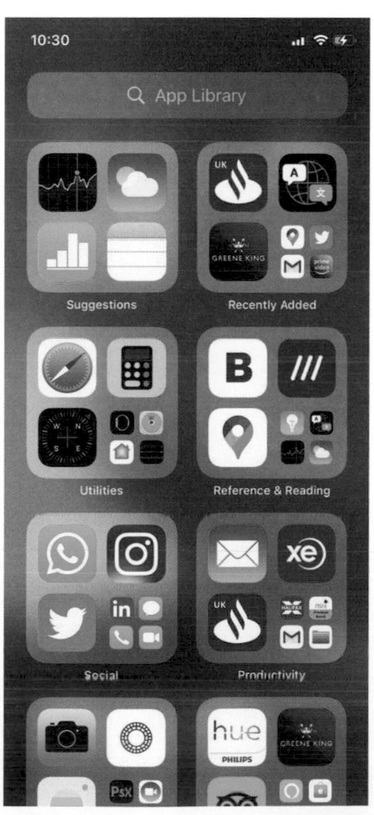

Several Home screens can be used as well as the App Library. However, the App Library can be used to make the overall use of your iPhone more streamlined, by removing Home screens so that there are fewer screens to swipe through to view all of your apps.

Working with Home Screens

The App Library is most effective when there are no additional Home screens, apart from the first one, so that all of the apps can be accessed from the App Library. This is done by hiding the existing Home screens. To do this:

NEW

Hiding Home screens is a new feature in iOS 14.

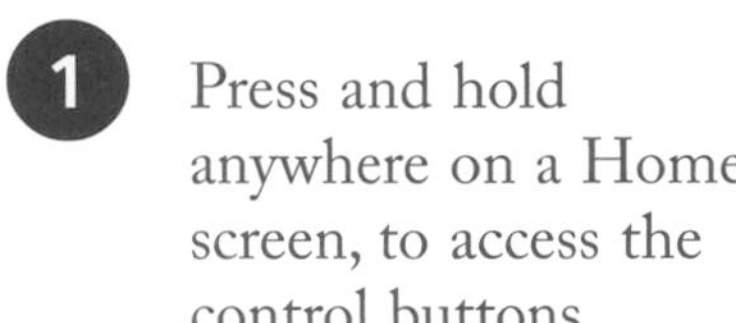

1. Press and hold anywhere on a Home screen, to access the control buttons

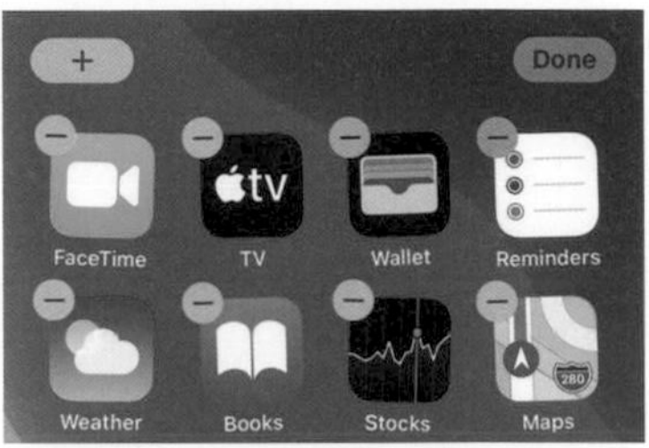

2. The number of Home screens in use is denoted by this bar toward the bottom of the screen

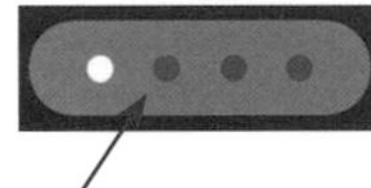

3. Tap once on the Home screen buttons bar to access the editing area

The number of dots on the Home screen buttons bar indicates the number of available Home screens and the App Library, which is denoted by the dot at the far right-hand side of the bar. So, the example in Step 3 includes three Home screens and the App Library.

4. The editing area displays all of the currently-available Home screens

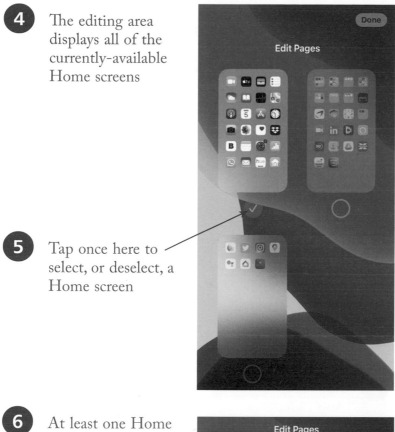

Hot tip

If the tick symbol is visible below a Home screen, this means that the Home screen will be available.

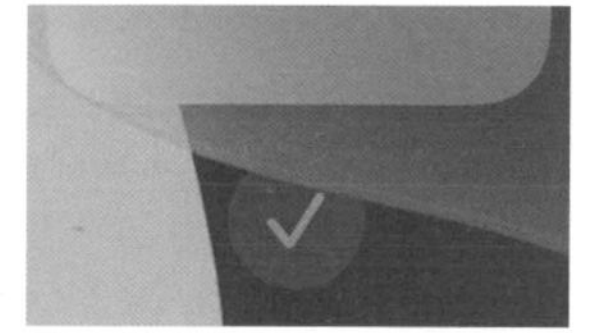

5. Tap once here to select, or deselect, a Home screen

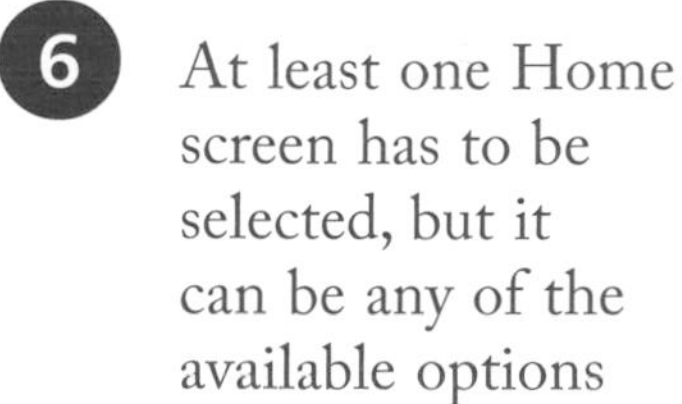

6. At least one Home screen has to be selected, but it can be any of the available options

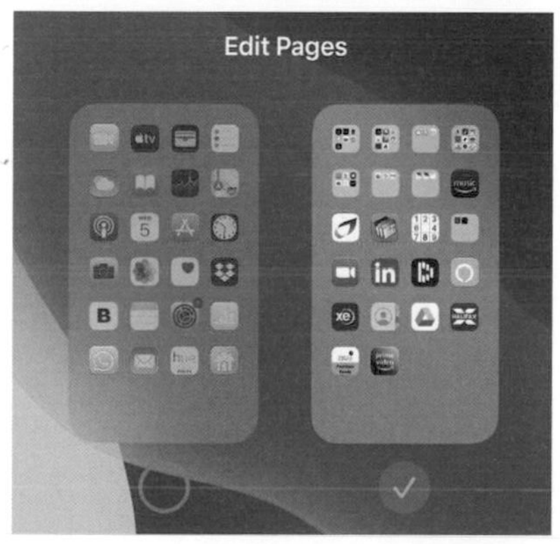

Once a Home screen has been hidden, the apps within it will not be visible, but they can be accessed from the App Library.

7. Tap once on the **Done** button to apply the Home screen changes, and tap once on the **Done** button on the Home screen to complete the editing process

Done

Using the App Library

The App Library automatically arranges apps into folders, based on their categories. Apps can be opened and deleted directly from the App Library. To use the App Library to work with and manage the apps on your iPhone:

1. Move to the final Home screen in use. This is indicated by the dots toward the bottom of the Home screen. If there is only one Home screen in use (i.e. the other Home screens have been hidden as shown on pages 34-35) then there will only be two dots, one for the Home screen and one for the App Library

2. Swipe from right to left on the Home screen to access the App Library

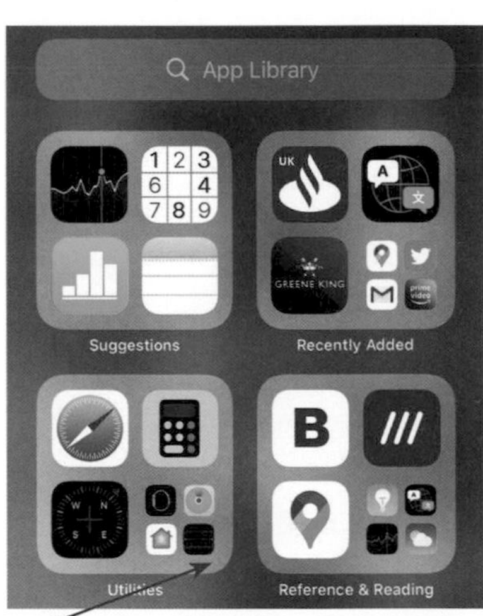

3. Apps in the App Library are automatically organized into appropriate folders. Tap once on an app in a folder to open it

4. If a folder has four or fewer apps, they are all displayed. If there are more than four apps, tap once on the bottom right-hand corner of a folder to view all of the apps within it

The order of the folders in the App Library cannot be changed; i.e. you cannot move them around within the App Library.

5. Press and hold anywhere on the App Library page to access the control buttons

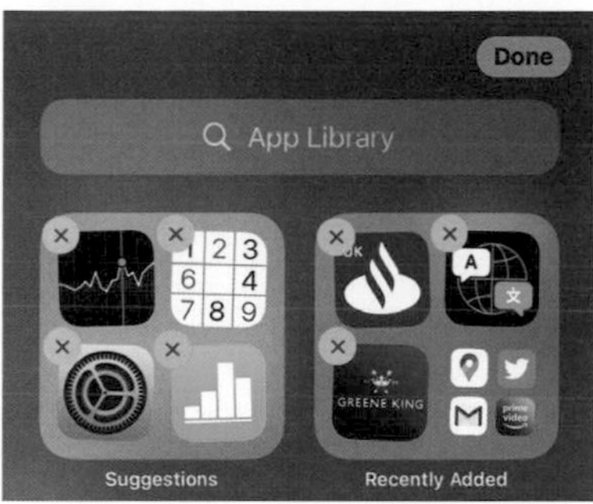

6. Tap once on this button to delete an app from your iPhone

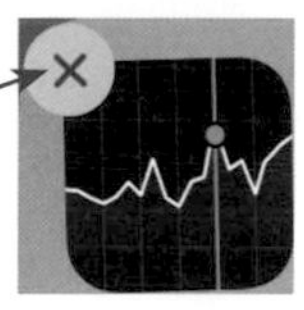

Viewing apps

To view all of the apps in the App Library:

1. Swipe downwards anywhere within the App Library
2. All of the available apps are listed alphabetically

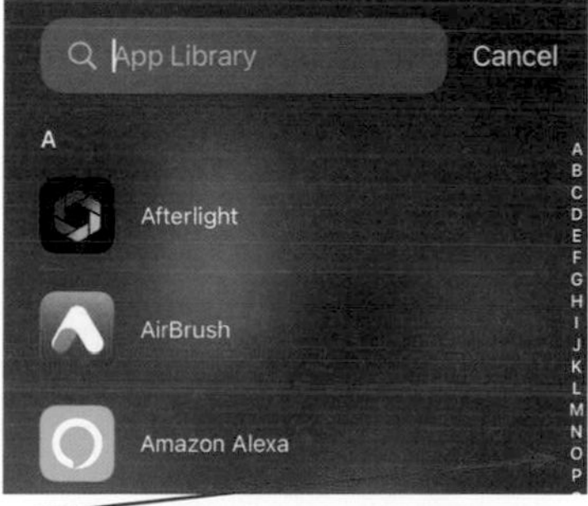

3. Swipe up and down to view all of the available apps, or tap on the alphabetic sidebar to move to that section
4. Use the Search box at the top of the App Library window to search for specific apps. As you type, matching apps will appear below the Search box

When an app is deleted as in Step 6, a confirmation dialog box will ask if you want to delete the app. Tap once on the **Delete** button if you do. Deleted apps can be reinstated from the App Store at any time.

Apps can be deleted from a Home screen in the same way as deleting them in the App Library.

The more letters used in the Search box in Step 4, the more defined the search results will become. For instance, "ca" will produce more results than "cal".

Today View Panel

The Today View panel can be used to display information from some of your favorite and most-used apps. It is accessed from the first Home screen. To use Today View:

The Today View panel has been updated in iOS 14.

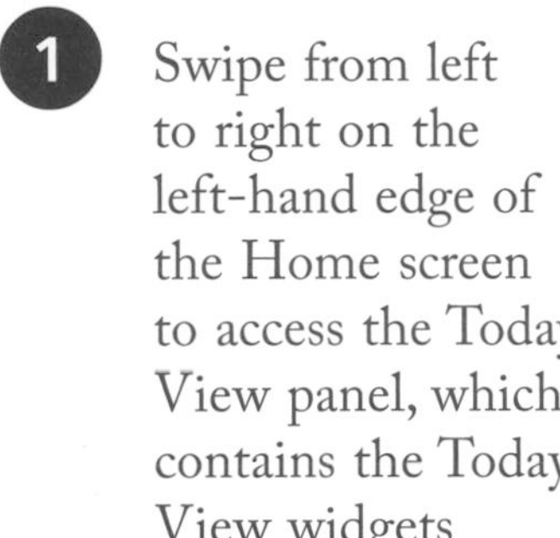

1. Swipe from left to right on the left-hand edge of the Home screen to access the Today View panel, which contains the Today View widgets

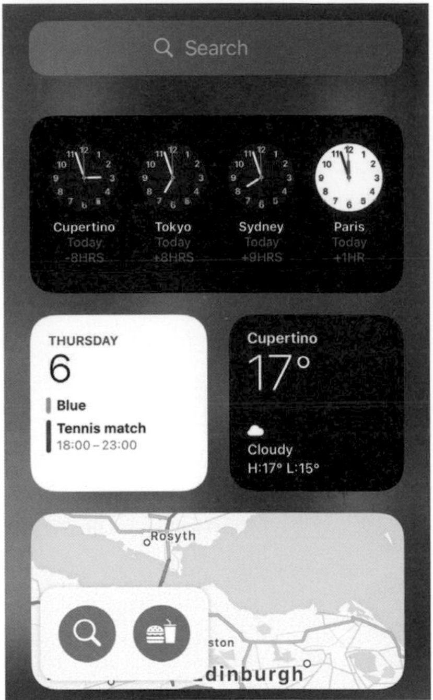

Swipe from right to left on the Today View panel to hide it.

2. Swipe up on the Today View panel to see all of the widgets currently in it. Tap on a widget to open it in its related app

3. Press and hold anywhere within the Today View panel to access its editing controls

4. Tap once on this icon in the top left-hand corner of a widget

5. Tap once on the **Remove** button to remove it from Today View

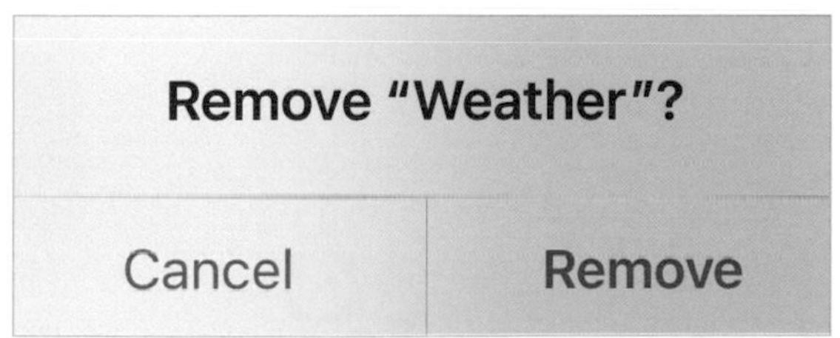

Widgets can also be removed from the Today View panel by pressing and holding on a widget within the panel. Tap once on the **Remove Widget** button and tap once on the **Remove** button.

iPhone Widgets

The iOS widgets can be added to the Today View panel, and some of them can also be edited to change their functionality.

Adding widgets

To add widgets to the Today View panel:

NEW

The widgets in the Today View panel have been updated in iOS 14.

1. Press and hold anywhere within the Today View panel and tap once on this button at thc top of the Today View panel

2. The Today View widgets are displayed

3. Swipe up the panel to view the full list of available widgets

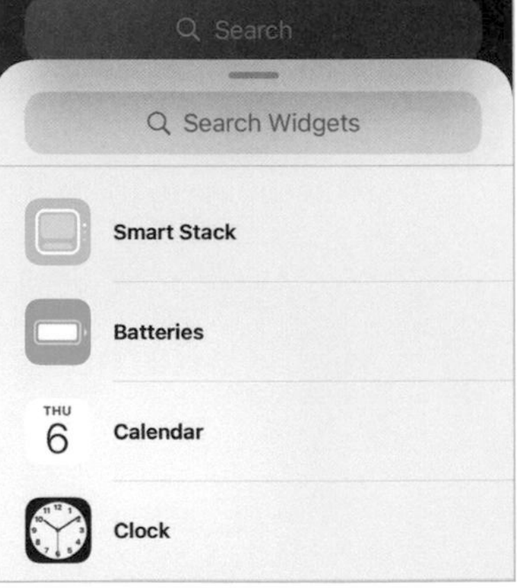

The widgets in the Today View panel can be moved around, so you can order the panel exactly how you want. To do this: press and hold on a widget in the Today View panel until the Today View controls appear. Drag the widget into a new position. Widgets remain at their selected sizes and other widgets will be reordered to accommodate the moved widget accordingly.

4. Tap once on a widget to add it to the Today View panel

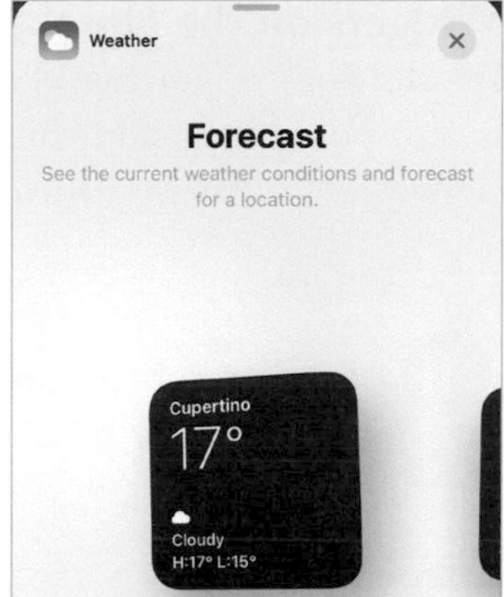

Being able to select widgets at different sizes is a new feature in iOS 14.

5. Swipe from right to left, or tap on the dots toward the bottom of the window, to access the different sizes at which the widget can be used. The sizes are small, medium or large

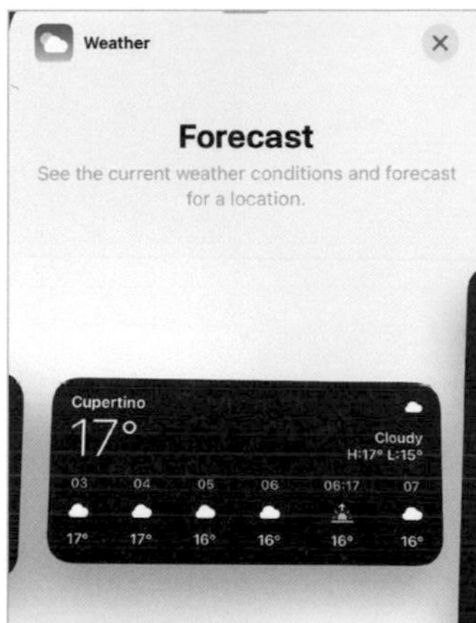

Several instances of the same widget can be added to the Today View panel. This can be useful if the widget is editable (see page 43) and so multiple instances can display different information. For instance, if you add several versions of the Weather widget, they can all display weather forecasts from different locations.

6. Tap once on the **Add Widget** button

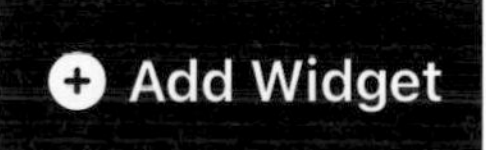

7. The widget is added to the Today View panel, at the size selected in Step 5

Widgets on the Home screen

In addition to viewing widgets in the Today View panel, it is also possible to add them to the Home screen, so they are right there when you turn on your iPhone. To do this:

Some of the widgets that can be added to the Today View panel are real-time widgets. This means that the information they display changes when there are updated details. An example of this is the Google Traffic widget, which can display travel information between two locations.

1. Press and hold anywhere within the Today View panel and tap once on this button at the top of the Today View panel

2. The Today View widgets are displayed

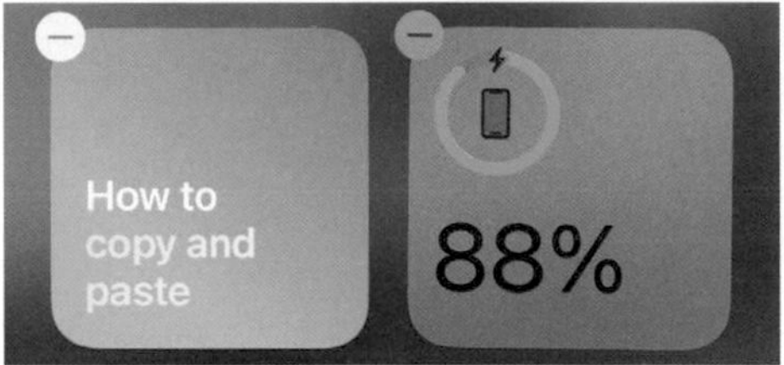

3. Press and hold on the required widget and drag it onto the Home screen. The other apps will move automatically to accommodate the widget. Tap once on this button to remove a widget from the Home screen

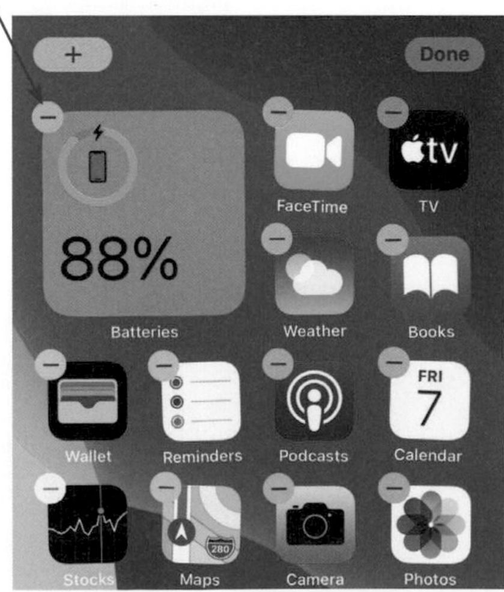

The button in Step 1 can also be accessed by pressing and holding on a free space on the Home screen.

Tap once on the **Done** button in Step 3 to complete the process for adding a widget to the Home screen.

Editing widgets

Some of the widgets in the Today View panel can be edited within the panel. The widgets with this functionality include: Calendar; News; Notes; Reminders; Stocks; and Weather. To edit a widget in the Today View panel:

1. Press and hold on a widget within the Today View panel and tap once on the **Edit Widget** button

2. Edit the widget as required. For instance, for the Weather widget, tap once on the **Location** button

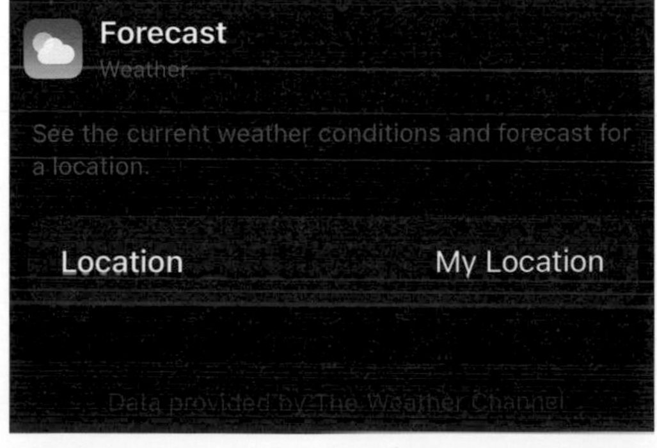

Editable widgets in the Today View panel is a new feature in iOS 14.

If a widget is not editable, the **Edit Widget** option will not be available in Step 1.

Several versions of the Weather app can be included in the Today View panel, to view forecasts from multiple locations.

Smart Stack widgets

Since the amount of space in the Today View panel is limited, it is important to have as much information in each widget as possible. This is where Smart Stack widgets come into their own. Smart Stacks are widgets that contain several elements; e.g. Photos, News, Calendar and Notes. Each item can be scrolled through within the Smart Stack widget. To use Smart Stacks:

Smart Stack widgets in the Today View panel is a new feature in iOS 14.

1. Press and hold anywhere within the Today View panel and tap once on this button at the top of the Today View panel

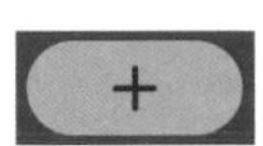

2. In the widgets window, tap once on the **Smart Stack** widget

3. Select the required size for the Smart Stack and tap once on the **Add Widget** button at the bottom of the screen to add the Smart Stack widget to the Today View panel

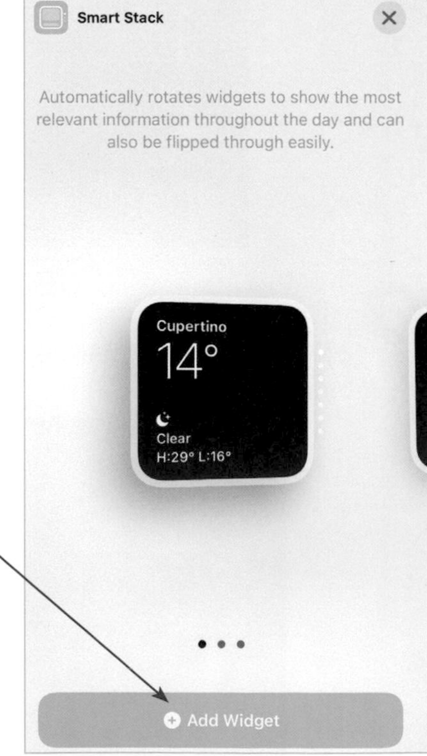

Swipe left or right on the icon in Step 3 to select the size for the Smart Stack.

The number of elements in the Smart Stack widget is indicated by the dots to the right of the widget. Swipe up on the Smart Stack to view the items.

Editing a Smart Stack widget

Once a Smart Stack has been added to the Today View panel it can be edited in various ways:

1. Press and hold on a Smart Stack widget and tap once on the **Edit Stack** button (or tap once on the **Remove Stack** button)

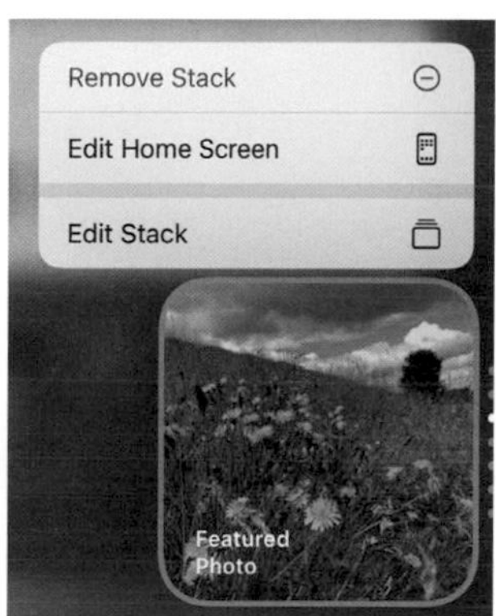

2. The items within the Smart Stack are displayed. Tap the **Smart Rotate** button **On** to enable the items within the Smart Stack to be displayed in the correct way for viewing

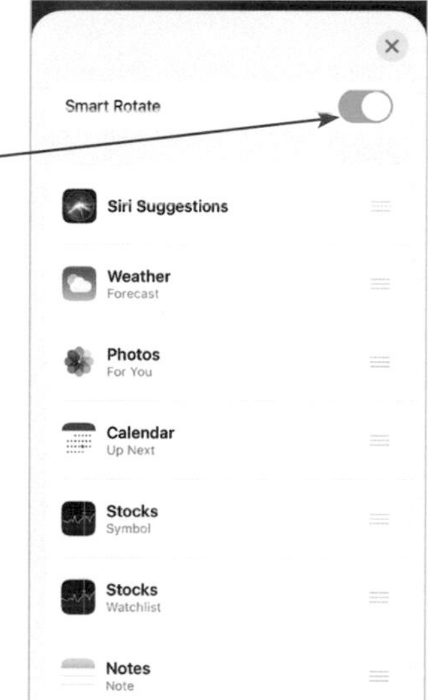

3. Press and hold here and drag an item to change its order within the Smart Stack

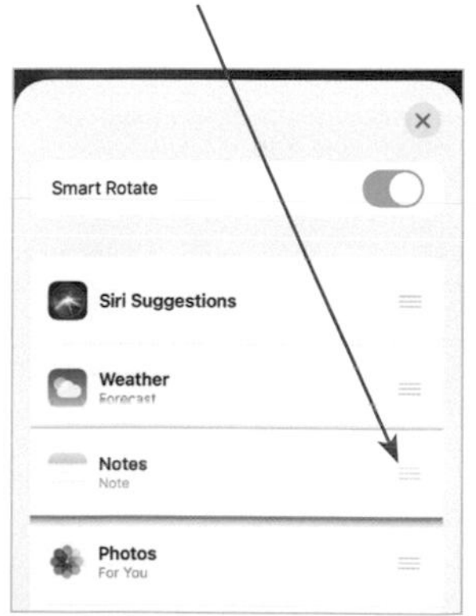

Swipe from right to left on a widget in Step 2 and tap once on the **Delete** button to remove it from the Smart Stack.

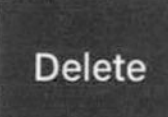

Using the Dock

By default, there are four apps on the Dock at the bottom of the iPhone's screen. These are the four that Apple thinks you will use most frequently:

- **Phone**, for making and receiving calls.
- **Safari**, for web browsing.
- **Messages**, for text messaging.
- **Music**.

With iOS 14, some of the pre-installed (built-in) apps can be deleted from your iPhone. These are indicated by a cross in the top left-hand corner when you press and hold on an app.

You can rearrange the order in which the Dock apps appear:

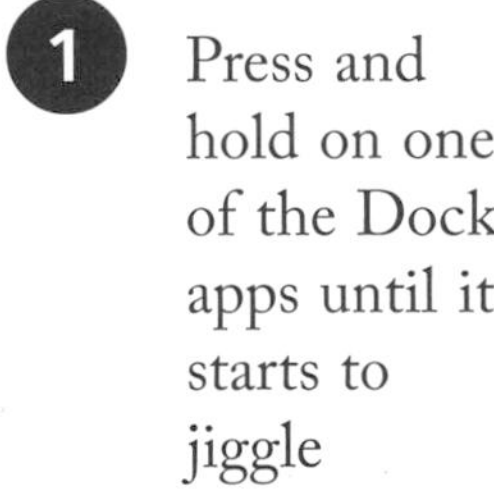

1. Press and hold on one of the Dock apps until it starts to jiggle

2. Drag the app into its new position

3. Swipe up from the bottom of the screen to exit editing mode

Just above the Dock is a line of small white dots. These indicate how many screens of content there are on the iPhone. Tap on one of the dots to go to that screen. (If the App Library is being used instead of separate Home screens – see pages 36-37 – there will only be two dots.)

Adding and removing Dock apps

You can also remove apps from the Dock and add new ones:

1. To remove an app from the Dock, press and hold it, and drag it onto the main screen area

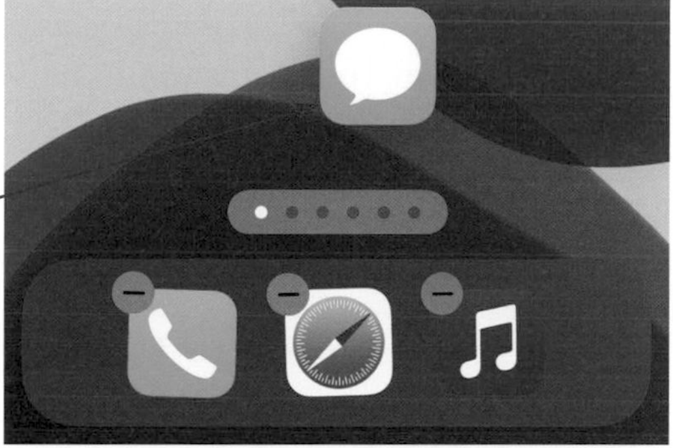

If items are removed from the Dock they are still available in the same way from the main screen.

2. To add an app to the Dock, press and hold it, and drag it onto the Dock

Editing mode can also be exited by tapping on the **Done** button in the top right-hand corner of the screen.

Done

3. The number of items that can be added to the Dock is restricted to a maximum of four, as the icons do not resize

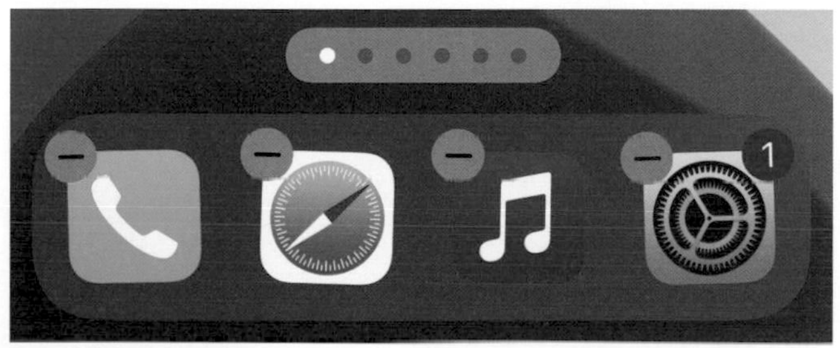

For older iPhones that have a physical Home button and run iOS 14, press the Home button to exit editing mode for the Dock.

4. Swipe up from the bottom of the screen to exit editing mode

Using the Control Center

The Control Center is a panel containing some of the most commonly-used options within the **Settings** app.

Accessing the Control Center

The Control Center can be accessed with one swipe from any screen within iOS 14, and it can also be accessed from the Lock screen. To set this up:

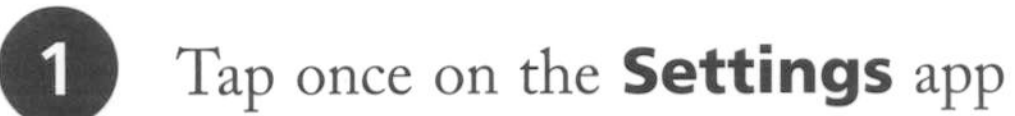

1. Tap once on the **Settings** app

2. Tap once on the **Control Center** tab, and drag the **Access Within Apps** button On or Off to specify if the Control Center can be accessed from there (if it is Off, it can still be accessed from any Home screen)

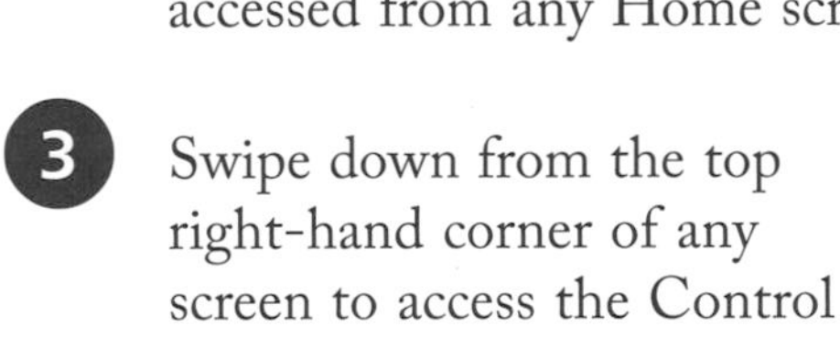

3. Swipe down from the top right-hand corner of any screen to access the Control Center

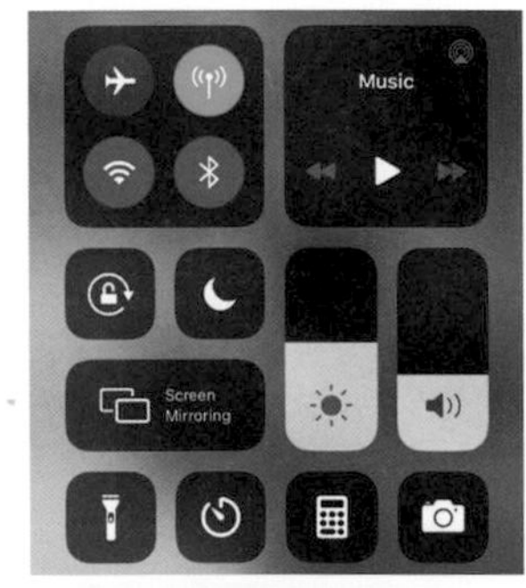

Control Center functionality

The Control Center contains items that have differing formats and functionality. To access these:

1. Press and hold on the folder of four icons in the top left-hand corner, to access the **Airplane Mode**, **Cellular Data**, **Wi-Fi**, **Bluetooth**, **AirDrop**, and **Personal Hotspot** options

For older iPhones that have a physical Home button and run iOS 14, access the Control Center by swiping up from the bottom of the screen.

AirDrop is the functionality for sharing items wirelessly between compatible devices. Tap once on the **AirDrop** button in the Control Center and specify whether you want to share with **Receiving Only**, **Contacts Only** or **Everyone**. Once AirDrop is set up, you can use the **Share** button in compatible apps to share items such as photos with any other AirDrop users in the vicinity.

2 Press on the **Music** button to expand the options for music controls, including playing or pausing items and changing the volume. Tap once on this icon to send music from your iPhone to other compatible devices, such as AirPod headphones or HomePods, Apple's wireless speakers

3 Tap once on individual buttons to turn items On or Off (they change color depending on their state)

4 Drag on these items to increase or decrease the screen brightness and the volume

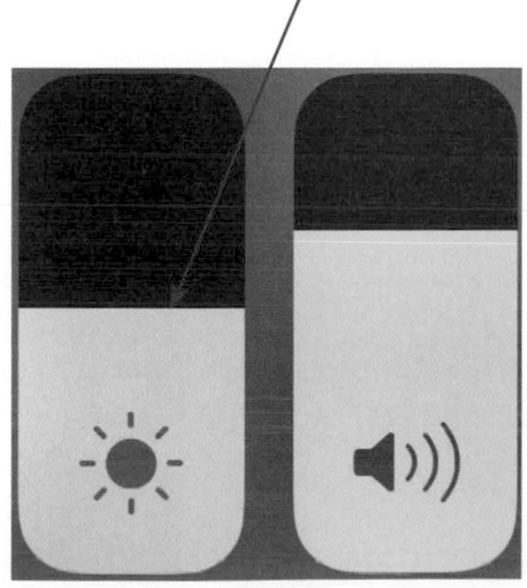

The Control Center cannot be disabled from being accessed from the Home screen.

...cont'd

Control Center controls

Access the items in the Control Center as follows:

- Tap once on this button to turn **Airplane Mode** On or Off, for network connections.

- Tap once on this button to turn **Cellular Data** On or Off, for cellular networks.

- Tap once on this button to turn **Wi-Fi** On or Off.

- Tap once on this button to turn **Bluetooth** On or Off.

- Tap once on this button to activate **AirDrop** for sharing items with other AirDrop users.

- Tap once on this button to turn **Personal Hotspot** On or Off, to use your iPhone as a hotspot for connecting another device like an iPad or Mac computer to the internet.

- Tap once on this button to **Lock** or **Unlock** screen rotation. If it is locked, the screen will not change when you change the orientation.

- Tap once on this button to turn **Do Not Disturb** mode On or Off.

- Tap once on this button to turn on the **Flashlight**. Press on the button to change the intensity of the flashlight.

- Tap once on this button to access the **Clock**, including a stopwatch and timer. Press on the button to access a scale for creating reminders.

- Tap once on this button to open the **Calculator** app.

- Tap once on this button to open the **Camera** app.

Hot tip

Bluetooth can be used to connect to other compatible devices, using radio waves over short distances up to approximately 20 meters. Both devices must have Bluetooth turned On and be "paired" with each other. This links them together so that content such as photos can be shared between them.

Press and hold on the Camera button to access options for taking a "selfie" (a self-portrait), recording a video, taking a portrait or taking a portrait selfie.

Customizing the Control Center

The Control Center can be customized so that items can be added or removed. To do this:

1. Tap once on the **Settings** app

2. Tap once on the **Control Center** tab

3. Drag the **Access Within Apps** button **On**, to enable the Control Center to be accessed from any open app

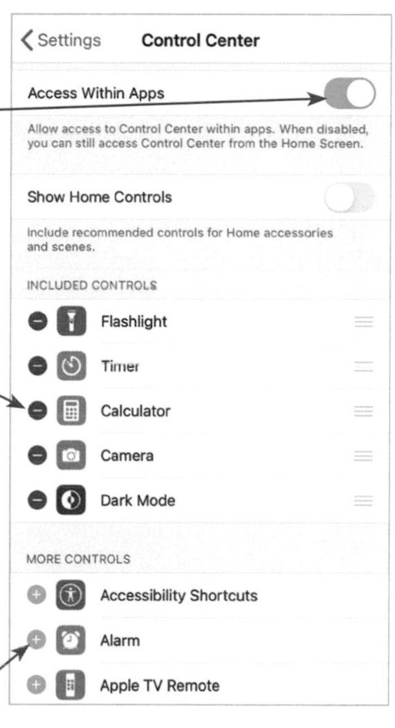

4. The items currently in the Control Center are shown at the top of the window; those that can be added are below them. Tap once on a red icon to remove an existing item, or tap once on a green icon to add new items to the Control Center

5. Items that are added in Step 4 are included in the Control Center, and can be accessed from here

Dark Mode can be activated by tapping on this button in the Control Center.

If the button is not visible by default in the Control Center, access **Settings** > **Control Center** > **Customize Controls** and tap once on the green button next to **Dark Mode**.

The flashlight and the camera can both be accessed directly from buttons on the Lock screen too.

Setting Up Siri

Siri is the iPhone's voice assistant that provides answers to a variety of verbal questions by looking at content in your iPhone and also web services. You can ask Siri questions relating to the apps on your iPhone, and also general questions such as weather conditions around the world or sports results. Initially, Siri can be set up within the **Settings** app:

Hot tip

Siri can be used to translate English words or phrases into different languages. More languages have been added in iOS 14, and there are now over 65 different language pairs.

1. Tap once on the **Settings** app

2. Tap once on the **Siri & Search** tab

Options for Siri

Within the Siri settings there are options for its operation:

Translations can also be done with the Translate app. This is a new feature in iOS 14.

1. Drag the **Listen for "Hey Siri"** button **On** if you want to be able to access Siri just by saying **Hey Siri**

2. Make selections here for the language, voice type, feedback and your own details to use with Siri

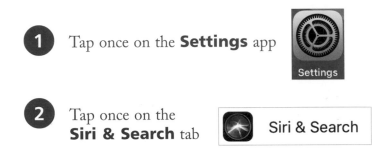

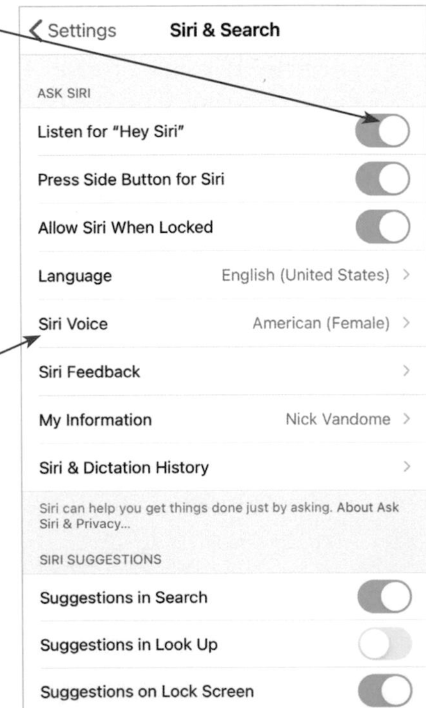

3. If using "Hey Siri", it has to be set up by training it for your voice. Tap once on the **Continue** button

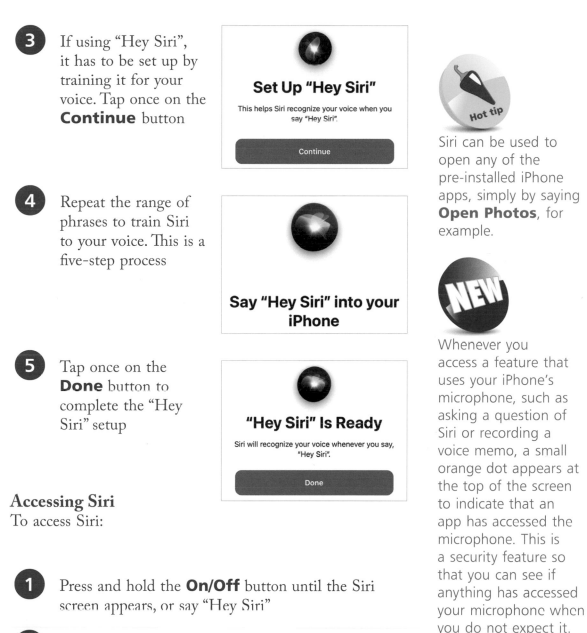

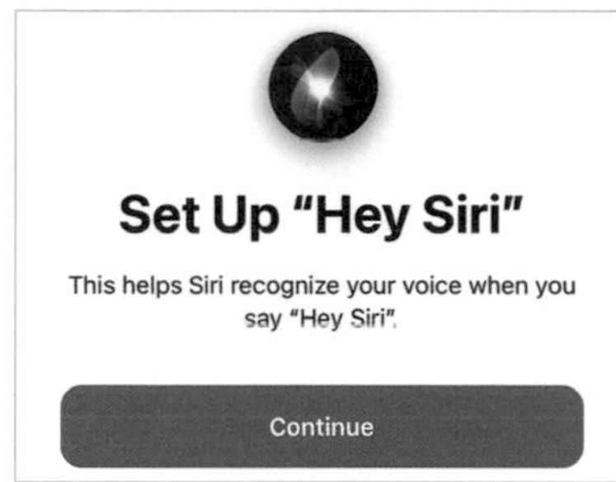
Set Up "Hey Siri"
This helps Siri recognize your voice when you say "Hey Siri".
Continue

4. Repeat the range of phrases to train Siri to your voice. This is a five-step process

Say "Hey Siri" into your iPhone

5. Tap once on the **Done** button to complete the "Hey Siri" setup

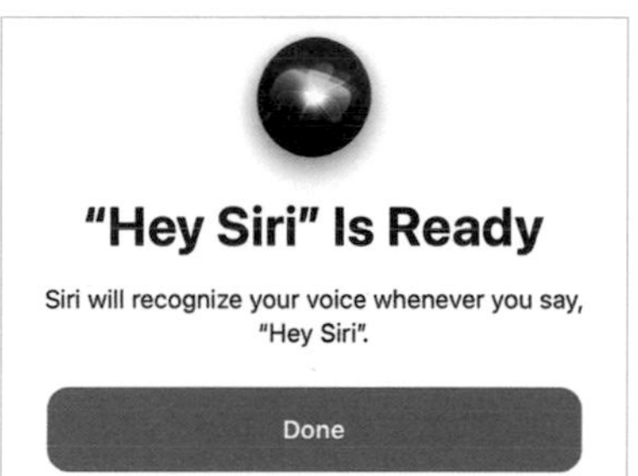
"Hey Siri" Is Ready
Siri will recognize your voice whenever you say, "Hey Siri".
Done

Accessing Siri

To access Siri:

1. Press and hold the **On/Off** button until the Siri screen appears, or say "Hey Siri"
2. The Siri icon appears at the bottom of the screen. Ask your question to Siri. After the reply, tap once on this icon to ask another question

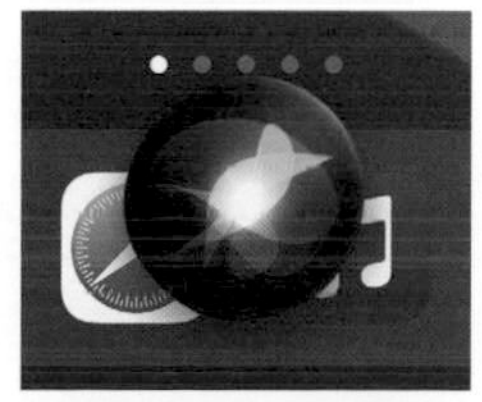

Hot tip

Siri can be used to open any of the pre-installed iPhone apps, simply by saying **Open Photos**, for example.

NEW

Whenever you access a feature that uses your iPhone's microphone, such as asking a question of Siri or recording a voice memo, a small orange dot appears at the top of the screen to indicate that an app has accessed the microphone. This is a security feature so that you can see if anything has accessed your microphone when you do not expect it. This is a new feature in iOS 14.

Finding Things with Siri

Siri is very versatile and can be used for a wide range of functions, including finding things on your iPhone, searching the web, getting weather forecasts, finding locations, and even playing music.

Hot tip

Siri can also display specific contacts. Say **Show me...** followed by the person's name to view their details (if they are in your contacts – see pages 80-81).

Accessing your apps

To use Siri to find things on your iPhone:

1. Access Siri as shown on page 53

2. To find something from your iPhone apps, ask a question such as **Open my contacts**

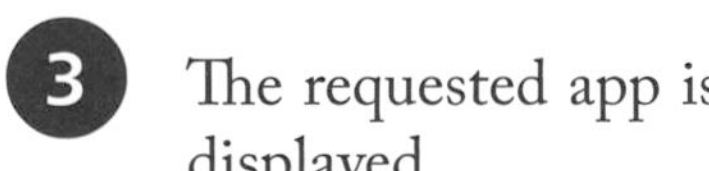

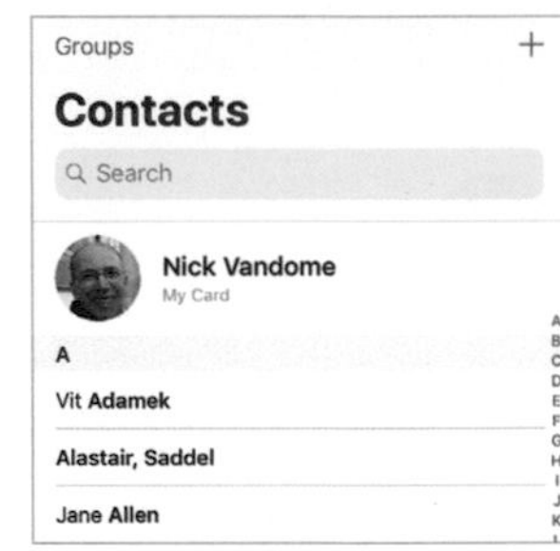

3. The requested app is displayed

Hot tip

Siri can also read out your information: open an item such as calendar appointments and then say **Read appointment**.

Getting the weather

You can ask Siri for weather forecasts for locations around the world. Simply ask for the weather in a certain city or location. The current weather details are displayed. Tap once on this to view a more extensive forecast.

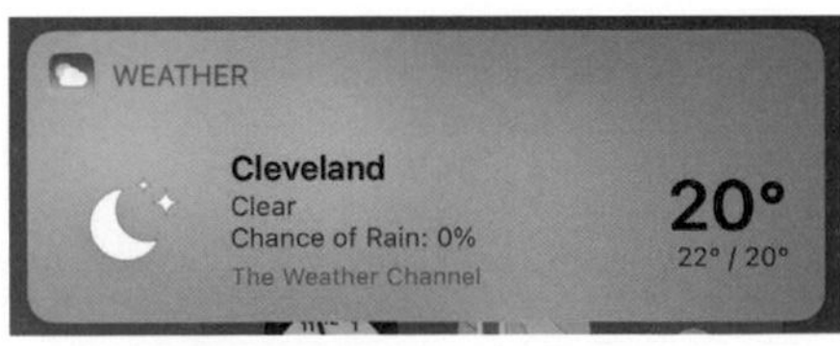

Don't forget

You can ask for weather forecasts for specific periods such as **Today** or **This Week**. However, Siri's power of forecasting only stretches to 10 days in the future.

Finding locations

Siri is also effective for viewing locations within the Maps app. This can be done on an international, national or city level. Siri can also be used to get directions.

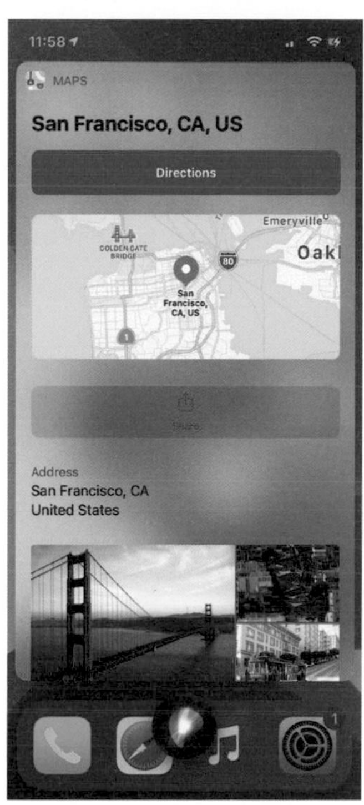

Searching locally

If Location Services is turned On for Siri, then you can ask for local information such as **Show the nearest Italian restaurants**. Siri can also be used to call restaurants and provide directions.

Playing music

You can use Siri to play any of the music that you have in the Music app. Simply ask Siri to play a track and it will start playing. (Music can be downloaded from the iTunes Store app; see pages 163-165 for more details.) To stop a song, simply say **Stop playing**.

Siri can be used with certain third-party apps to perform tasks such as booking a taxi or a restaurant table.

Items can also be searched for using the Spotlight Search option. This can be accessed by swiping downwards on the Home screen and entering a keyword or phrase in the Search box at the top of the window. Items can be searched for on your iPhone (including apps), or use the **Search Web** button at the bottom of the window to search the web.

Siri can also play a whole album as well as individual tracks.

Reachability

Because of the size of the iPhone 12, the iPhone 12 mini, the iPhone 12 Pro, and the iPhone 12 Pro Max, it is not always easy to access all items with one hand. This is overcome by a feature known as Reachability, which can be accessed from any screen of the iPhone. This moves the items on the screen to the bottom half, and they can all be accessed from here.

Hot tip

If the Reachability function is not turned On by default, go to **Settings** > **Accessibility** > **Touch** and drag the **Reachability** button **On**, underneath the **Interaction** heading.

1. By default, all items on the screen take up the whole area
2. Swipe down on the bottom edge of the screen

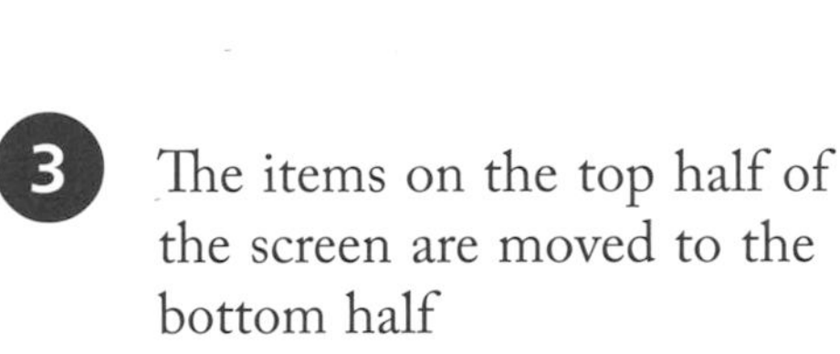

3. The items on the top half of the screen are moved to the bottom half

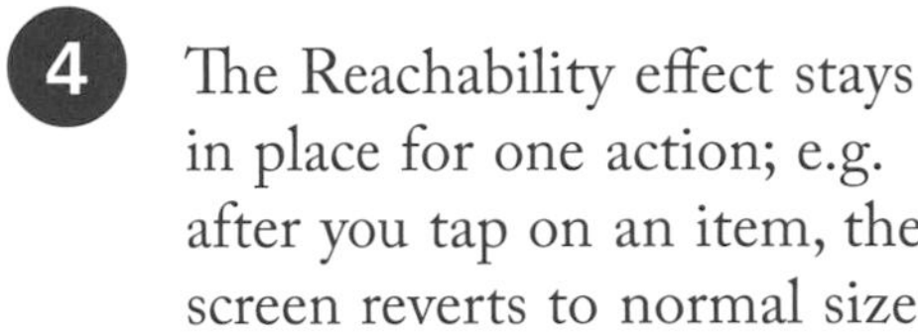

4. The Reachability effect stays in place for one action; e.g. after you tap on an item, the screen reverts to normal size

The **Display & Brightness** settings can also be used to increase the text size for supported apps. Tap once on the **Text Size** button to access a slider with which you can set the required text size.

Night Shift

Getting a good night's sleep is becoming increasingly recognized as a vital and often overlooked element of our overall health and wellbeing. One of the biggest obstacles to this is the amount of artificial lighting that we experience at night time, such as street lighting, lighting in the home, and the light emitted from mobile devices such as iPhones. This type of light is known as "blue light", and it is one of the most restrictive in terms of getting a good night's sleep, as it is the type of light that instructs the body that it is time to be awake and alert. One option to reduce the impact of blue light from your iPhone is to use the Night Shift option, which reduces the amount of blue light that is emitted.

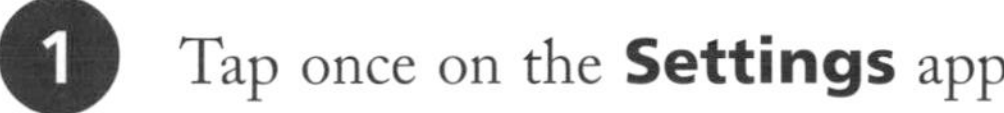

1. Tap once on the **Settings** app

2. Tap once on the **Display & Brightness** tab

3. Tap once on the **Night Shift** button

Night Shift Off

4. Drag the **Scheduled** button **On** and tap once on the **From/To** option to set a time period for when Night Shift is applied

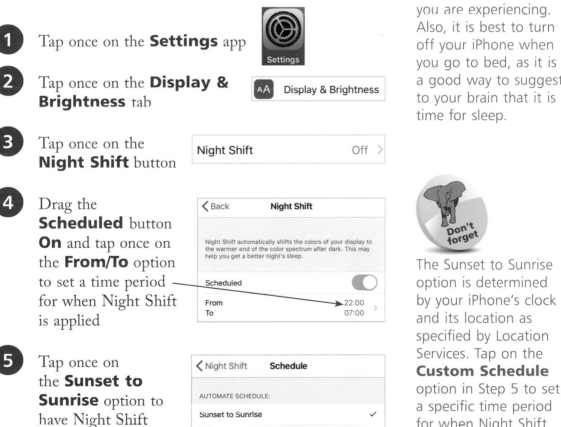

Back Night Shift

Night Shift automatically shifts the colors of your display to the warmer end of the color spectrum after dark. This may help you get a better night's sleep.

Scheduled

From 22:00
To 07:00

5. Tap once on the **Sunset to Sunrise** option to have Night Shift applied for this period

Night Shift Schedule

AUTOMATE SCHEDULE:

Sunset to Sunrise ✓

Custom Schedule

Try not to use your iPhone, or other mobile devices, for prolonged periods just before you go to bed, to reduce the amount of artificial light that you are experiencing. Also, it is best to turn off your iPhone when you go to bed, as it is a good way to suggest to your brain that it is time for sleep.

The Sunset to Sunrise option is determined by your iPhone's clock and its location as specified by Location Services. Tap on the **Custom Schedule** option in Step 5 to set a specific time period for when Night Shift operates.

Do Not Disturb

The iPhone is excellent for keeping up-to-date with calls and notifications from apps, so you never miss an important call or message. However, there can be times when constant notifications can be too intrusive, and you may wish to have a period of quiet without having to turn off notifications completely. This can be achieved with the Do Not Disturb feature. To use this:

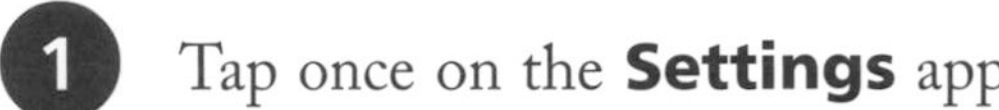

1. Tap once on the **Settings** app

2. Tap once on the **Do Not Disturb** tab

3. Drag the **Do Not Disturb** button **On** to activate **Do Not Disturb**, so that calls and notifications will be muted

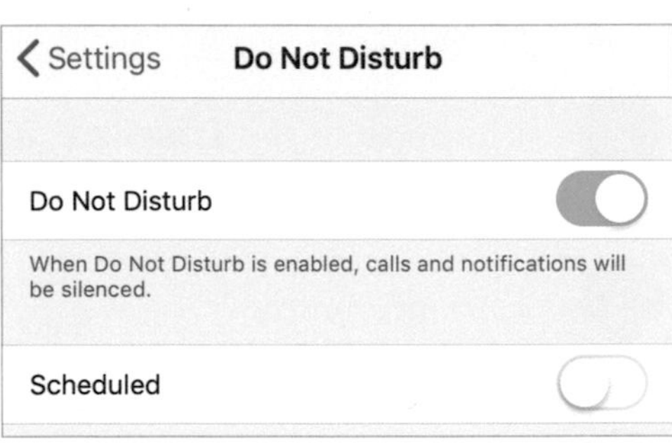

4. Drag the **Scheduled** button **On** to set a specific time period for Do Not Disturb to be applied

5. Drag the **Dim Lock Screen** button **On** to darken the Lock screen and send any notifications to the Notifications Center

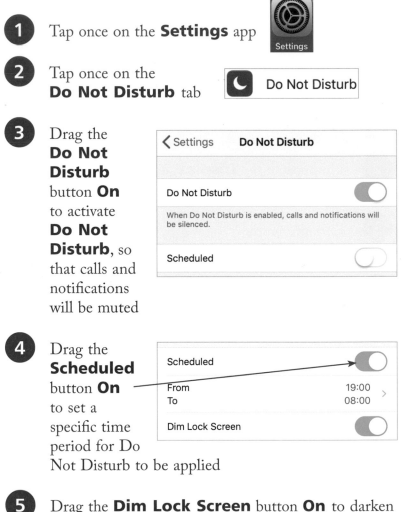

Tap once on the **From/To** option in Step 4 to set the time period for Do Not Disturb.

Using Haptic Touch

One of the features using touch on the iPhone is Haptic Touch. This can be used to activate different options for certain apps, depending on the length of the press on an item. For instance, a single press or tap can be used to open an app. However, if you press for longer (long press) on the app then different options appear in a Quick Actions menu:

Quick Actions

Quick Actions can be used to perform actions without opening an app first (this is for the Camera app):

1. Press and hold on an app until the Quick Actions menu is displayed. For the **Camera** app this includes options for taking a selfie, recording a video, taking a portrait, or taking a selfie portrait

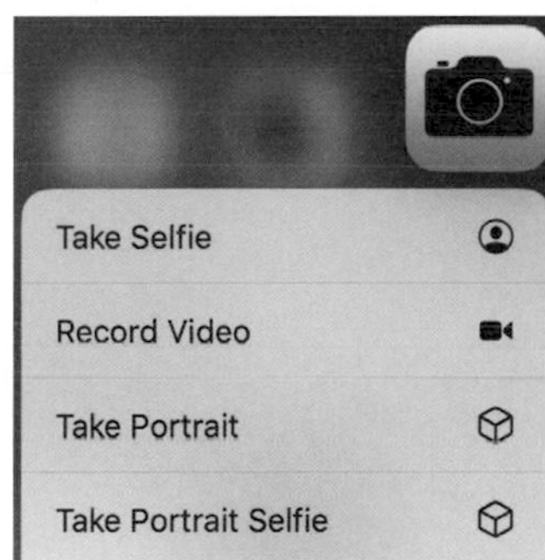

Using Haptic Touch within apps

Haptic Touch can also be used to quickly access menus for selected items within compatible apps. To do this, using the Photos app:

1. Open the Photos app and press and hold on a photo
2. The photo is displayed, along with the Quick Actions menu with options relating to the photo

Other apps that use Haptic Touch and Quick Actions include: Safari and Mail. In the Safari app, perform a long press on a web page link to view a preview of the page and a Quick Actions menu. In the Mail app, perform a long press on an email in your Inbox to access options for replying to or organizing the email message.

Screen Time

The amount of time that we spend on our digital devices is a growing issue in society, and steps are being taken to let us see exactly how much time we are spending looking at our cellular phone screens. In iOS 14, a range of screen-use options can be monitored with the Screen Time feature. To use this:

1. Select **Settings** > **Screen Time**

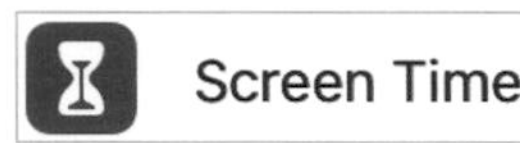

2. Tap once on the **Turn On Screen Time** button

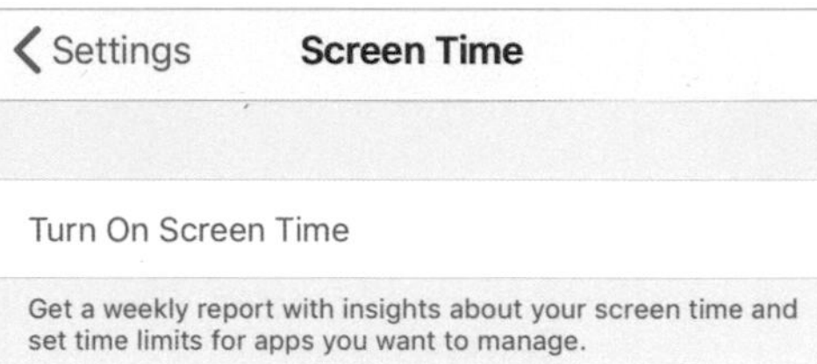

3. Options for using Screen Time are displayed

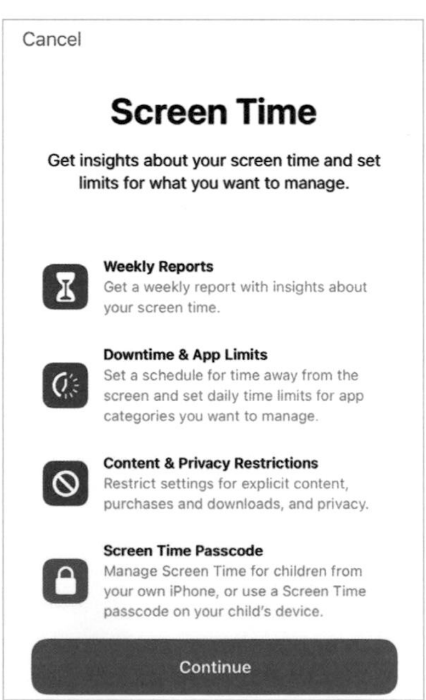

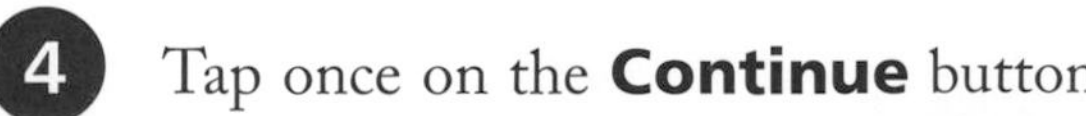

4. Tap once on the **Continue** button

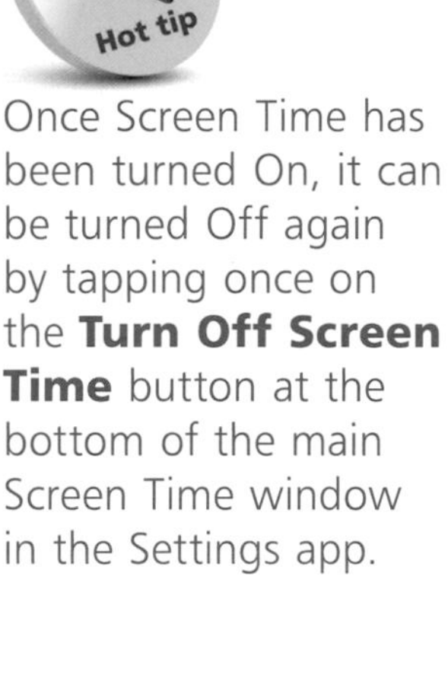

Once Screen Time has been turned On, it can be turned Off again by tapping once on the **Turn Off Screen Time** button at the bottom of the main Screen Time window in the Settings app.

5. Screen Time can be set up for your own use, or on a child's iPhone. If it is set up for a child, there will be more parental control options for controlling the type of content that is available. Tap once on the required option

6. The current Screen Time usage is shown at the top of the Screen Time settings screen. More Screen Time options are shown below – see pages 62-63

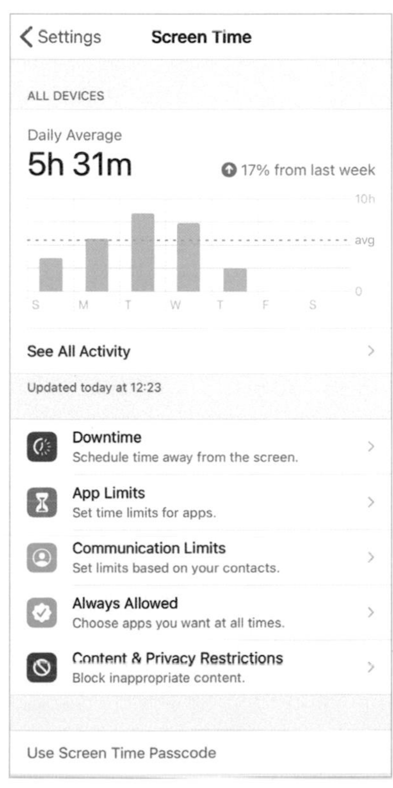

If Screen Time is set up for a child (**This is My Child's iPhone** option in Step 5), you can create a parental passcode that is required for a child to continue using the iPhone once one of the Screen Time restrictions have been reached. (See pages 64-65 for details.)

Each week, the Screen Time option produces a report based on the overall usage, as shown in Step 6. The report is identified with a notification when it is published each week.

Options for Screen Time

Within the Screen Time settings there are options for viewing apps and content on your iPhone. Each of these is accessed on the main Screen Time settings page:

For each Screen Time option, the main Screen Time page can be reached by tapping once on the back arrow at the top of the relevant window.

1. Tap once on **Downtime**

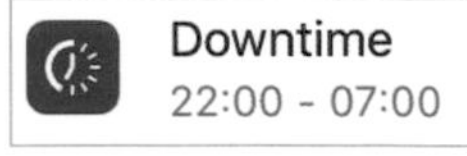

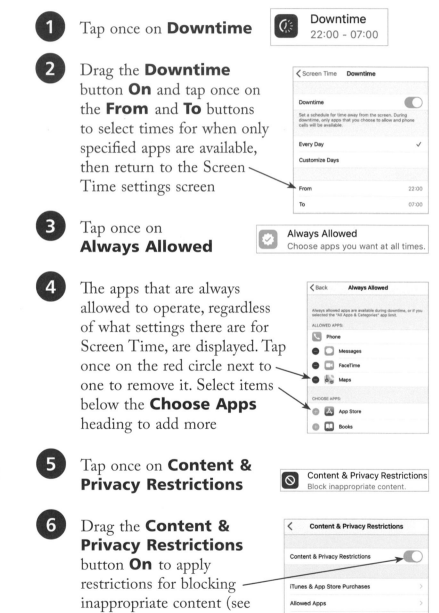

2. Drag the **Downtime** button **On** and tap once on the **From** and **To** buttons to select times for when only specified apps are available, then return to the Screen Time settings screen

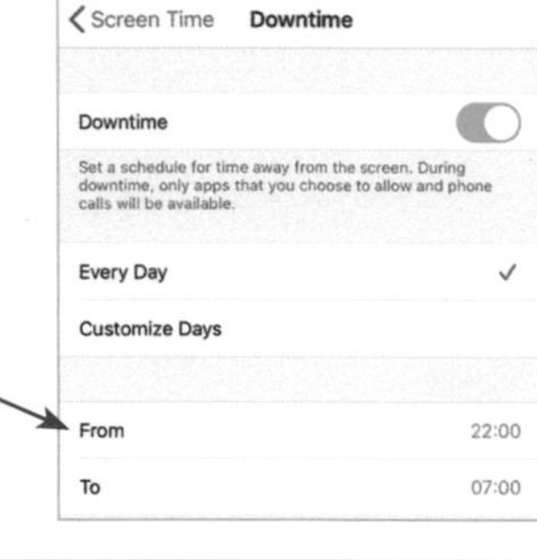

3. Tap once on **Always Allowed**

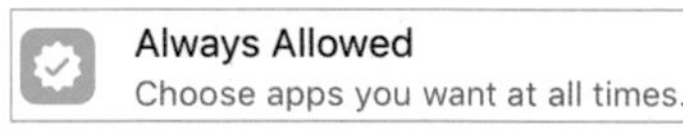

4. The apps that are always allowed to operate, regardless of what settings there are for Screen Time, are displayed. Tap once on the red circle next to one to remove it. Select items below the **Choose Apps** heading to add more

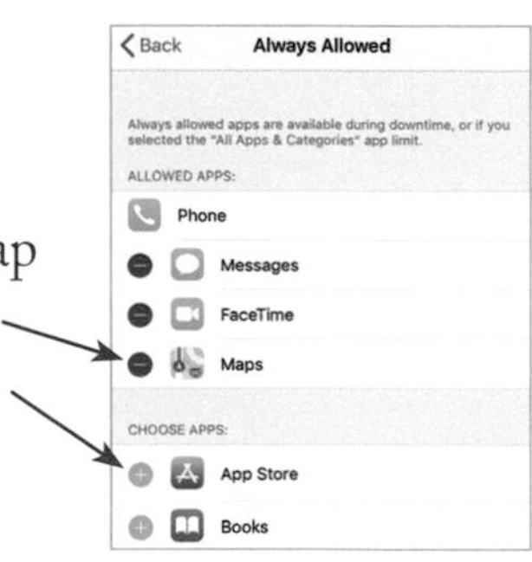

5. Tap once on **Content & Privacy Restrictions**

6. Drag the **Content & Privacy Restrictions** button **On** to apply restrictions for blocking inappropriate content (see page 65 for details)

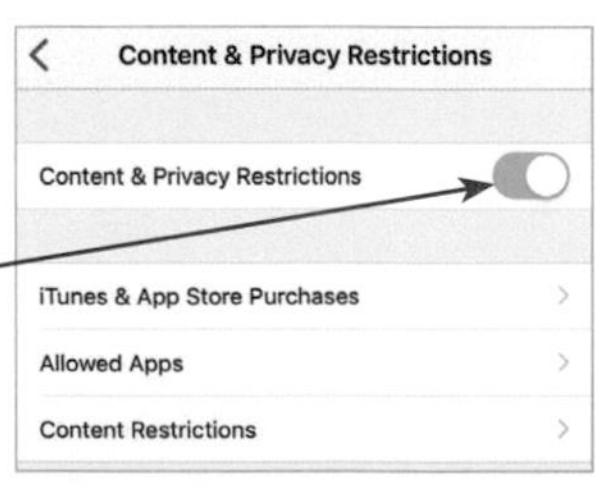

Content restrictions can be applied for content from the iTunes Store (such as age ratings for movies and TV shows), web content, and search content accessed by Siri, the iPhone's digital voice assistant.

7. Tap once on **App Limits**

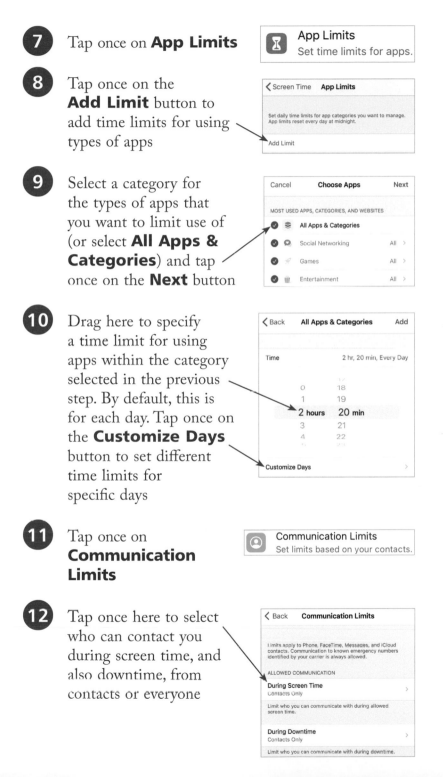

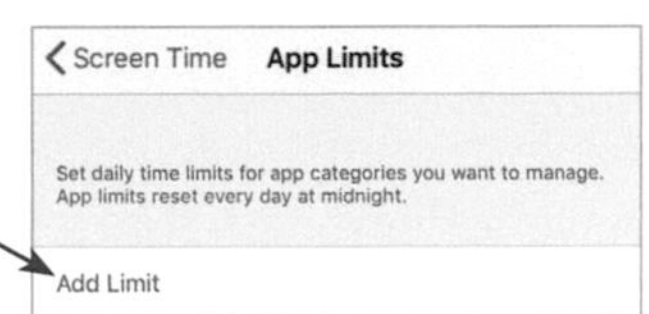

8. Tap once on the **Add Limit** button to add time limits for using types of apps

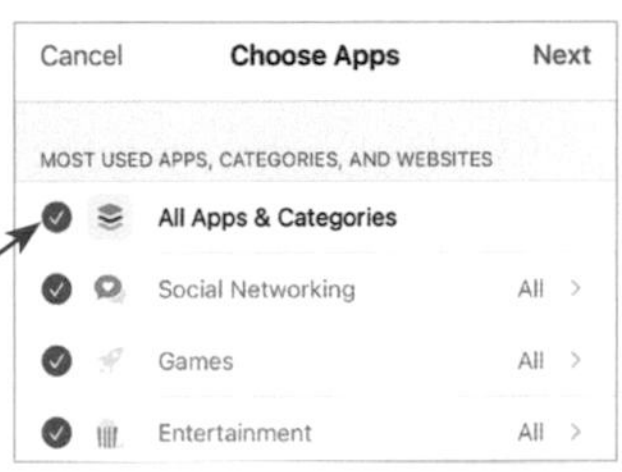

Set daily time limits for app categories you want to manage. App limits reset every day at midnight.

9. Select a category for the types of apps that you want to limit use of (or select **All Apps & Categories**) and tap once on the **Next** button

2 hr, 20 min, Every Day

10. Drag here to specify a time limit for using apps within the category selected in the previous step. By default, this is for each day. Tap once on the **Customize Days** button to set different time limits for specific days

11. Tap once on **Communication Limits**

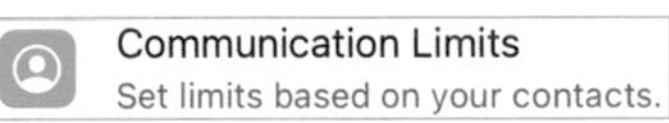

Set limits based on your contacts.

12. Tap once here to select who can contact you during screen time, and also downtime, from contacts or everyone

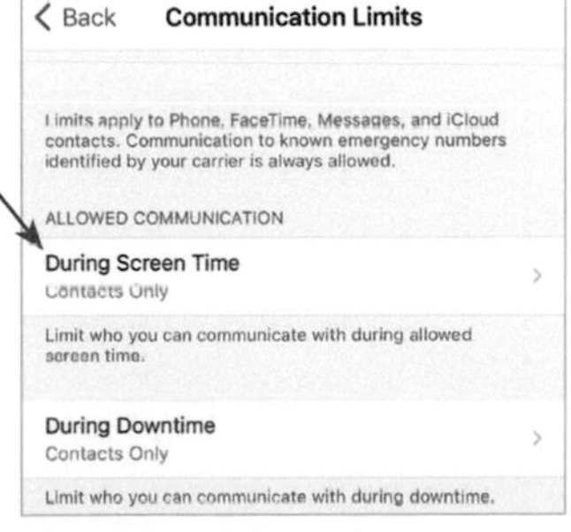

Limits apply to Phone, FaceTime, Messages, and iCloud contacts. Communication to known emergency numbers identified by your carrier is always allowed.

Limit who you can communicate with during allowed screen time.
During Downtime

Limit who you can communicate with during downtime.

The time limit for using apps is only a suggestion, and the apps do not stop operating when the limit is reached. Instead, a notification appears to alert you to the fact that the time limit has been reached. Tap once on the **Ignore Limit** button to continue using the app.

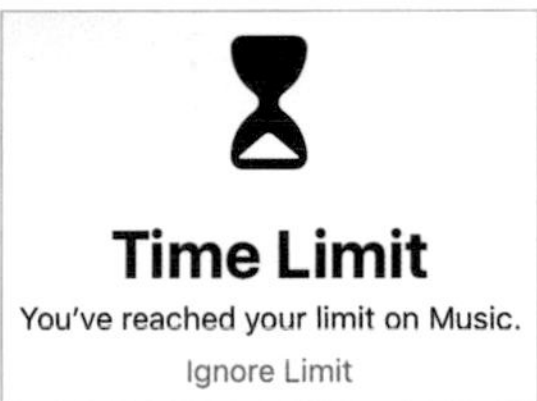

You've reached your limit on Music.

Select an option for how long you want to ignore the time limit.

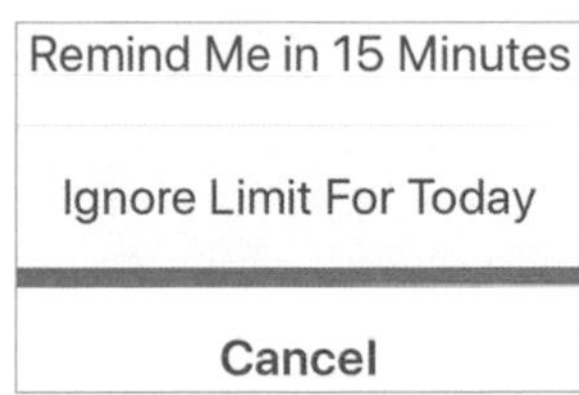

Remind Me in 15 Minutes

Restrictions for Children

If children or grandchildren have access to an iPhone, this can raise genuine concerns about the type of content that they may be accessing, and also the amount of time that they spend on the device. The Screen Time options can be used to apply specific settings for a child, so that you can have a degree of control over what they are using. These are similar to the standard Screen Time options, but they can be set up with an initial selection of wizards, and it is also possible to include a parental passcode that has to be entered when limits are reached. To set up restrictions for children:

Don't forget

A wizard is a feature that guides you through the installation or setup of a software program or hardware device.

1. Access Screen Time options as shown on page 60, and tap once on the **This is My Child's iPhone** button

Back
Is This iPhone for Yourself or Your Child?
Screen time for a child's iPhone lets you set up additional parental controls.
This is My iPhone
This is My Child's iPhone

2. Select options for **Downtime**, for when the device cannot be used, by tapping on the **Start** and **End** options and specifying a time for each. Tap once on the **Set Downtime** button to apply these times

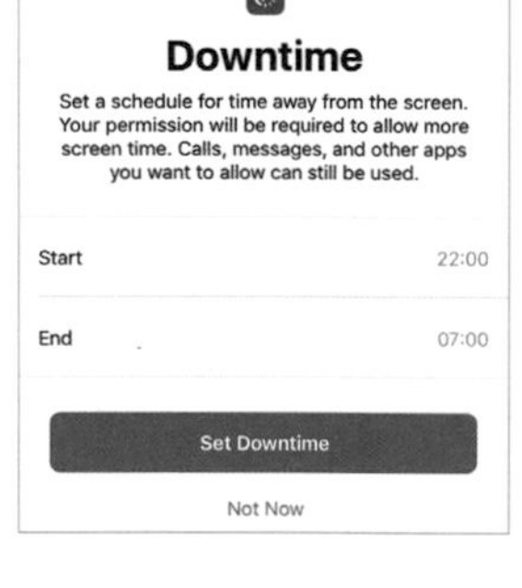
Downtime
Set a schedule for time away from the screen. Your permission will be required to allow more screen time. Calls, messages, and other apps you want to allow can still be used.
Start
22:00
End
07:00
Set Downtime
Not Now

Hot tip

Drag the **Block At End of Limit** button **On** on the App Limits page that is accessed from Step 3, to ensure that apps cannot continue to be used after the time limit unless a parental passcode is entered.

Block At End of Limit 

3. On the **App Limits** screen, tap once on the category of apps that you want to restrict and tap once on the **Set App Limit** button. Enter time controls as shown in Step 10 on page 63

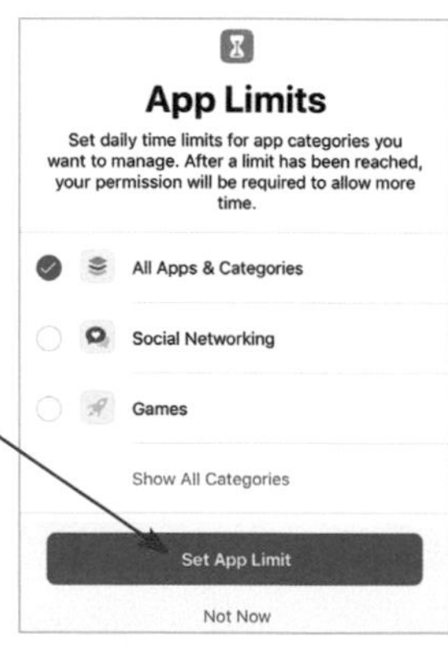
App Limits
Set daily time limits for app categories you want to manage. After a limit has been reached, your permission will be required to allow more time.
All Apps & Categories
Social Networking
Games
Show All Categories
Set App Limit
Not Now

4. On the **Content & Privacy** screen, tap once on the **Continue** button

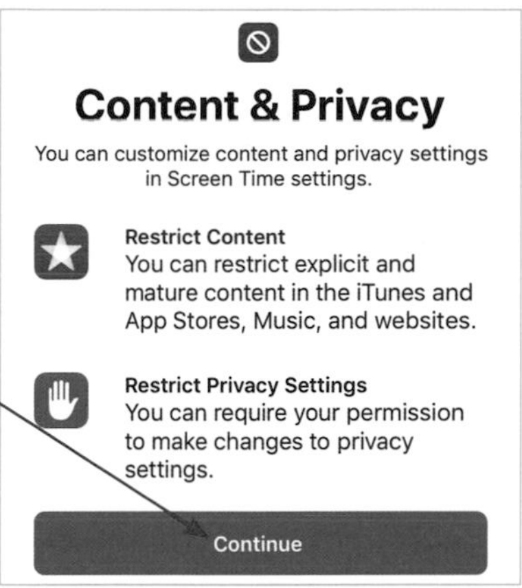

Content & Privacy
You can customize content and privacy settings in Screen Time settings.
Restrict Content
You can restrict explicit and mature content in the iTunes and App Stores, Music, and websites.
Restrict Privacy Settings
You can require your permission to make changes to privacy settings.
Continue

5. Create a parental passcode that will be required to access any restricted content, or override a time limit once it has been reached

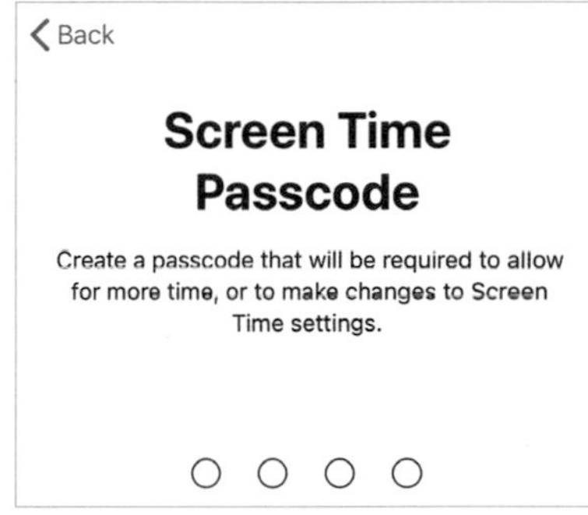

6. Tap once on the **Content & Privacy Restrictions** option, as shown on page 62. Drag the **Content & Privacy Restrictions** button **On** to access the available options. These include options for limiting **iTunes & App Store Purchases**, specifying **Allowed Apps**, and selecting **Content Restrictions** for media such as movies, TV shows, music, and books that have been downloaded from the iTunes Store

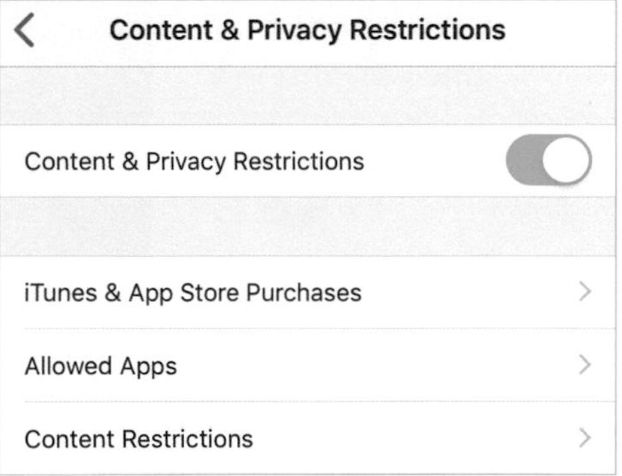

A passcode can also be created for your own Screen Time settings. This prevents anyone else from changing these settings, and can be used to allow more time once a time limit is reached.

If you are setting restrictions for a child or a grandchild, tell them about it and explain what you are doing and why.

About Apple Pay

Apple Pay is Apple's service for mobile, contactless payment. It can be used by adding credit, debit, and store cards to your iPhone via the Wallet app, and then paying for items by using your Face ID (or Touch ID for older iPhones) as authorization for payment. Credit, debit, and store cards have to be issued by banks or retailers that support Apple Pay, and there are an increasing number that do so, with more joining on a regular basis. Outlets also have to support Apple Pay but this, too, is increasing and, given the success of the iPhone, is likely to grow at a steady rate.

Cards can also be added to the Wallet at any time from **Settings** > **Wallet & Apple Pay** > **Add Card**. This can also be used to create cash payments to people, using the Messages app. See page 103 for details.

Setting up Apple Pay

To use Apple Pay you have to first add your cards to your iPhone (and be signed in to iCloud):

1. Tap once on the **Wallet** app

2. Tap once on the **Add Credit or Debit Card** link, or tap once on this button

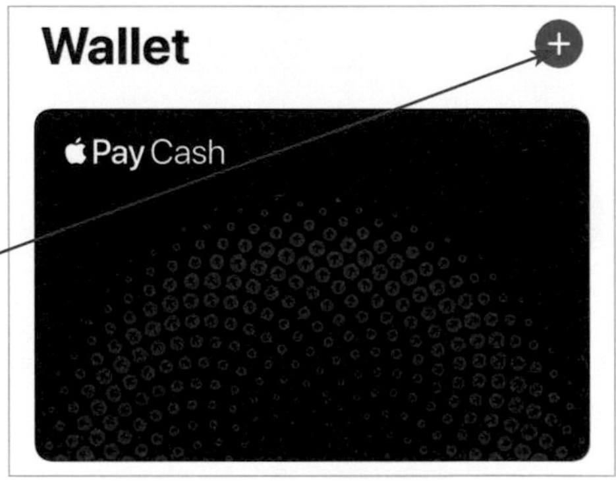

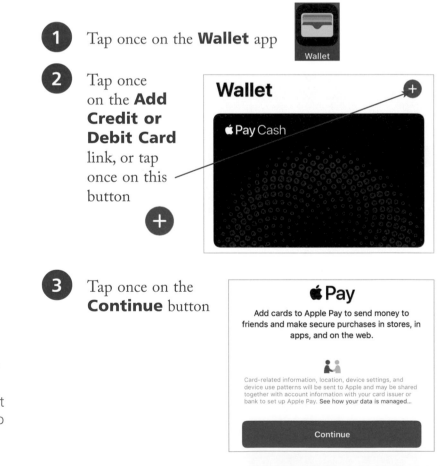

3. Tap once on the **Continue** button

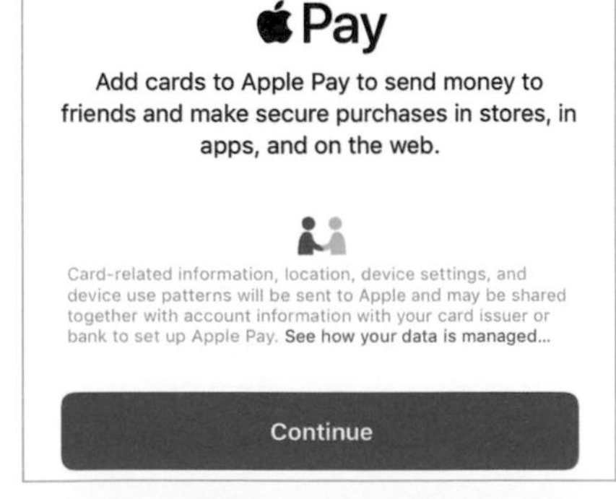

Pay
Add cards to Apple Pay to send money to friends and make secure purchases in stores, in apps, and on the web.
Card-related information, location, device settings, and device use patterns will be sent to Apple and may be shared together with account information with your card issuer or bank to set up Apple Pay. See how your data is managed...
Continue

If your bank does not yet support Apple Pay then you will not be able to add your credit or debit card details to the Wallet app.

4. The card details can be added to the Wallet app by taking a photo of the card. Place the card on a flat surface, and position it within the white box. The card number is then added automatically. Alternatively, tap once on **Enter Card Details Manually**

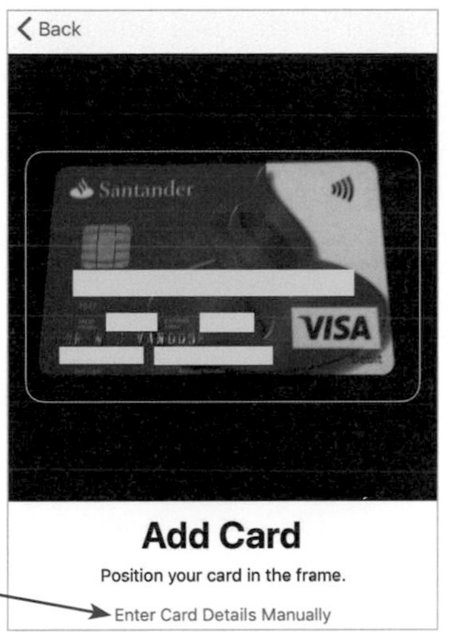

5. Once the card details have been added, your bank or store card issuer has to verify your card. This can be done either by a text message or a phone call

6. Once the Apple Pay wizard is completed, details of the card appear in the Wallet app

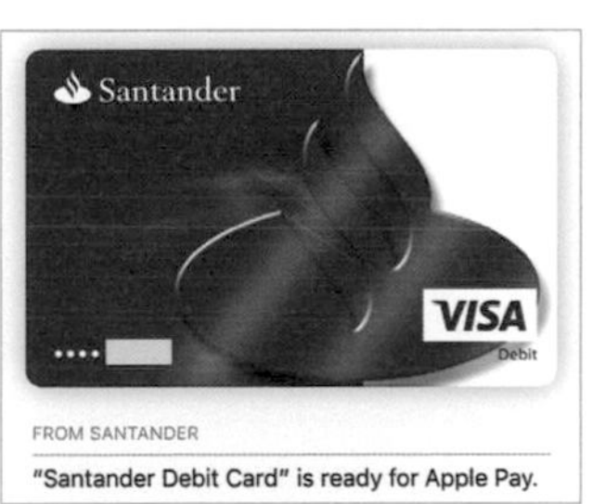

7. To pay for items with Apple Pay, open the **Wallet** app and tap once on the card you want to use. Hold your iPhone up to the contactless payment card reader. Press the **On/Off** button twice and look at the phone screen to authorize the payment with Face ID. (Retailers must have a contactless card reader in order for Apple Pay to be used)

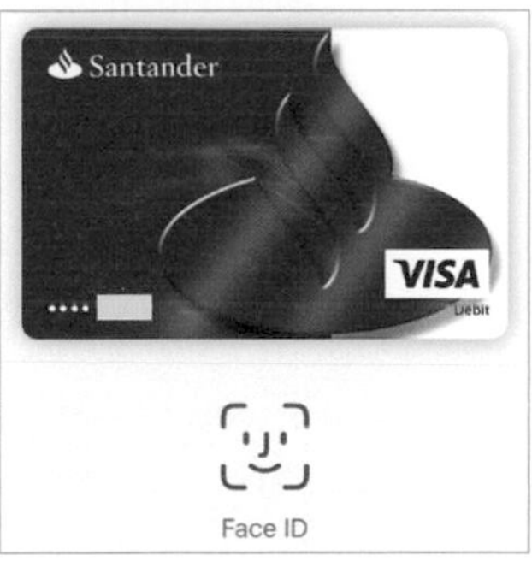

Obtaining your card number using the camera is not always completely accurate. Take the photo in good light, always check the number afterwards, and amend it if necessary.

Although no form of contactless payment is 100% secure, Apple Pay does offer some security safeguards. One is that no card information is passed between the retailer and the user; the transaction is done by sending an encrypted token that is used to authorize the payment. Also, the use of the Face ID process ensures another step of authorization that is not available with all other forms of contactless payment.

Using the EarPods

There are no EarPods provided with the iPhone 12 models. If an existing pair of EarPods is used with an iPhone 12, it will need to be one with a Lightning Connector, since the iPhone 12 does not have a separate headphone connection.

The iPhone EarPods are not only an excellent way to listen to music and other audio on your iPhone; they can also be used in a variety of ways with the phone function.

The EarPods contain three main controls:

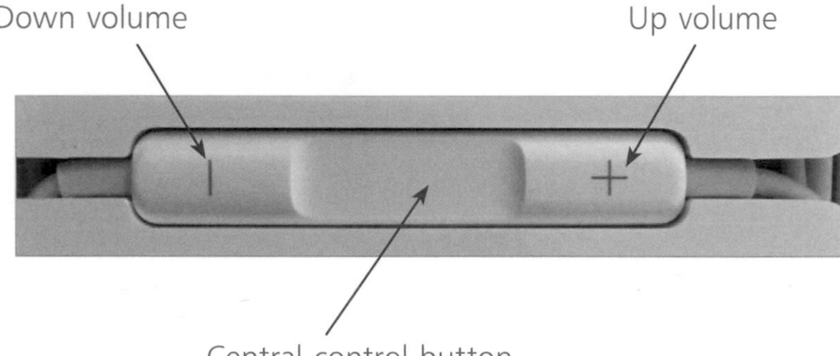

- Plug in the EarPods to use them to hear someone who is calling you. Speak normally, and the other person will be able to hear you via the EarPods' in-built microphone.
- Click once in the middle of the control button to answer an incoming call.
- Press and hold in the middle of the control button for a couple of seconds (until you hear two beeps) to decline an incoming call.
- Click once in the middle of the control button to end the current call.
- If you are on a call and receive another one, click once in the middle of the control button to put the first call on hold and activate the second call.
- Press and hold in the middle of the control button to dial a number using Voice Control, whereby you can speak the required number.
- Click on the control button when playing a music track to pause it. Click again to restart it. Double-click on the control button to move to the next track. Triple-click on the control button to move back to the previous track.

All models of the iPhone can be used with AirPods, the wireless headphones from Apple.

3 Head in the iCloud

iCloud, the online storage service, is at the heart of the iPhone for backing up your content and sharing it with other family members.

What is iCloud?

iCloud is the Apple online storage and backup service that performs a number of valuable functions:

- It makes your content available across multiple devices. The content is stored in the iCloud and then pushed out to other iCloud-enabled devices, including the iPad, iPod Touch, and other Mac or Windows computers.
- It enables online access to your content via the iCloud website. This includes your iCloud email, photos, contacts, calendar, reminders, and documents.
- It can back up the content on your iPhone.

To use iCloud you must have an Apple ID. This can be done when you first set up your iPhone, or at a later date. Once you have registered for and set up iCloud, it works automatically so you do not have to worry about anything.

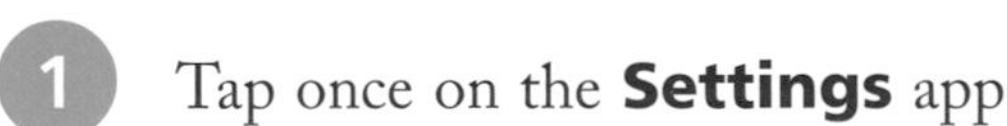

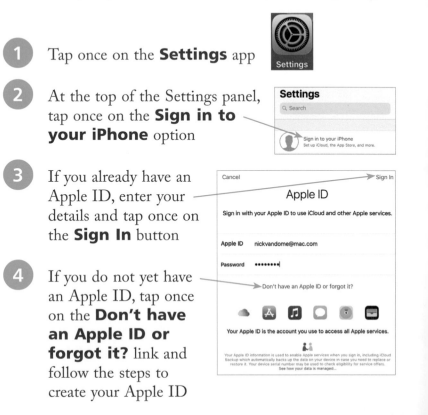

1. Tap once on the **Settings** app

2. At the top of the Settings panel, tap once on the **Sign in to your iPhone** option

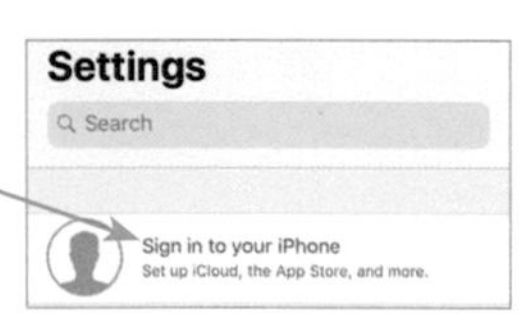

3. If you already have an Apple ID, enter your details and tap once on the **Sign In** button

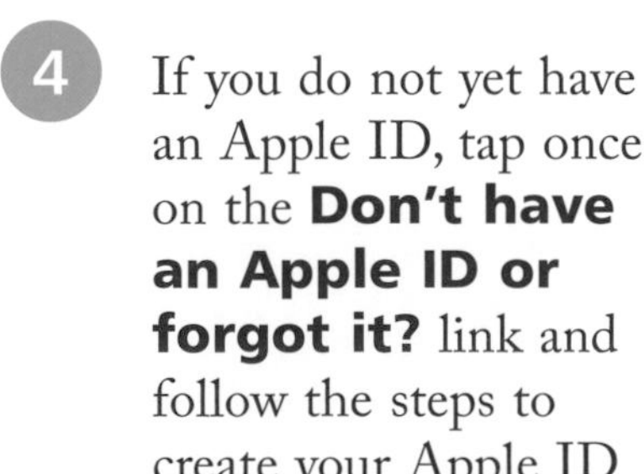

4. If you do not yet have an Apple ID, tap once on the **Don't have an Apple ID or forgot it?** link and follow the steps to create your Apple ID

Don't forget

It is free to register for and set up a standard iCloud account.

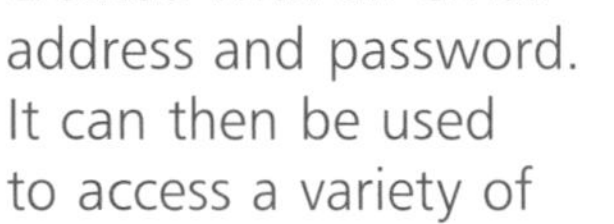

Don't forget

An Apple ID can be created with an email address and password. It can then be used to access a variety of services, including the iTunes Store, the Book Store, and the App Store.

Hot tip

To access your iCloud account through the website, access www.icloud.com and enter your Apple ID details.

iCloud Settings

Once you have set up your iCloud account, you can then apply settings for how it works. Once you have done this, you will not have to worry about it again:

1. Tap once on the **Apple ID** section in the Settings app

2. Tap once on the **iCloud** button

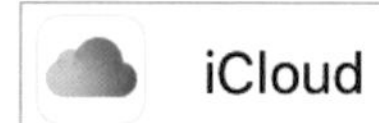

3. Drag these buttons **On** for each item that you wish to be included in iCloud. Each item is then saved and stored in the iCloud and made available to your other iCloud-enabled devices

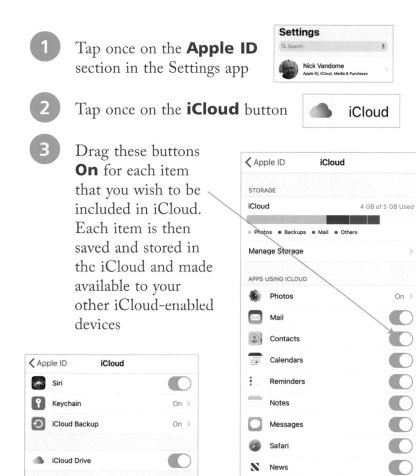

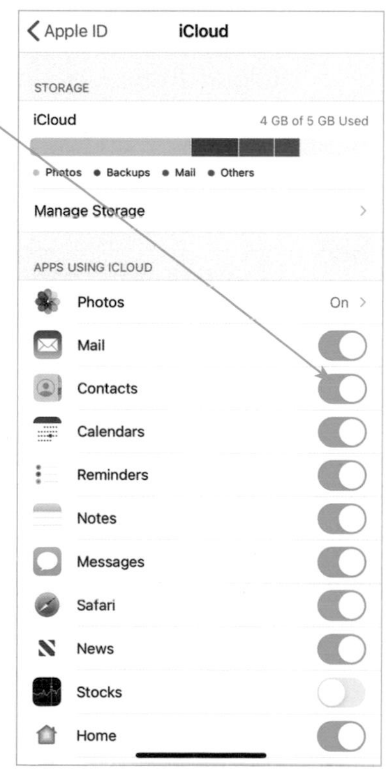

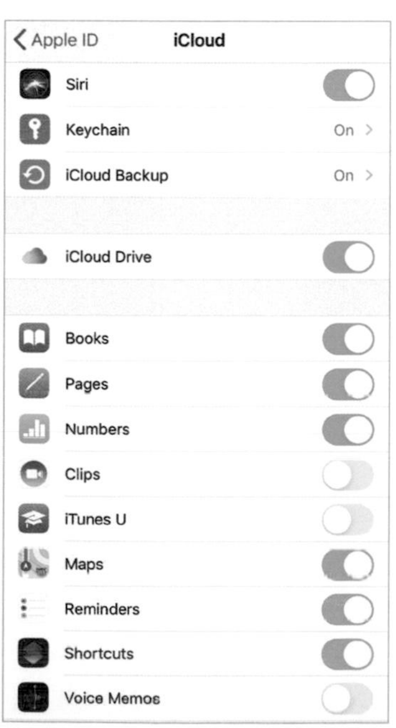

Adding iCloud Storage

By default, you get 5GB of free storage space with an iCloud account. However, you can upgrade this if you want to increase the amount of storage. To do this:

If you have a lot of photos stored in iCloud then you may want to consider increasing your amount of storage.

1. Access **iCloud** in Settings, as shown on page 71

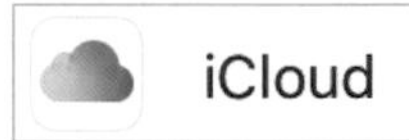

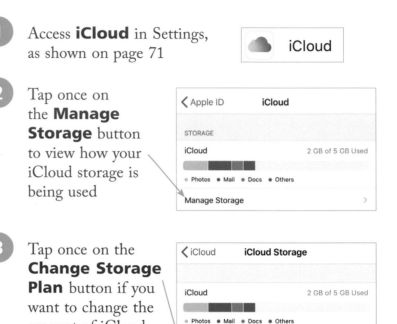

2. Tap once on the **Manage Storage** button to view how your iCloud storage is being used

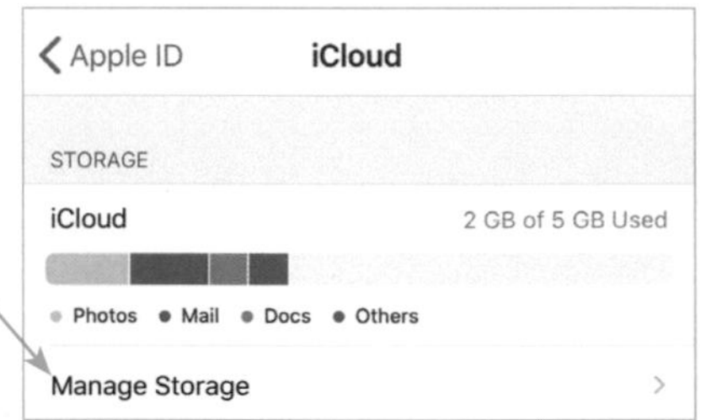

3. Tap once on the **Change Storage Plan** button if you want to change the amount of iCloud storage

4. Tap once on one of the storage options to buy this amount of iCloud storage. (Note: charges appear in your local currency.) Tap once on the amount of storage you require, to complete the change of storage

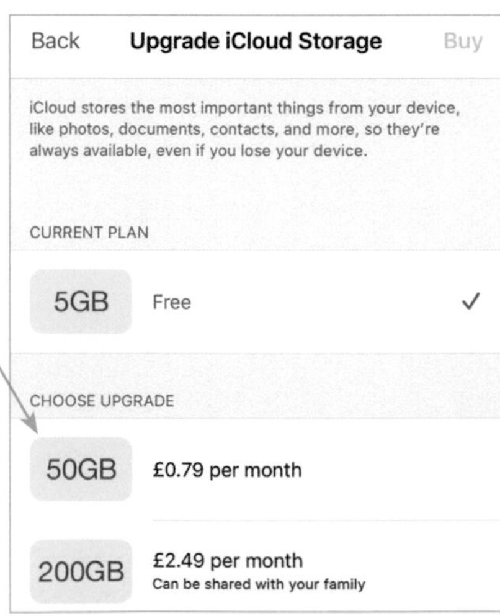

Backing Up with iCloud

All of the items that you have assigned to iCloud (see page 71) should be backed up there automatically. However, if this is not happening you may need to turn on the iCloud Backup. To do this:

1. Within the iCloud section of the Settings app, tap once on the **iCloud Backup** button, if it is **Off**

iCloud Backup Off >

2. The iCloud Backup button will be **Off**

< iCloud Backup

BACKUP

iCloud Backup

Automatically back up data such as your photo library, accounts, documents, Home configuration, and settings when this iPhone is plugged in, locked, and connected to Wi-Fi. Learn more...

3. Drag the **iCloud Backup** button **On** to enable automatic backup for iCloud. This has to be done over Wi-Fi, with the iPhone locked and plugged in

< iCloud
Backup
BACKUP
iCloud Backup
Automatically back up data such as your photo library, accounts, documents, Home configuration, and settings when this iPhone is plugged in, locked, and connected to Wi-Fi. Learn more...
Back Up Now
iCloud Backup will occur later when plugged-in, locked, and connected to Wi-Fi.

4. You can also back up manually at any time by tapping once on the **Back Up Now** button

Hot tip

Another useful iCloud function is the iCloud Keychain (**Settings** > **Apple ID** > **iCloud** > **Keychain**). If this is enabled, it can keep all of your passwords and credit card information up-to-date across multiple devices and remember them when you use them on websites. The information is encrypted and controlled through your Apple ID.

About Family Sharing

As everyone gets more and more digital devices it is becoming increasingly important to be able to share content with other people, particularly family members. In iOS 14, the Family Sharing function enables you to share items that you have downloaded from the App Store, such as music and movies, with up to six other family members, as long as they have an Apple ID. Once this has been set up, it is also possible to share items such as family calendars and photos, and even see where family members are on a map. To set up and start using Family Sharing:

If children are using Family Sharing you can specify that they have to ask permission before downloading content from the iTunes Store, the App Store or the Book Store. To do this, select them in the **Family Sharing** section of the **iCloud** settings and drag the **Ask To Buy** button **On**. For each purchase you will be sent a notification asking for approval.

1. Access the Apple ID section within the Settings app, as shown on page 71

2. Tap once on the **Family Sharing** button

3. Tap once on the **Set Up Your Family** button

4. Tap once on the **Invite People** button to invite family members, or friends, to join your Family Sharing. This includes music, storage plans, iTunes and App Store purchases, and location sharing for finding a lost or stolen Apple device

Invite People

5. Complete the setup process by confirming your iCloud account, and specify a payment method for items that are purchased through Family Sharing

6. The available options are displayed on the Family Sharing page

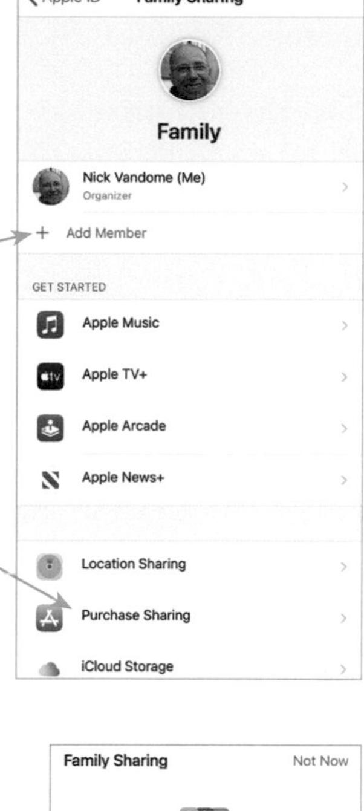

7. Tap once on the **Add Member** button to invite another family member

8. Tap once on the **Purchase Sharing** button to share your purchased content with members of your Family Sharing group

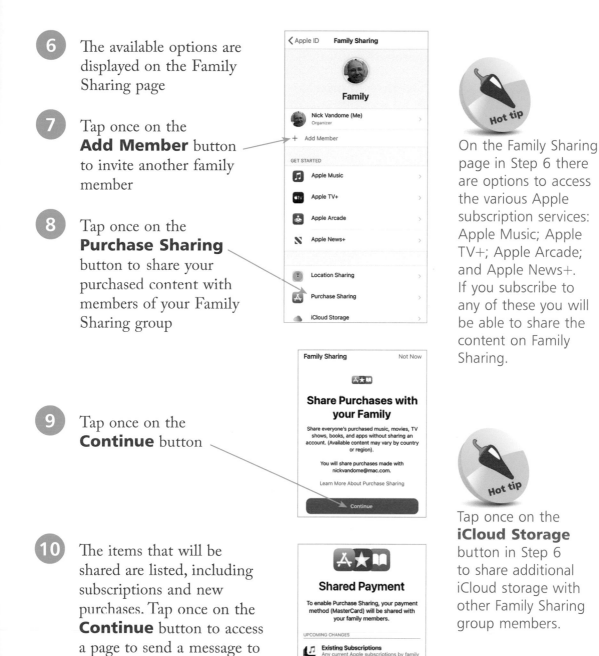

On the Family Sharing page in Step 6 there are options to access the various Apple subscription services: Apple Music; Apple TV+; Apple Arcade; and Apple News+. If you subscribe to any of these you will be able to share the content on Family Sharing.

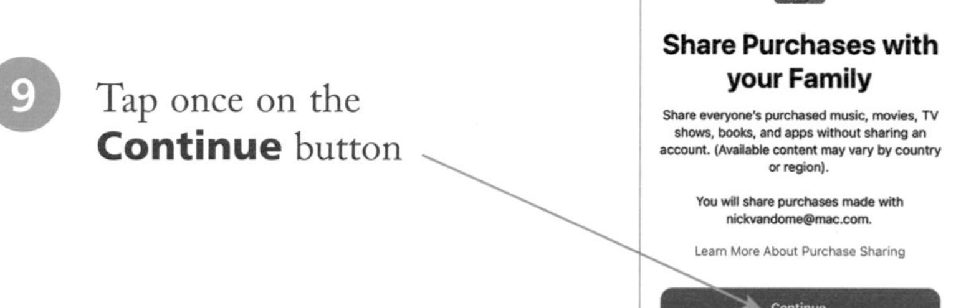

9. Tap once on the **Continue** button

Tap once on the **iCloud Storage** button in Step 6 to share additional iCloud storage with other Family Sharing group members.

10. The items that will be shared are listed, including subscriptions and new purchases. Tap once on the **Continue** button to access a page to send a message to all of the members of the Family Sharing group to let them know that you will pay for their purchases via Family Sharing

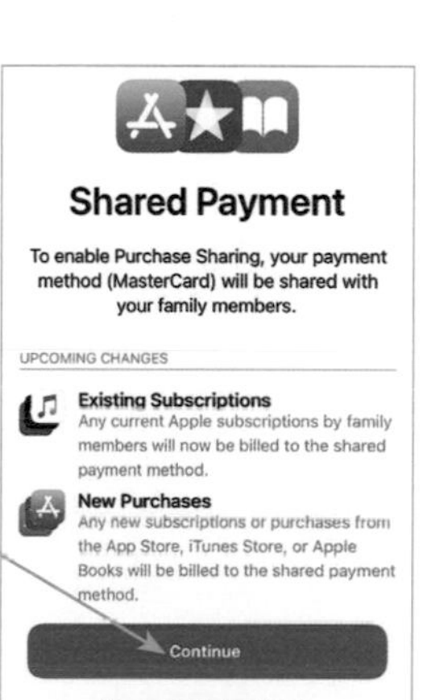

Using Family Sharing

Once you have set up Family Sharing and added family members, you can start sharing a selection of items.

Sharing photos

Photos can be shared with Family Sharing, with the Family album that is created automatically within the Photos app.

Photo Sharing has to be turned **On** to enable Family Sharing for photos (**Settings** > **Photos** > **Shared Albums**).

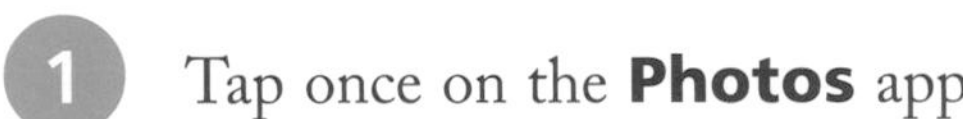

1. Tap once on the **Photos** app

2. Tap once on the **Albums** button on the bottom toolbar

3. The **Family** album is already available in the **Shared Albums** section. Tap once on the Family album

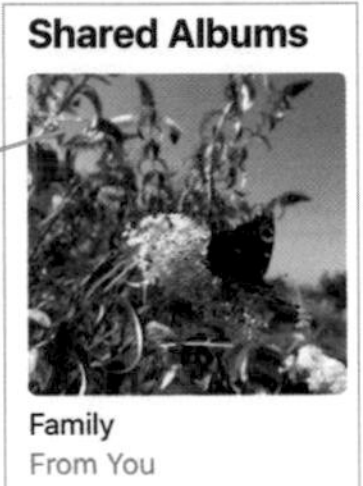

4. Tap once on this button to add photos to the album

5. Tap once on the photos you want to add, and tap once on the **Done** button

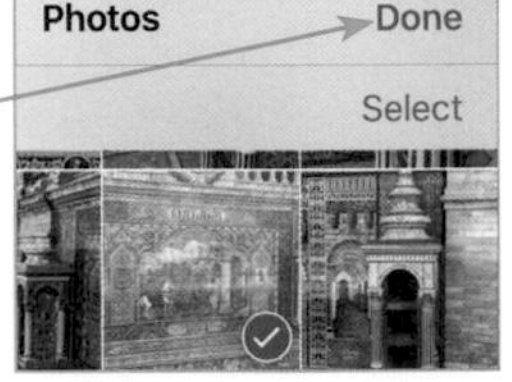

6. Make sure the **Family** album is selected as the Shared Album, and tap once on the **Post** button

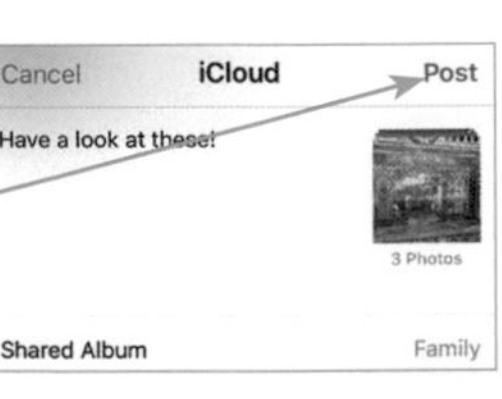

When someone else in your Family Sharing circle adds a photo to the Family album, you are notified in the Notification Center and also by a red notification on the Photos app.

Sharing calendars

Family Sharing also generates a Family calendar that can be used by all Family Sharing members:

1. Tap once on the **Calendar** app

2. Tap once on this button and create a new event, (see page 155). Select **Family** as the Calendar option to distribute the event to your Family Sharing members

Calendar • Family >

When someone in the Family Sharing circle adds an event to the Family calendar it will appear in your calendar with the appropriate tag. A red notification will also appear on the Calendar app, and it will appear in the Notification Center (if the Calendar has been selected to appear here).

Sharing apps, music, books and movies

Family Sharing means that all members of the group can share purchases from the iTunes Store, the App Store or the Book Store, accessed from within the Books app. This is done from the Purchased section of each app:

1. Open the relevant app and access the **Purchased** section. (For the **App Store**, tap once on the Account icon and tap once on the **Purchased** button; for the **iTunes Store**, tap once on the **Purchased** button on the bottom toolbar; for the **Books** app, tap once on the Account icon)

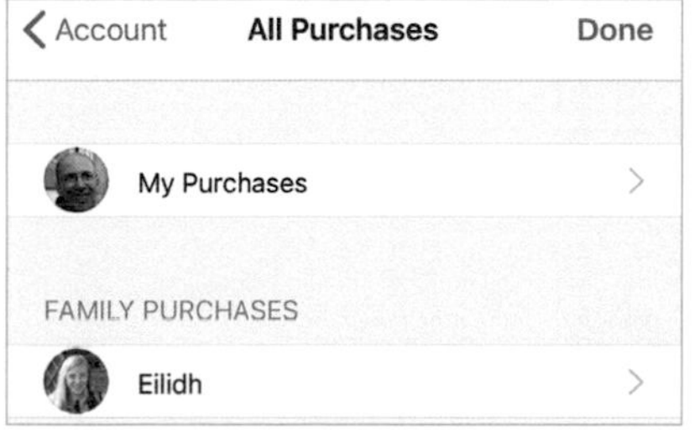

2. For all three apps, tap once on a member under **Family Purchases** to view their purchases and download them, if required, by tapping once on this button

Family Sharing makes it easy to keep in touch with the rest of the family and see exactly where they are. This can be done with the Find My app. The other person must have their Apple device turned On and be online. To find family members, tap once on the Find My app. The location of any people who are linked via your Family Sharing is displayed.

iCloud Drive and the Files App

One of the features of iCloud is the iCloud Drive, which can be used to store documents such as those created with the Apple suite of productivity apps (available in the App Store): Pages (word processing), Numbers (spreadsheets), and Keynote (presentations). These documents can then be accessed with the Files app.

The Files app can also be used with other online storage services such as Dropbox and Google Drive, if you have one of these accounts. If so, they will appear under the **Locations** section in Step 3.

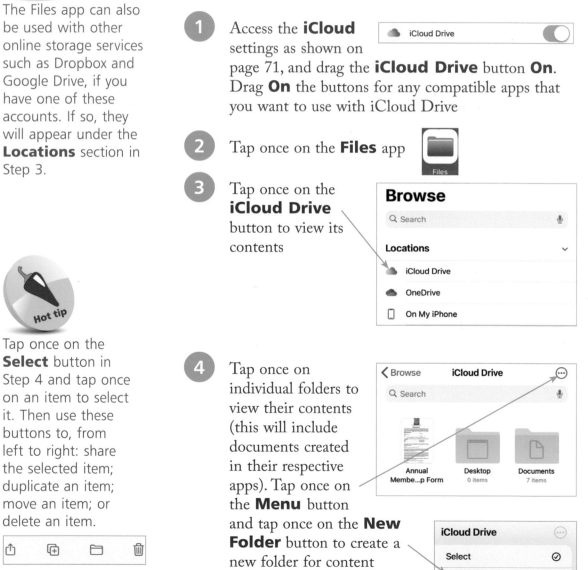

1. Access the **iCloud** settings as shown on page 71, and drag the **iCloud Drive** button **On**. Drag **On** the buttons for any compatible apps that you want to use with iCloud Drive

2. Tap once on the **Files** app

3. Tap once on the **iCloud Drive** button to view its contents

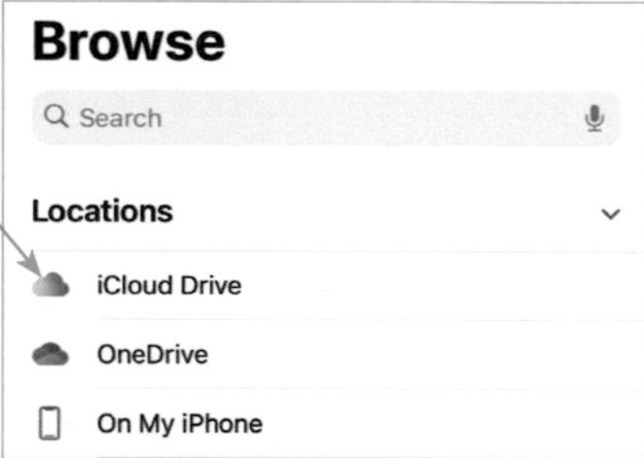

4. Tap once on individual folders to view their contents (this will include documents created in their respective apps). Tap once on the **Menu** button and tap once on the **New Folder** button to create a new folder for content

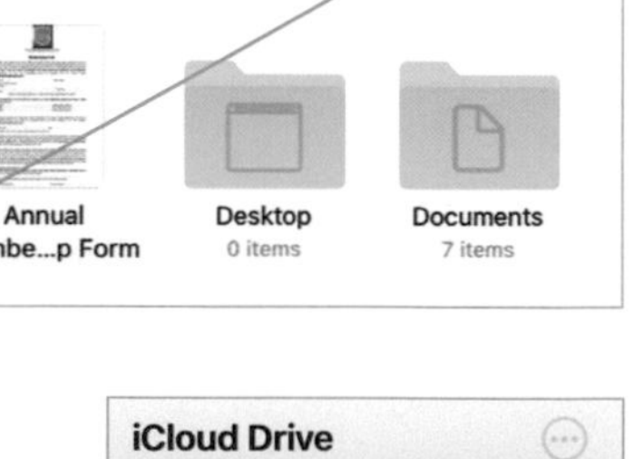

iCloud Drive

Select

New Folder

Hot tip

Tap once on the **Select** button in Step 4 and tap once on an item to select it. Then use these buttons to, from left to right: share the selected item; duplicate an item; move an item; or delete an item.

4 Calls and Contacts

One of the main uses for the iPhone is still to make and receive phone calls. This chapter shows what you need for this.

Adding Contacts

Because of its power and versatility, it is sometimes forgotten that one of the reasons for the iPhone's existence is to make phone calls. Before you start doing this, it is a good idea to add family and friends to the Contacts app. This will enable you to phone them without having to tap in their phone number each time. To add a contact:

1. Tap once on the **Contacts** app

2. Any contacts that you already have are displayed

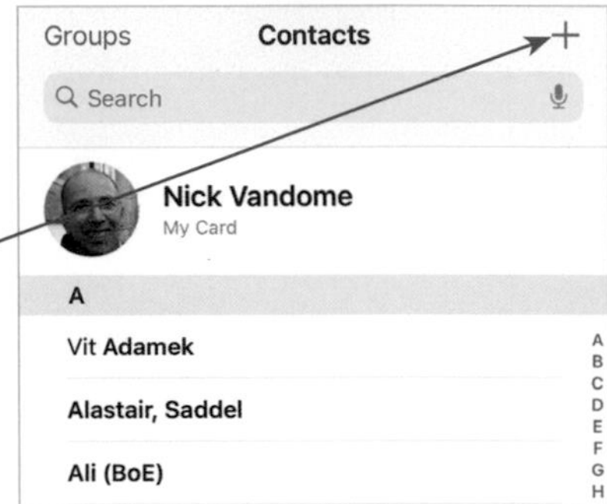

3. Tap once on this button to add a new contact

4. Enter the name for the contact at the top of the window, in the **First name** and **Last name** fields

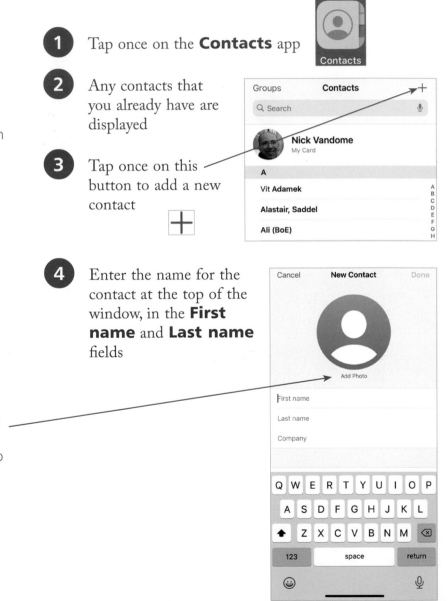

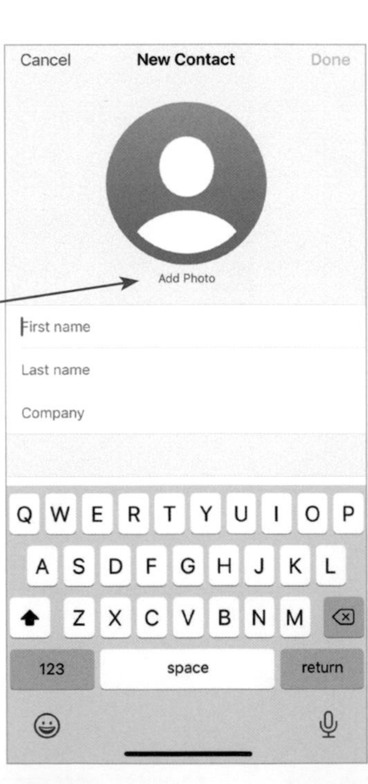

Tap once on the green button next to a field to add another field. Tap once on a red button to delete a field.

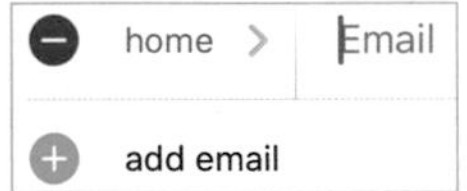

Tap once on the **Add Photo** option in Step 4 to add a photo for a new contact from your photos library or by taking one with the camera.

5 Tap once in one of the Phone fields, or tap once on the **add phone** button to add a new Phone field

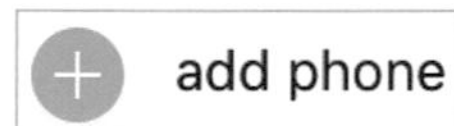

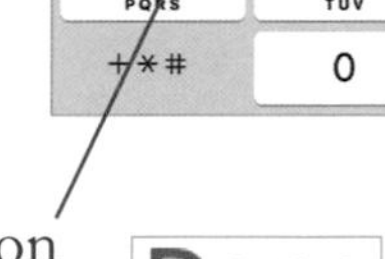

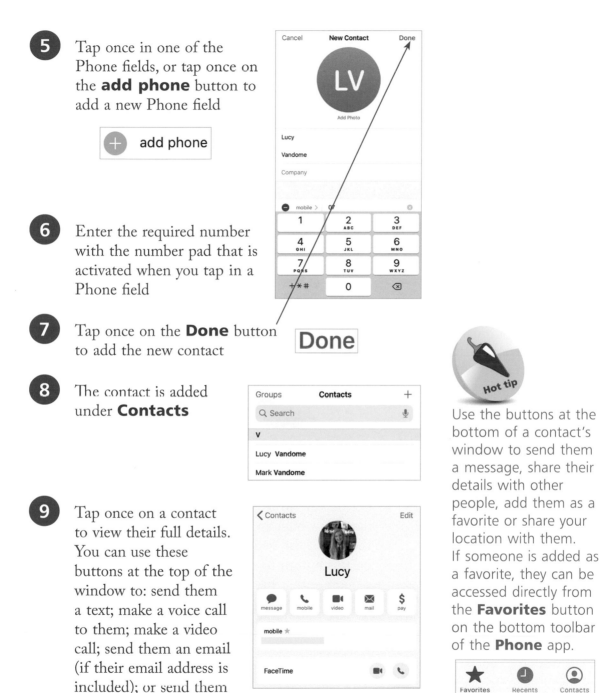

6 Enter the required number with the number pad that is activated when you tap in a Phone field

7 Tap once on the **Done** button to add the new contact

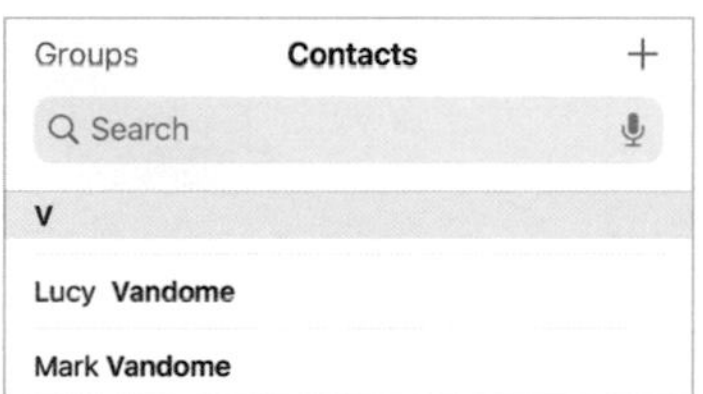

8 The contact is added under **Contacts**

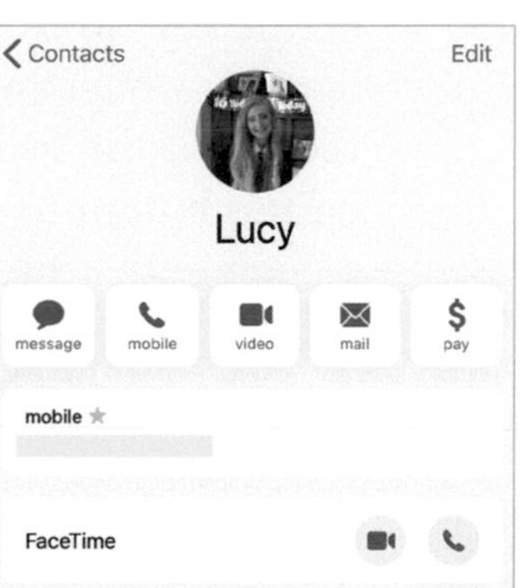

9 Tap once on a contact to view their full details. You can use these buttons at the top of the window to: send them a text; make a voice call to them; make a video call; send them an email (if their email address is included); or send them money via Apple Pay (if this is available)

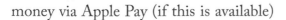

Hot tip

Use the buttons at the bottom of a contact's window to send them a message, share their details with other people, add them as a favorite or share your location with them. If someone is added as a favorite, they can be accessed directly from the **Favorites** button on the bottom toolbar of the **Phone** app.

Making a Call

The iPhone can be used to make calls to specific phone numbers that you enter manually, or to contacts in your Contacts app.

Dialing a number

To make a call by dialing a specific number, first tap once on the **Phone** app.

1. Tap once on the **Keypad** button at the bottom of the window

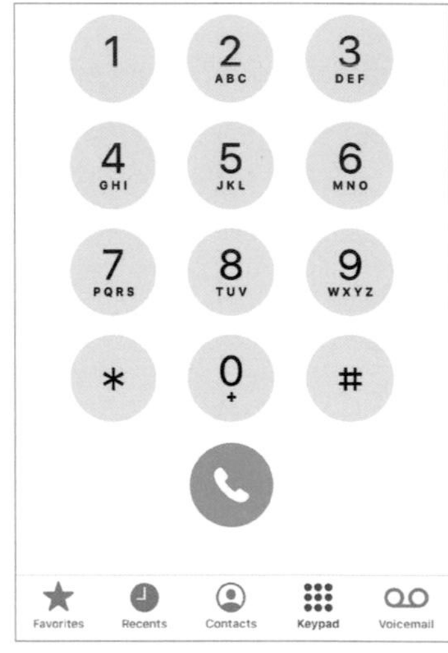

2. Tap on the numbers on the keypad to enter the number, which appears at the top of the window. Tap on this button to delete a number that has been entered

3. Tap once on this button to make the call

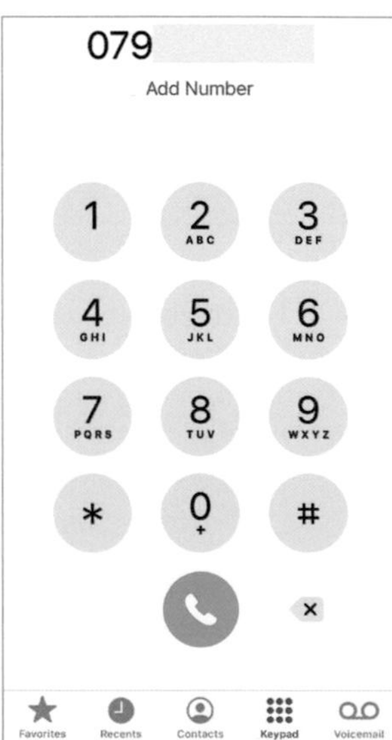

Don't forget

You must have a SIM card inserted in your iPhone and an appropriate cellular/mobile service provider in order to make a call with the **Phone** app, unless it is through an app that uses Wi-Fi, such as FaceTime – see pages 132-133.

Tap once on the **Voicemail** button on the bottom toolbar to view any messages here. If you have any, there will be a red notification icon on the Voicemail button.

Calling a contact

To call someone who has been added to the Contacts app:

1. Open the **Phone** app, and tap once on the **Contacts** button at the bottom of the window. The Contacts app opens, with the Phone toolbar still visible at the bottom of the window

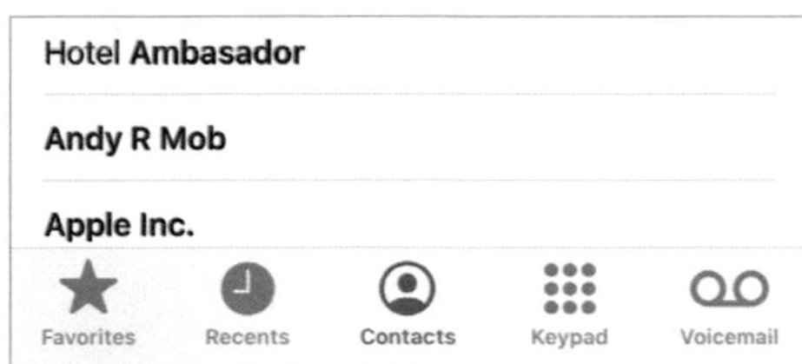

2. Tap once on a contact

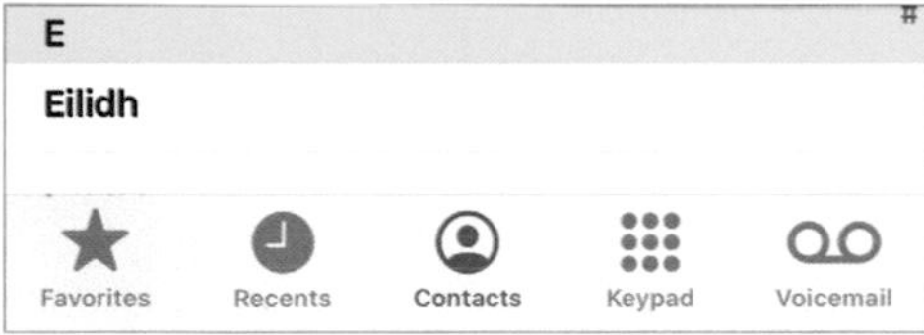

3. The full details for the contact are displayed. Tap once on the **mobile** button at the top of the window to call the number of the contact

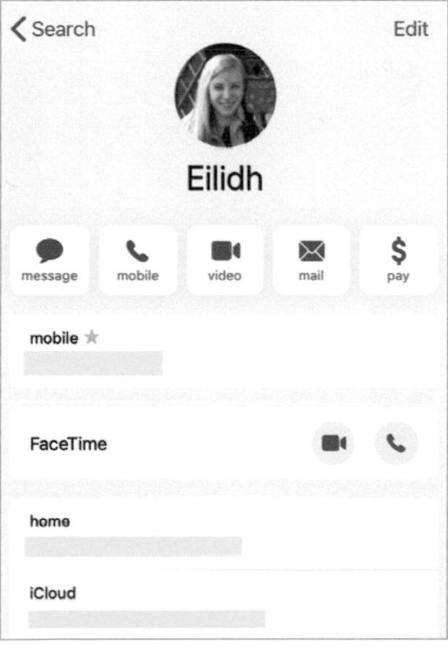

To find someone in the Contacts app (either directly from the app, or from the **Contacts** button in the Phone app), swipe up and down on the screen; enter a name in the Search box at the top of the window; or tap on a letter on the alphabetic list down the right-hand side.

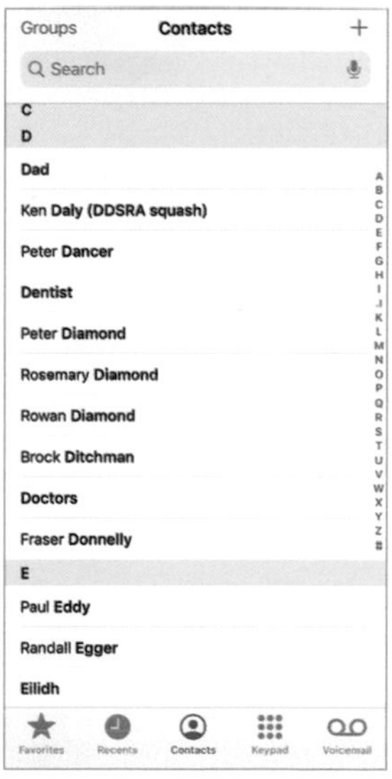

Receiving a Call

When you receive a call, there are two main options:

Calls when the iPhone is unlocked

1. When you receive a call, the person's name and photo (if they have been added to your contacts) or number appears in a banner at the top of the screen

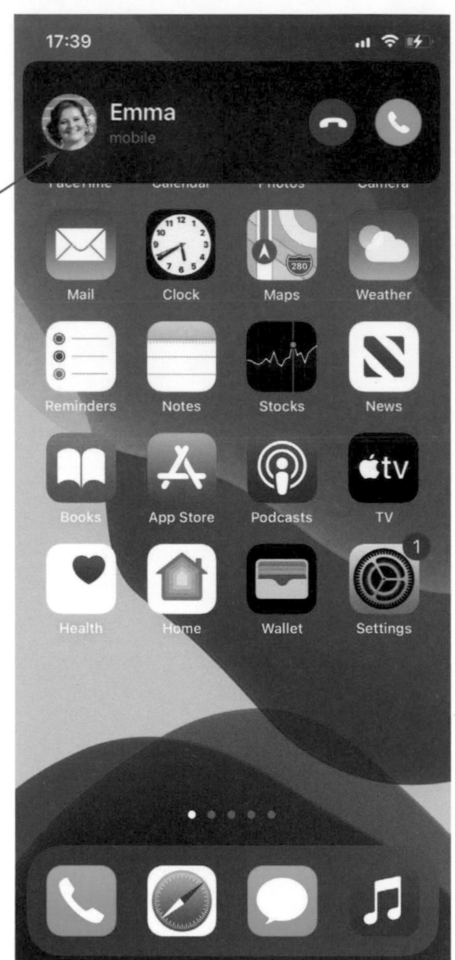

2. Tap once on this button to take the call

3. Tap once on this button to decline the call

NEW

The banner in Step 1 is known as a Compact Call and is a new feature in iOS 14.

When a call is connected, tap on the banner and the following buttons appear on the screen. Use them to: mute a call; access the keypad again, in case you need to add any more information such as for an automated call; access the speaker so you do not have to keep the phone at your ear; add another call to create a conference call; make a FaceTime call to the caller (if they have this facility); or access your Contacts app.

Calls when the iPhone is locked

If you receive a call while your iPhone is locked, it will be displayed on the Lock screen. If this happens, there are various options on the Lock screen in terms of what can be done with the call:

1. Swipe this button from left to right to answer the call

2. Tap once on the **Remind Me** button to decline the call but set a reminder

3. Tap once on one of the options for when you are reminded about the call. The options are for **In 1 hour** or **When I leave** (if Location Services is turned On in **Settings** > **Privacy**)

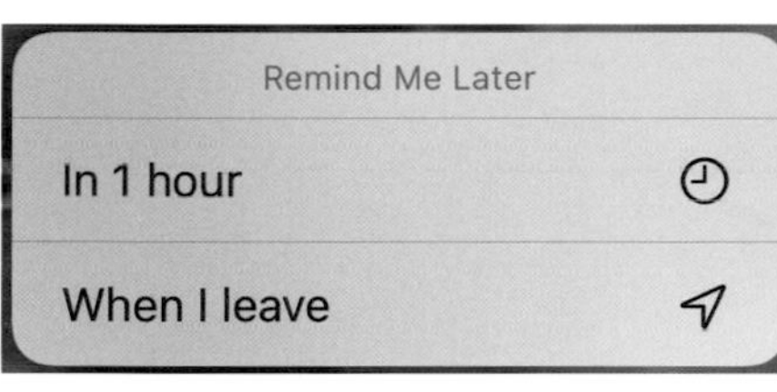

4. Tap once on the **Message** button to decline the call but send the person a text message instead

5. Tap once on the text message that you want to send

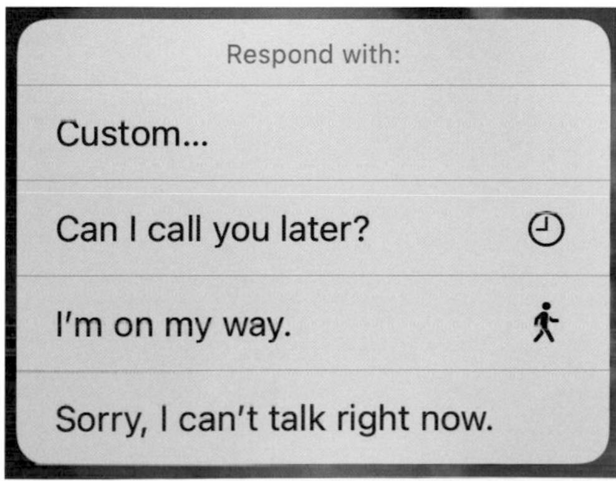

The reminder in Step 3 will appear on the Lock screen at the specified time.

Tap once on the **Custom...** button in Step 5 to create your own customized text message to send to the caller.

Saving Phone Contacts

Another quick way to add a contact is to ask someone to phone you so that you can then copy their number directly from your phone to your contacts. You do not even have to answer the phone to do this.

Information from a caller can also be added to an existing contact. For instance, if one of your contacts calls you from a different phone, these details can be added to their existing information. To do this, tap once on the **Add to Existing Contact** button in Step 5.

To block a number from contacting you, tap once on the **Block this Caller** button in Step 5.

1. Once someone has phoned, tap once on the **Phone** app

2. Tap once on the **Recents** button at the bottom of the window

3. The call will be displayed. Tap once on the **i** symbol

4. Information about the call is displayed, including the number

5. Tap once on the **Create New Contact** button

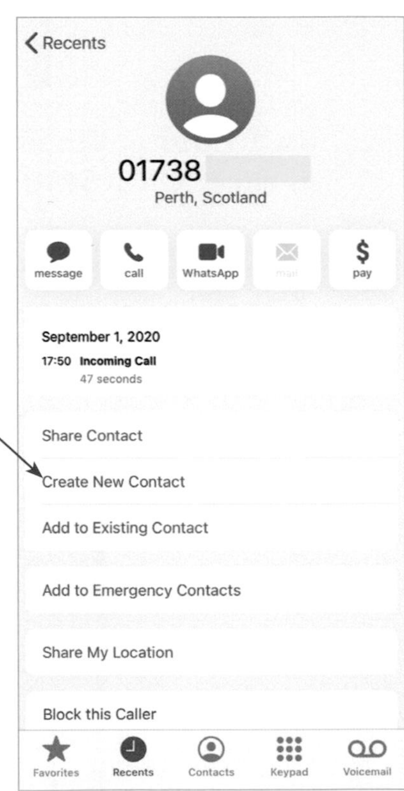

6. The **New Contact** window opens, with the number already pre-inserted

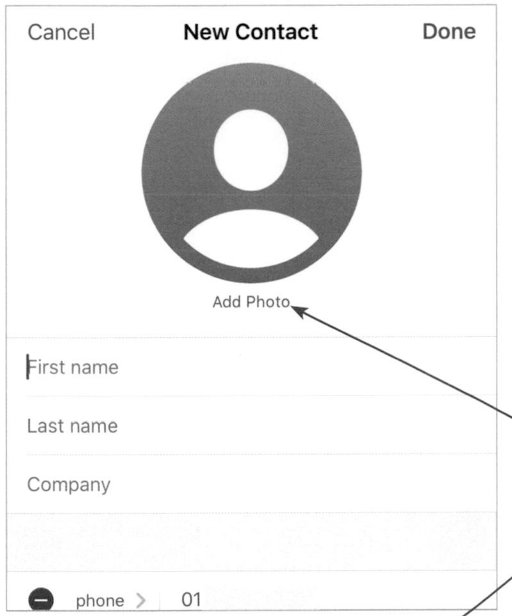

7. Add information for the contact as required, such as name, any additional phone numbers, and email

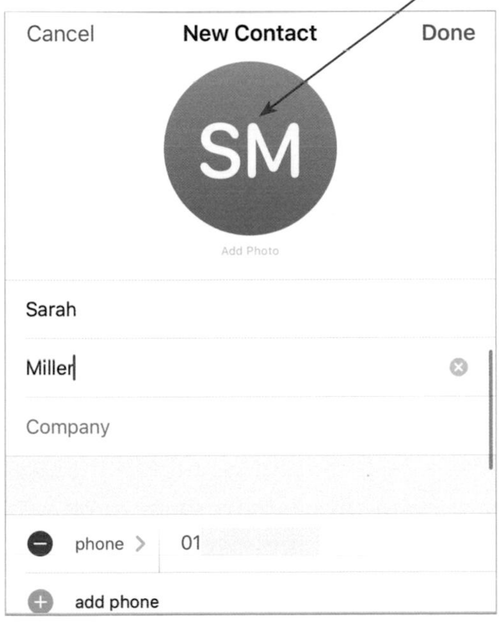

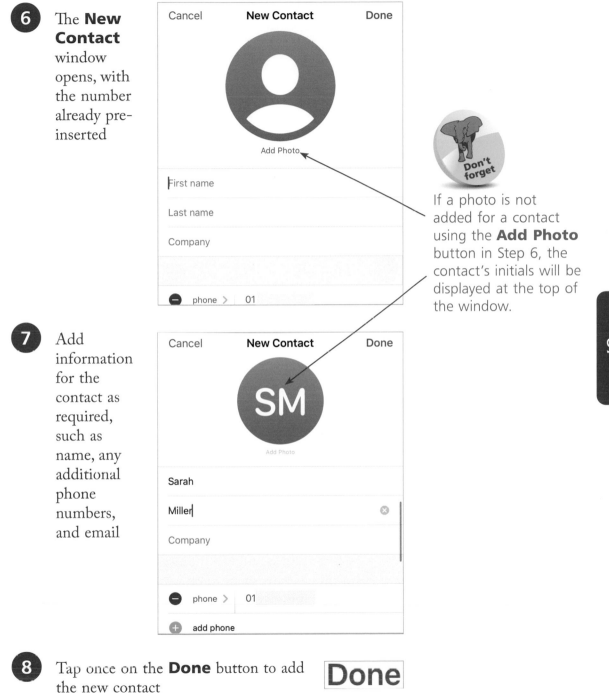

If a photo is not added for a contact using the **Add Photo** button in Step 6, the contact's initials will be displayed at the top of the window.

8. Tap once on the **Done** button to add the new contact

Setting Ringtones

Ringtones were one of the original "killer apps" for mobile/cell phones: the must-have accessory that helped transform the way people looked at these devices. The iPhone has a range of ringtones that can be used, and you can also download and install thousands more. To use the default ringtones:

1. Tap once on the **Settings** app

2. Tap once on the **Sounds & Haptics** tab

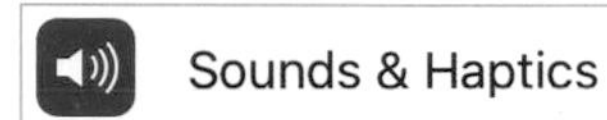

3. Tap once on the **Ringtone** link under **Sounds and Vibration Patterns** to select ringtones for when you receive a phone call

4. Tap once on one of the options to hear a preview and select it

5. Sounds and vibrations can also be selected for a range of other items such as text messages, email, and calendar and reminder alerts, by going back to the **Sounds and Vibration Patterns** section and choosing a tone for each item

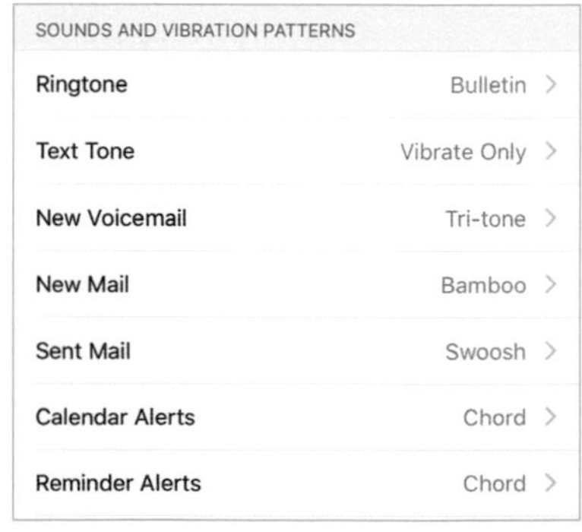

Tap once on the **Tone Store** button in the Ringtone window to go to the iTunes Store, where you can download more ringtones, from the **Tones** button.

Tone Store

If the Ringer button on the side of the iPhone is turned **Off**, the iPhone can still be set to vibrate if a call or notification is received, using the **Vibrate on Silent** button at the top of the main **Sounds & Haptics** window (drag the button **On**).

Adding individual ringtones

It is also possible to set ringtones for individual people, so that you know immediately who a call is from.

1. Select a contact in the Contacts app, and tap on the **Edit** button

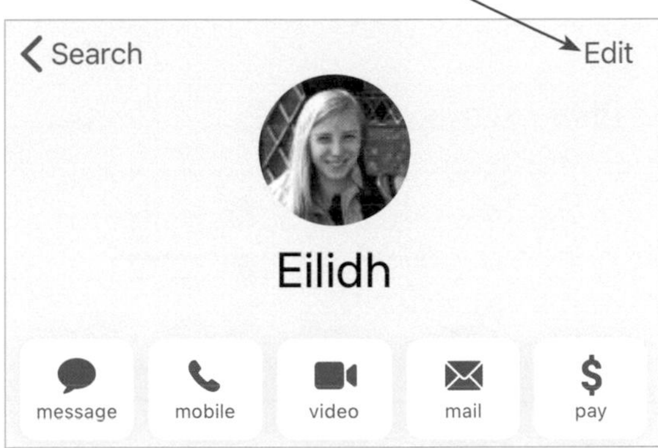

Only set ringtones for your most regular contacts, otherwise you may end up with too many variations.

2. Tap once on the **Ringtone** button

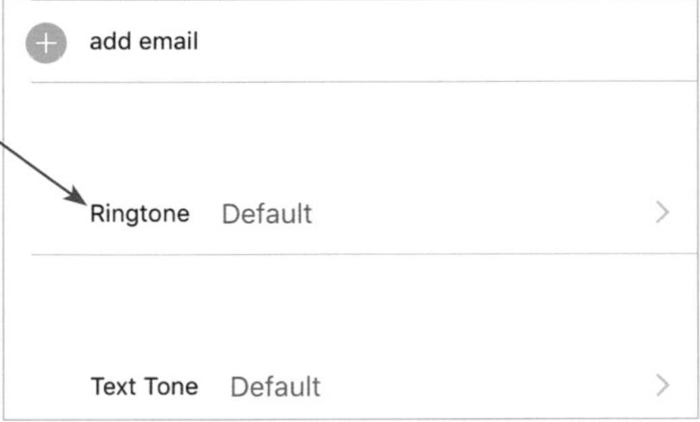

3. Tap once on a ringtone to assign this to the contact

If you are going to be using your iPhone around other people, consider turning the **Keyboard Clicks** option (at the bottom of the main **Sounds & Haptics** settings window) **Off**, as the noise can get annoying for those in the vicinity.

Phone Settings

As with most of the iPhone functions, there is a range of settings for the phone itself. To use them:

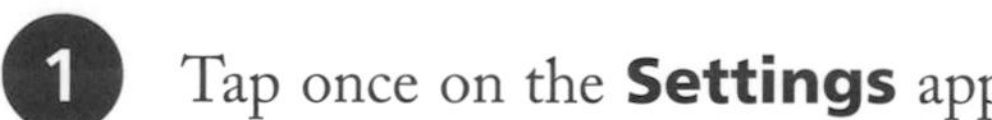

1. Tap once on the **Settings** app

2. Tap once on the **Phone** tab

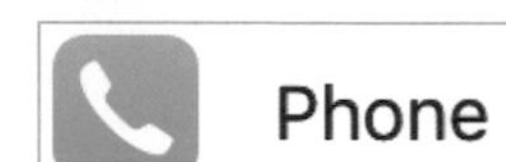

3. The Phone settings have options for responding with a text to a call that you do not take (see next step); call forwarding; call waiting; and silencing the phone's ringer when it receives an unknown number (see bottom tip)

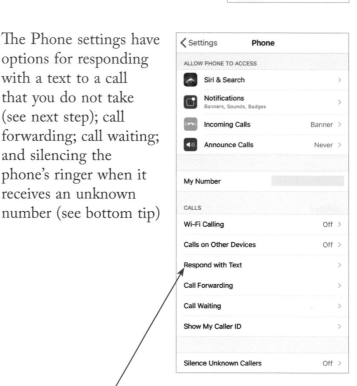

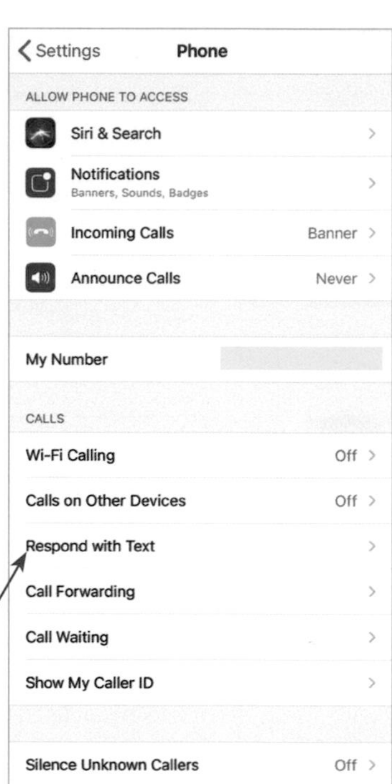

4. Tap once on the **Respond with Text** button to create a text message that can be sent if you do not want to answer a call when it is received

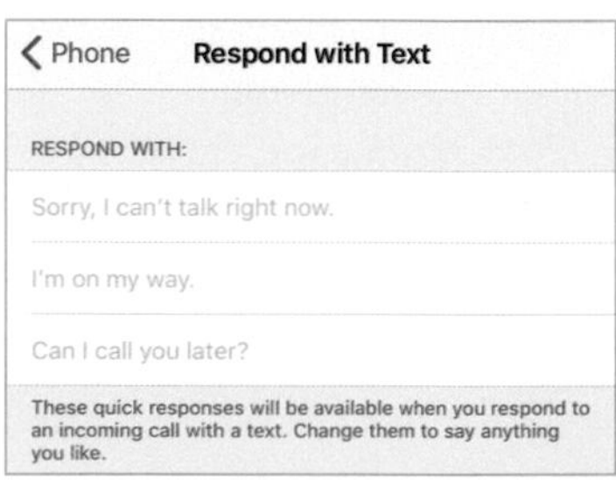

Use the options for **Cellular** (**Mobile**) settings for items specific to your phone service provider.

Drag the **Silence Unknown Callers** button **On** in Step 3 to ensure that any calls from numbers that you do not recognize (those not in your contacts) are silenced; i.e. the phone will not ring.

Silence Unknown Callers 

5 Typing and Texts

This chapter shows how to use the iPhone keyboard to add text, and also shows the range of items that can be added to messages with iOS 14, including animated Animojis and Memojis.

The iPhone Keyboard

The keyboard on the iPhone is a virtual one; i.e. it appears on the touchscreen whenever text or numbered input is required for an app. This can be for a variety of reasons:

- Entering text with a word processing app, or into an email or an organizing app such as Notes.
- Entering a web address in a web browser such as the Safari app.
- Entering information into an online form.
- Entering a password.

Hot tip

In some apps such as Notes, Mail and Messages, it is possible to change the keyboard into a trackpad for moving the cursor. To do this, press and hold firmly on the keyboard, and then swipe over the trackpad to move the cursor around.

Viewing the keyboard

When you attempt one of the actions above, the keyboard appears so that you can enter any text or numbers:

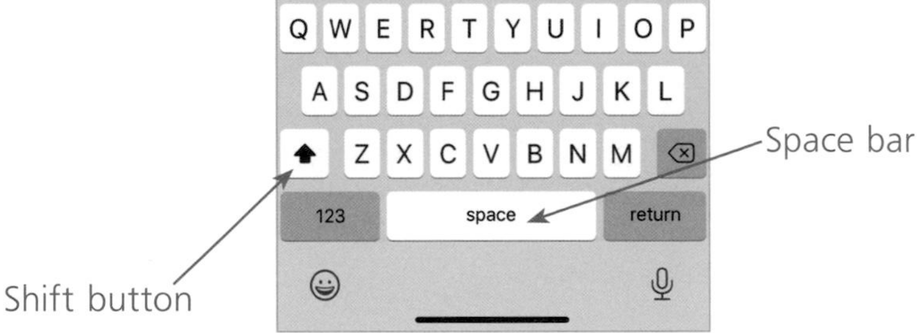

It is possible to increase the size of view of the iPhone keyboard with the **Zoom** feature within the Accessibility settings. See pages 182-183 for details.

Around the keyboard

To access the various keyboard controls:

1. Tap once on the **Shift** button to create a **Cap** (capital) text letter

2. Double-tap on the **Shift** button to enable **Caps Lock**

3. Tap once on this button to back-delete an item

To return from Caps Lock, tap once on the **Caps** button.

4. Tap once on this button to access the **Numbers** keyboard option

5. From the Numbers keyboard, tap once on this button to access the **Symbols** keyboard

If you are entering a password, or details into a form, the keyboard will have a **Go** or **Send** button that can be used to activate the information that has been entered.

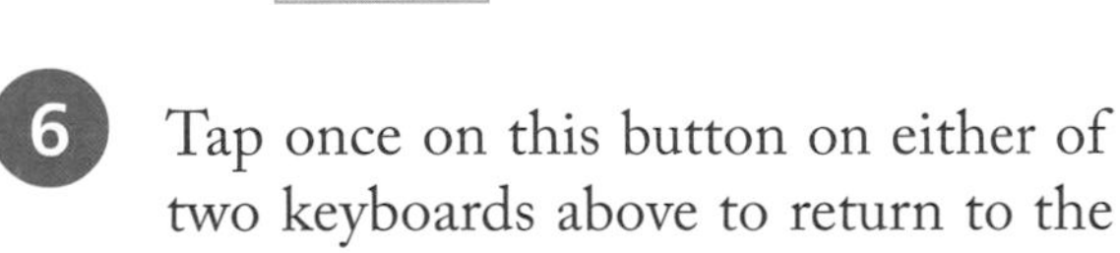

6. Tap once on this button on either of the two keyboards above to return to the standard QWERTY option

Several keys have additional options that can be accessed by pressing and holding on the key. A lot of these are letters that have accented versions in different languages; e.g. a, e, i, o and u. Swipe across a letter to add it.

Shortcut keys

Instead of having to go to a different keyboard every time you want to add punctuation (or numbers), there is a shortcut for this:

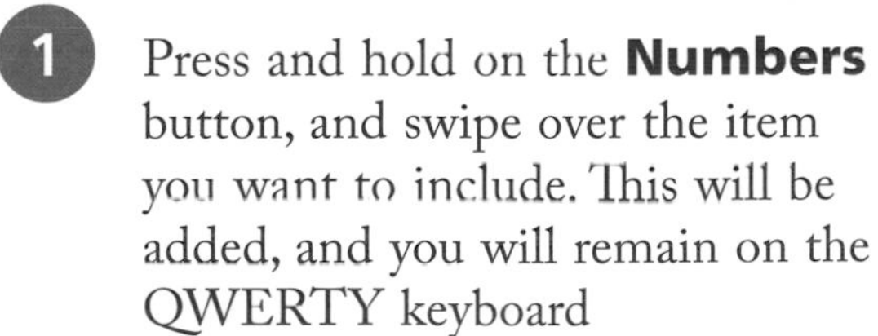

1. Press and hold on the **Numbers** button, and swipe over the item you want to include. This will be added, and you will remain on the QWERTY keyboard

Keyboard Settings

Settings for the keyboard can be determined in the General section of the Settings app. To do this:

Drag the **Predictive** button **On** to enable predictive texting (see pages 96-97). Drag the **Character Preview** button **On** to show a magnified example of a letter or symbol when it is pressed, to ensure that the correct one is selected.

The Auto-Correction function works as you type a word, so it may change a number of times depending on the length of the word you are typing.

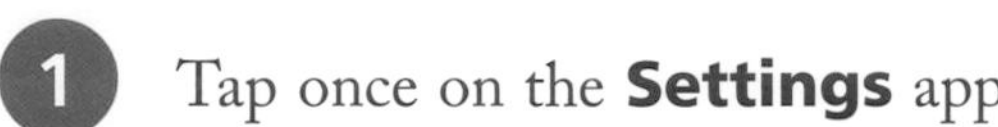

1. Tap once on the **Settings** app

2. Tap once on the **General** tab

3. Tap once on the **Keyboard** link

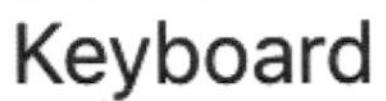

4. Drag the **Auto-Capitalization** button **On** to automatically capitalize letters at the beginning of a sentence

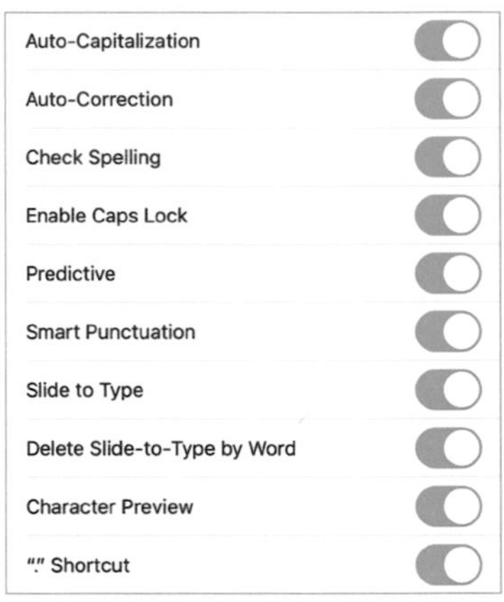

5. Drag the **Auto-Correction** button **On** to enable suggestions for words to appear as you type, particularly if you have mistyped a word
6. Drag the **Check Spelling** and **Smart Punctuation** buttons **On** to identify misspelled words and add punctuation
7. Drag the **Enable Caps Lock** button **On** to enable this function to be performed
8. Drag the **"." Shortcut** button **On** to add a period (full stop) and a space to start a new sentence by just tapping the space bar twice

9. Tap once on the **Text Replacement** link to view existing text shortcuts and also to create new ones

10. Tap once on this button to create new shortcuts

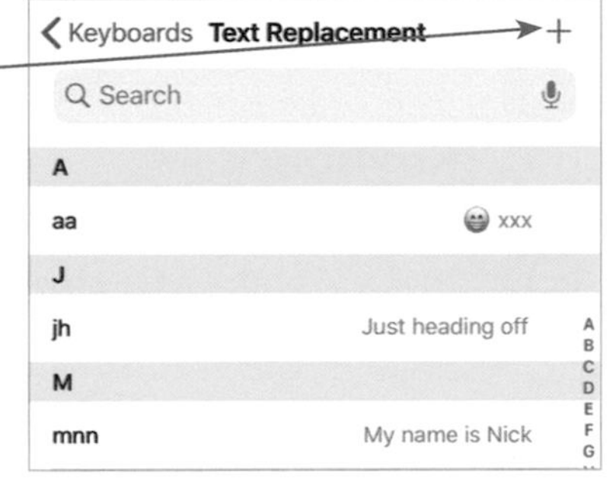

11. Enter a phrase and the shortcut you want to use to create it when you type. Tap once on the **Save** button

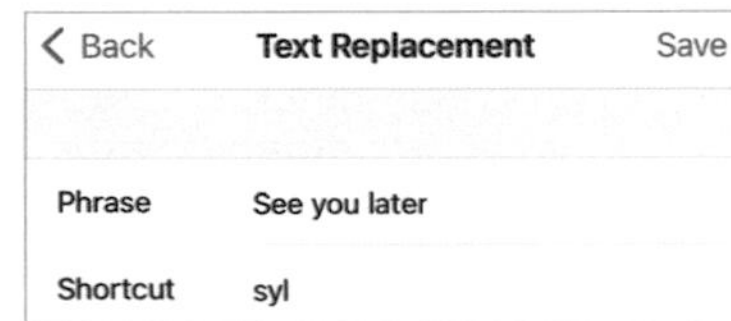

12. Tap once on the **Keyboards** button in Step 9 to add a new keyboard

13. Tap once on the **Add New Keyboard...** button

14. Tap once on a keyboard to add it. The keyboard will be available by selecting the globe icon (see the Don't forget tip)

With iOS 14, third-party keyboards can be downloaded from the App Store and used instead of the default one. One to look at is Microsoft SwiftKey Keyboard.

By default, two keyboards are installed: one for the language of your region, and the emoji one. If more keyboards are added, this symbol will appear on the keyboard. Press on it to select another keyboard from the one being used. If only the two default keyboards are installed, this symbol will be the emoji one.

Using Predictive Text

Predictive text tries to guess what you are typing, and also predicts the next word following the one you have just typed. It is excellent for text messaging. To use it:

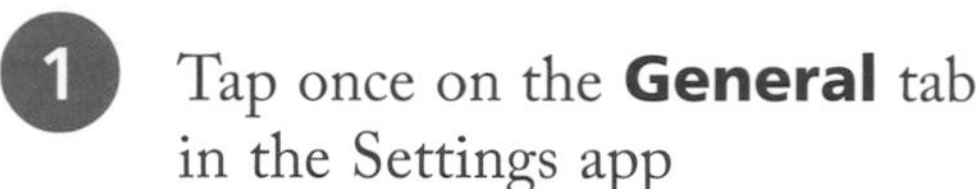

1. Tap once on the **General** tab in the Settings app

2. Tap once on the **Keyboard** link

3. Drag the **Predictive** button **On**

4. When predictive text is activated, the QuickType bar is displayed above the keyboard. Initially, this has a suggestion for the first word to include. Tap on a word or start typing

5. As you type, suggestions appear. Tap on one to accept it. Tap on the word within the quotation marks to accept exactly what you have typed

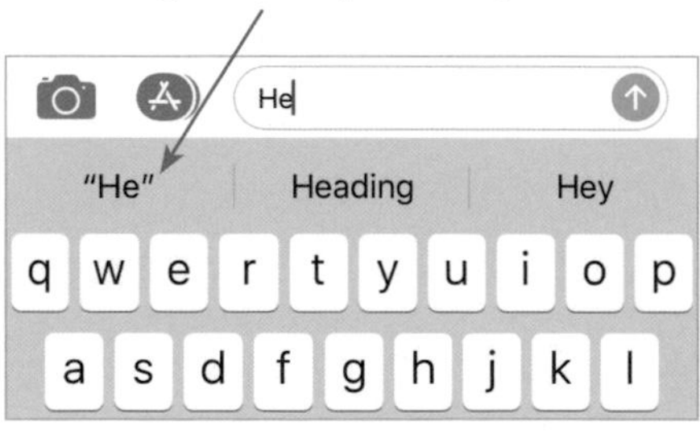

Predictive text learns from your writing style as you write, and so gets more accurate at predicting words. It can also recognize a change in style for different apps such as Mail and Messages.

6. If you continue typing, the predictive suggestions will change as you add more letters

7. After you have typed a word, a suggestion for the next word appears. Tap on one of the suggestions or start typing a new word, which will then also have predictive suggestions as you type

It is also possible to create text by swiping over letters on the keyboard. This is known as QuickPath Typing. To set this up, access **Settings** > **General** > **Keyboard** and turn **Slide to Type On**. Text can then be created by sliding your fingers over the required letters, rather than tapping on them individually.

Toggling predictive text from the keyboard

You can also toggle predictive text On or Off from the keyboard. To do this:

1. Press and hold on this button on the keyboard

2. Tap once on the **Keyboard Settings...** button to access the **Predictive** setting, from where it can be turned **On** or **Off**

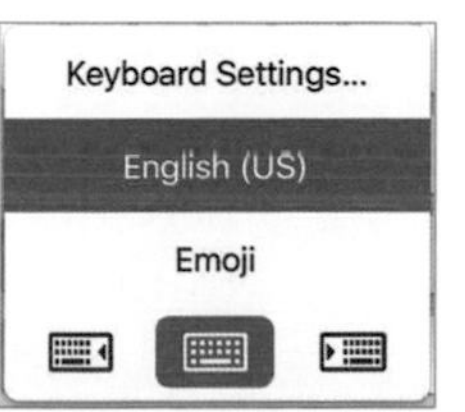

Tapping the button in Step 1 allows you to add emojis, which are symbols used in text messages to signify happiness, surprise, sadness, etc. (See page 104 for details.)

One Handed Keyboard

When typing with the iPhone, this is frequently done with one hand. To make this easier, there is an option for formatting the keyboard for one handed typing. To do this:

1. Open the **General** tab in the Settings app, and tap once on the **One Handed Keyboard** link

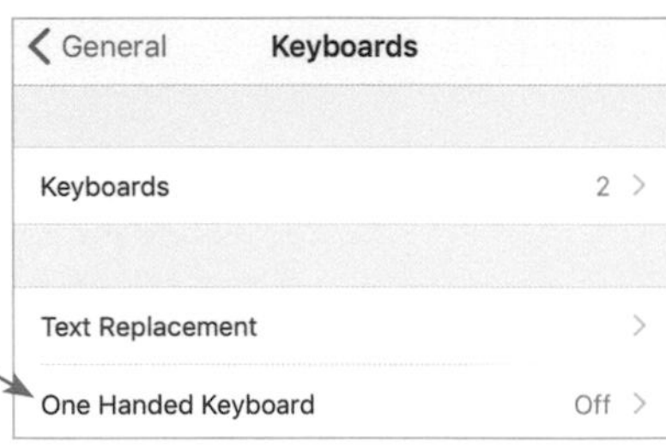

2. Select the **Left** or **Right** option for the keyboard

3. If more than one keyboard has been added (e.g. the emoji keyboard), press and hold on this button on the keyboard, and tap once on the options for moving the keyboard to the left or right

4. The keyboard is moved into the position selected in either Step 2 or 3. Tap once here to revert to the original keyboard

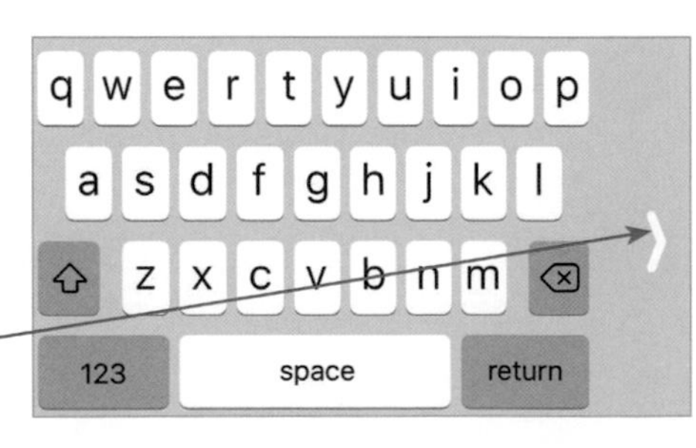

When using your iPhone one handed, make sure you keep a good hold on it so that it does not fall on the ground.

Entering Text

Once you have applied the keyboard settings that you require, you can start entering text. To do this:

1. Tap once on the screen to activate the keyboard from the app. Start typing with the keyboard. The text will appear at the point where you tapped on the screen

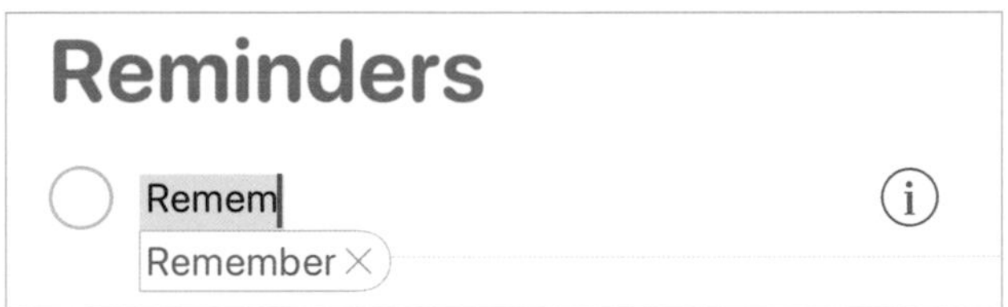

2. As you type, Auto-Correction comes up with suggestions (if it is turned On). Tap once on the space bar to accept the suggestion, or tap once on the cross next to it to reject it

3. If **Check Spelling** is enabled in the keyboard settings, any misspelled words appear highlighted. Press on the word to access a replacement word. Tap once on the replacement to use it, if required

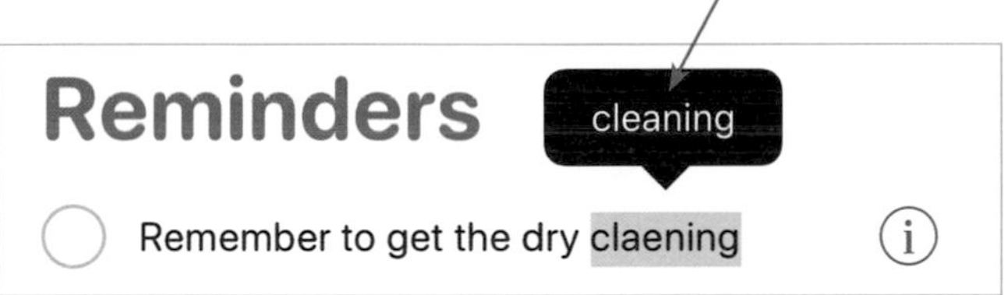

4. Double-tap the space bar to enter a period (full stop) and a space at the end of a sentence

If you keep typing as normal, the Auto-Correction suggestion will disappear when you finish the word.

If predictive text is turned **On** (**Settings** > **General** > **Keyboard** > **Predictive**), the Auto-Correction suggestions will appear on the QuickType bar above the keyboard, rather than below the word being typed, as in Step 1.

The **"." Shortcut** option has to be turned **On** (**Settings** > **General** > **Keyboard** > **"." Shortcut**) for the functionality in Step 4 to work (see page 94).

Editing Text

Once text has been entered it can be selected, copied, cut, and pasted. Depending on the app being used, the text can also be formatted, such as with a word processing app.

Managing text

To work with text in a document you have created:

Hot tip

Once the selection buttons have been accessed, tap once on **Select** to select the previous word, or **Select All** to select all of the text.

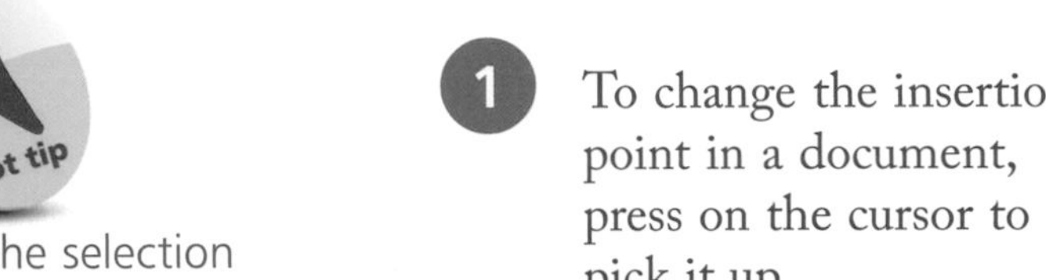

1. To change the insertion point in a document, press on the cursor to pick it up

2. Drag the cursor to move the insertion point

Moving the cursor.

3. Tap once at the insertion point to access the menu buttons

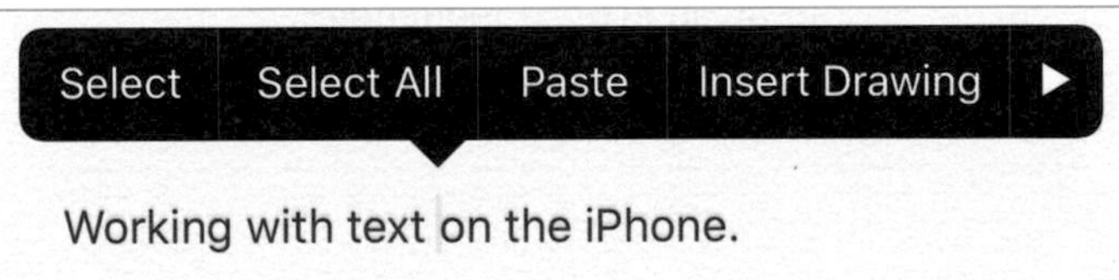

Hot tip

The menu buttons in Step 4 can be used to replace the selected word; add bold, italics or underlining to it; or view a definition of it (Look Up), accessed from the button in Step 5. Text menus vary depending on which app is being used.

4. Double-tap on a word to select it. Tap once on one of the menu buttons, as required

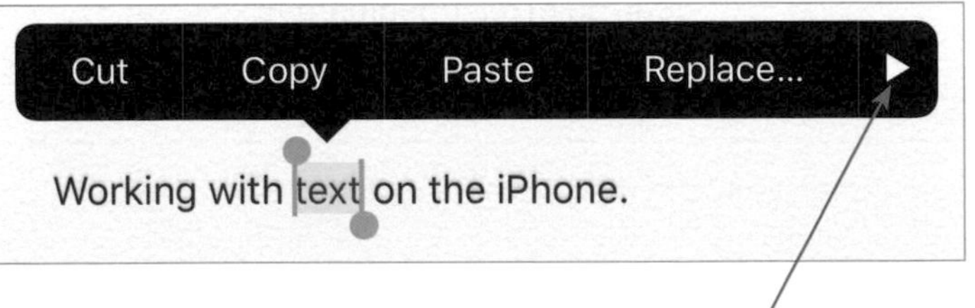

5. Tap once on this button to access more options for working with the selected text (see bottom tip)

Selecting text

Text can be selected using a range of methods:

1. Double-tap on a word to select it

   Once text has been entered with an app on the iPhone it can then be managed. This can involve editing the text. It can also include selecting text.

2. Drag the selection handles to increase or decrease the selection. This is a good way to select certain text within a sentence or within a paragraph

   Once text has been entered with an app on the iPhone it can then be managed. This can involve editing the text. It can also include selecting text.

3. Triple-tap on a word to select the whole of its related sentence

   Once text has been entered with an app on the iPhone it can then be managed. This can involve editing the text. It can also include selecting text.

4. Quadruple-tap on a word to select the whole of its related paragraph

   Once text has been entered with an app on the iPhone it can then be managed. This can involve editing the text. It can also include selecting text.

Once text has been selected, there is a range of gestures that can be used to copy and paste it, and also undo the previous action. To copy selected text: pinch inwards over the text with thumb and two fingers. To paste text: swipe outwards with thumb and two fingers, in a dropping motion. To undo the previous action: swipe from right to left with three fingers.

Text Messaging

Text messages sent with the Messages app can either be iMessages or SMS text messages, depending on how they are sent. iMessages are sent using Wi-Fi to other users with an Apple ID and using an iPhone, iPad, iPod Touch, or a Mac computer. SMS text messages are just sent via your cellular (mobile) carrier. When you send an iMessage, it appears in a blue bubble in the Messages app; when you send an SMS text, it appears in a green bubble.

Hot tip

You can also add someone from your contacts by typing their name into the **To:** field shown in Step 3. As you start typing, names will appear for you to select from. You can type the telephone number of anyone who isn't in your contacts here, too.

1. Tap once on the **Messages** app

2. Tap once on this button to create a new message and start a new conversation

3. Tap once on this button to select someone from your contacts

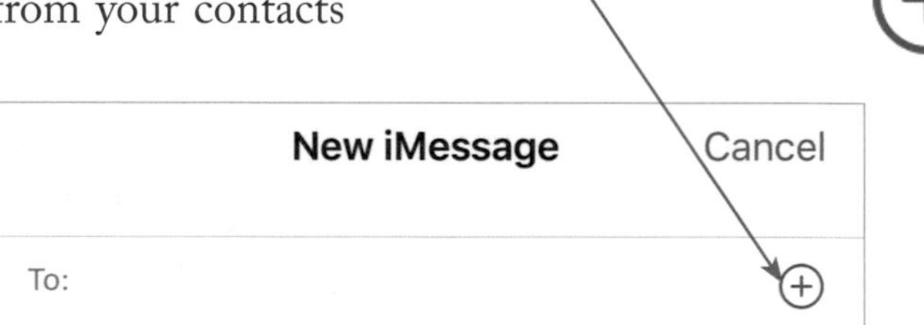

Hot tip

You can also send family and friends audio clips in an iMessage so that they can hear from you too. To do this, press and hold on the microphone icon at the right-hand side of the text box, and record your message.

4. Tap once on a contact to select them as the recipient of the new message

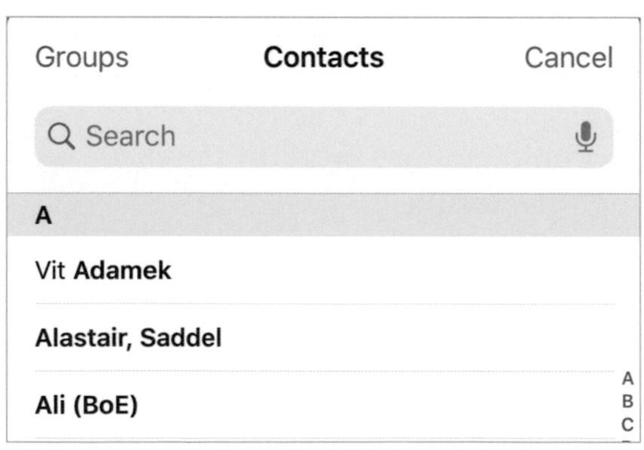

5 Tap once here, and type with the keyboard to create a message

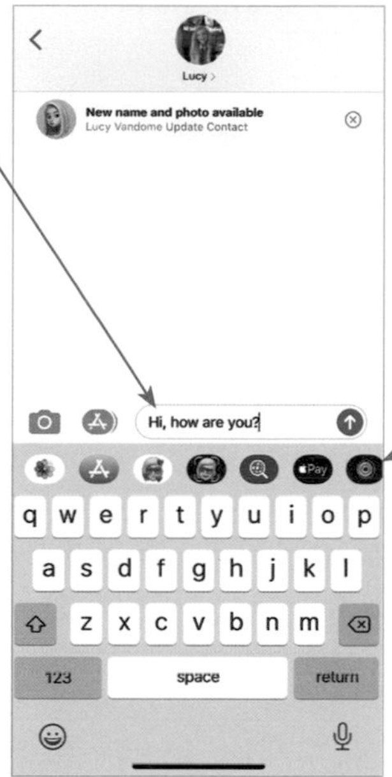

The App Strip, containing options for adding content to a text message, is available below the text box.

When a message has been sent, you are notified underneath it when it has been delivered.

6 Tap once on this button to send a message (it is not available until a message has been composed)

7 As the conversation progresses, each message is displayed in the main window

Money can be transferred to other people by tapping on this button on the App Strip. To use this service, Apple Pay and Apple Pay Cash have to be set up on your own iPhone and the recipient's. At the time of printing, this service is only available in the US.

Enhancing Text Messages

Adding Emojis

Emojis (small graphical symbols) are very popular in text messages, and there is now a huge range that can be included with iOS 14. To add these:

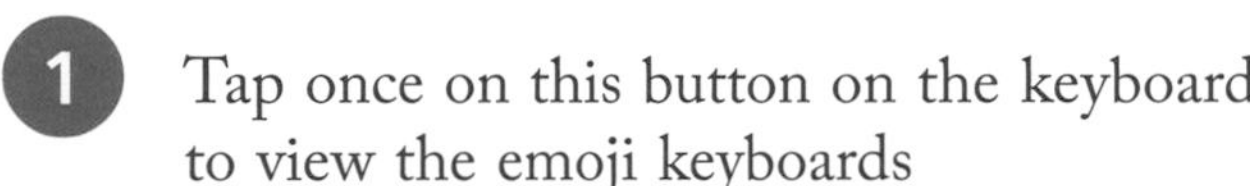

1. Tap once on this button on the keyboard to view the emoji keyboards

2. Swipe left and right to view the emoji options. Tap once on an emoji to add it to a message

Don't forget

Emojis are grouped together according to subject. These include Smileys & People; Animals & Nature; Food & Drink; Objects; and Flags.

Emojis can be added automatically from certain words:

Turn predictive text **On** in the Keyboard settings (see page 96) to get emoji suggestions as you type.

1. Add text, and tap once on the button in Step 1 above. The items that can be replaced are highlighted

2. Tap once on a highlighted word to see the emoji options. Tap once on one to add it to the message

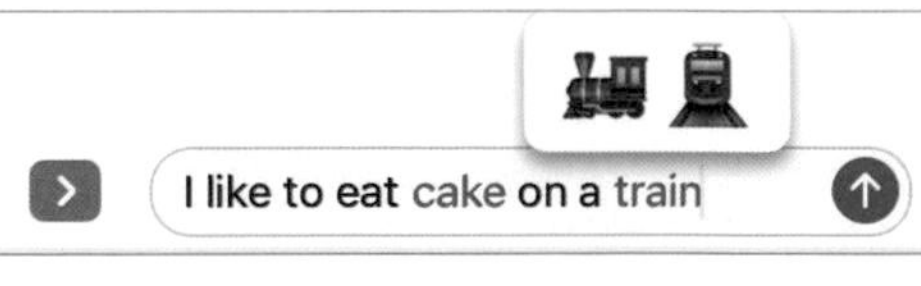

Adding Animojis

Introduced on the iPhone X with iOS 11, the Animoji feature is now available on all new models of iPhone. Animojis are animated stickers that can take on the expressions and voice of the person looking at the iPhone's camera:

1. Create a new message or open an existing conversation

2. Tap once on the **Animoji** icon, in the App Strip below the text box

3. Swipe left and right to select the Animoji icon, as required

4. Tap once on the **Record** button to record a facial expression for the Animoji

5. Tap once on this button to finish recording (The expressions for an Animoji can be recorded for up to 30 seconds.)

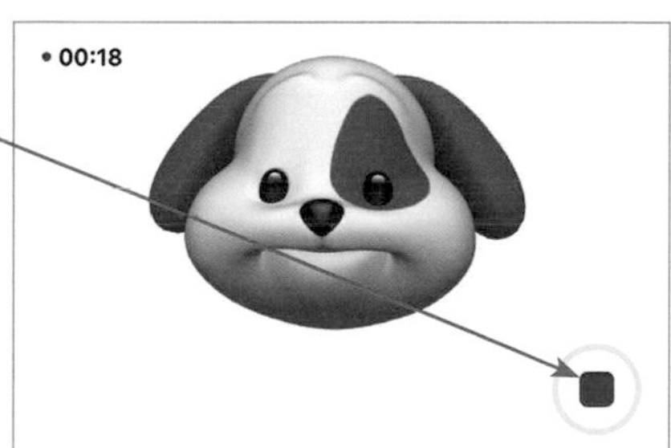

6. Tap once on the **Send** button to send the Animoji to the recipient of the message

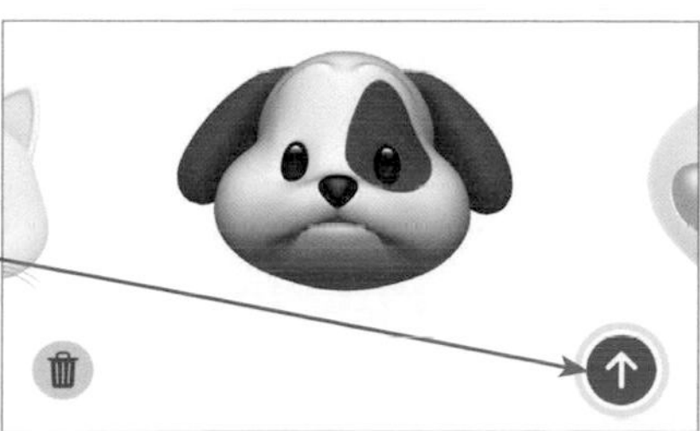

It is also possible to create animated avatars based on your own face. This is called a Memoji and it can be created by tapping once on the button in Step 2 and then tapping once on the **+** button. The Memoji is created using the avatar at the top of the window, which mirrors your expression as you look at it. A range of options, such as skin color, hairstyles, glasses and much more, can be added by swiping here and tapping once on the options below, to add them to the avatar.

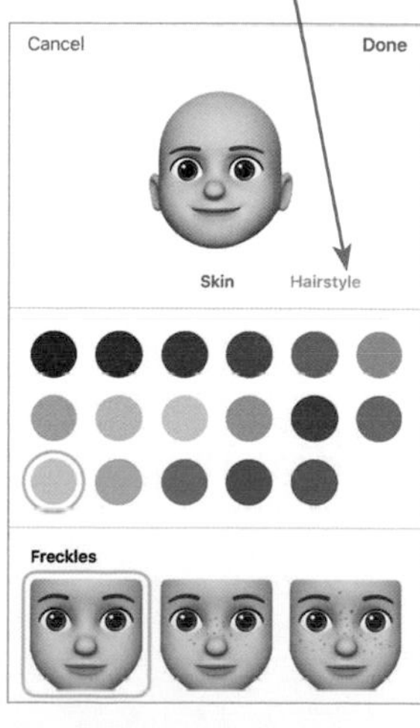

...cont'd

Full-screen messages

iMessages can also be sent with full-screen effects:

Once a Screen or Bubble effect has been added, tap once on this button to send the message.

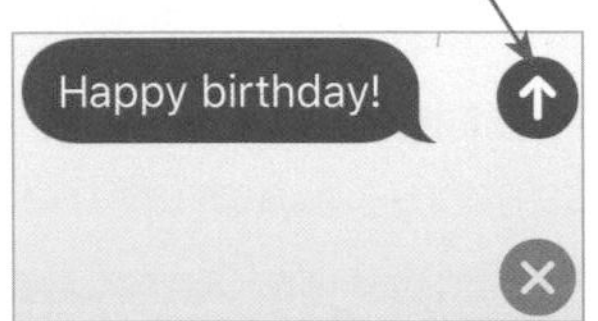

1. Write a message, and press and hold on this button 

2. Tap once on the **Screen** button at the top of the window

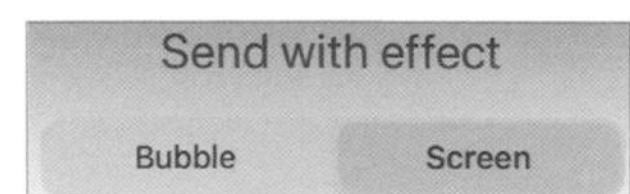

3. Different animated options can be selected to accompany the message

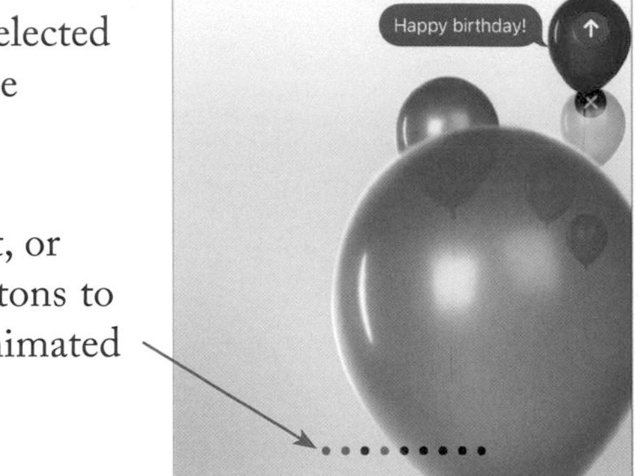

4. Swipe to the left, or tap on these buttons to view different animated effects

Bubble messages

A range of other effects can also be added to text messages:

Press and hold on a message that you have received, and tap once on one of these icons to send it as a reply. This is known as Tapback.

1. Tap once on the button in Step 1 for full-screen messages above and tap once on the **Bubble** button to create a message with one of the effects: **Slam**; **Loud**; **Gentle**; or **Invisible Ink**

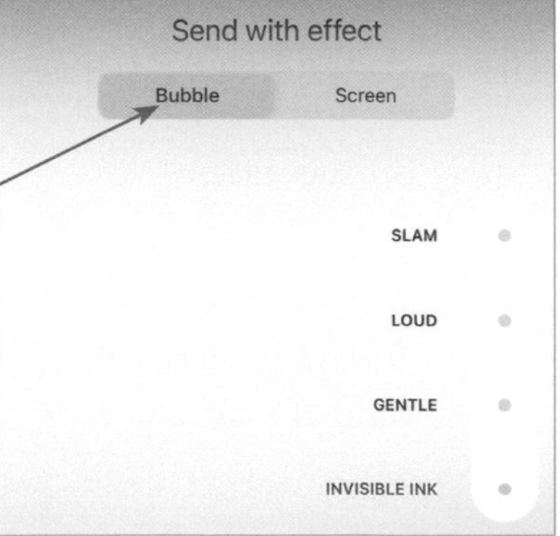

Pinning conversations

As more conversations are started with the Messages app, you may use some of them more than others. In cases such as this, it is possible to pin the most popular conversations at the top of the Messages window. To do this:

Pinning messages in the Messages app is a new feature in iOS 14.

1. Press and hold on an existing conversation with one of your contacts and tap once on the **Pin** button

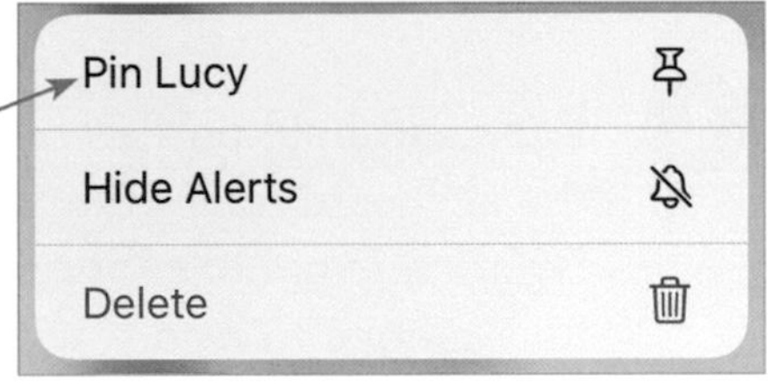

2. The conversation is pinned at the top of the window

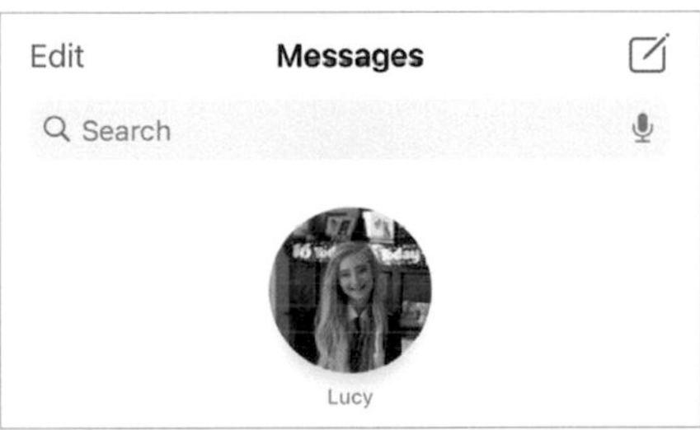

Replying within groups

Group conversations can be created in the Messages app by adding numerous recipients when the message is first created. Existing groups in the Contacts app can also be selected as the recipient for a conversation. When participating in a group conversation it can be useful to send replies to an individual, while still in the group conversation. This is known as an inline reply. To do this:

Using inline replies in the Messages app is a new feature in iOS 14.

1. Press and hold on a message in a group conversation and tap once on the **Reply** button

Voice Typing

On the keyboard there is also a voice-typing option, which enables you to enter text by speaking into a microphone, rather than typing on the keyboard. This is On by default.

Beware

Voice typing is not an exact science, and you may find that some strange examples appear. The best results are created if you speak as clearly as possible and reasonably slowly.

Using voice typing

Voice typing (dictation) can be used with any app with a text input function. To do this:

Dictation can be turned **On** or **Off** in **Settings** > **General** > **Keyboard** > **Enable Dictation**.

1. Press and hold on this button on the keyboard to activate the voice-typing microphone. Speak into the microphone to record text

2. As the voice-typing function is processing the recording, this screen appears

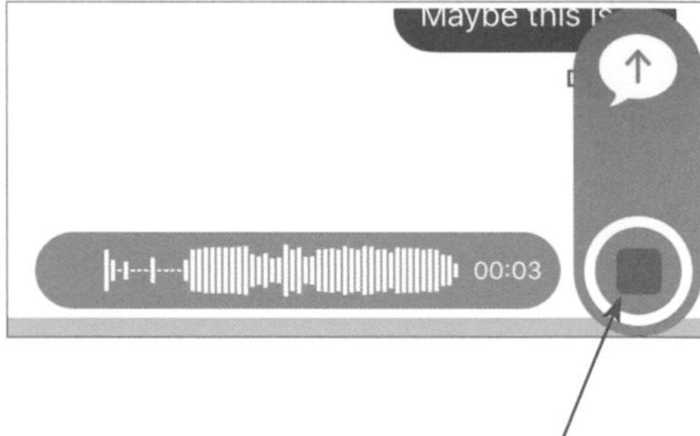

3. Tap once on this button to finish recording and return to the standard keyboard

4. Once the recording has been processed, the text appears in the app

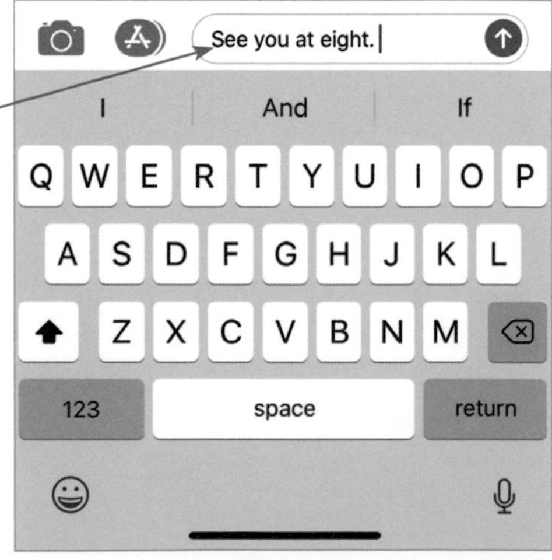

There are other voice-typing apps available from the App Store. One to try is Dragon Anywhere.

Managing Messages

Text conversations with individuals can become quite lengthy so it is sometimes a good idea to remove some messages, while still keeping the conversation going.

1. As a conversation with one person progresses, it moves downwards in the window

2. Press and hold on a message that you want to delete, and tap once on the **More...** button (pressing and holding on a message also activates the Tapback option; see page 106)

Reply

Copy

More...

3. Tap once next to any message that you want to delete, so that a white tick in a blue circle appears

4. Tap once on the Trash icon to delete the selected message(s)

You can copy a message by tapping once on the **Copy** button in Step 2 and then pasting it into another app, such as an email. To do this, press and hold on an open email, and tap once on the **Paste** button.

Settings for the Messages app can be applied in the Settings app. These include: **Send Read Receipts**, to indicate that you have read the message sent; and **Send as SMS**, to send a SMS message when iMessage is unavailable.

...cont'd

Whole conversations can also be deleted:

1. From a conversation, tap once on the **Back** button to view all of your conversations

2. Tap once on the **Edit** button

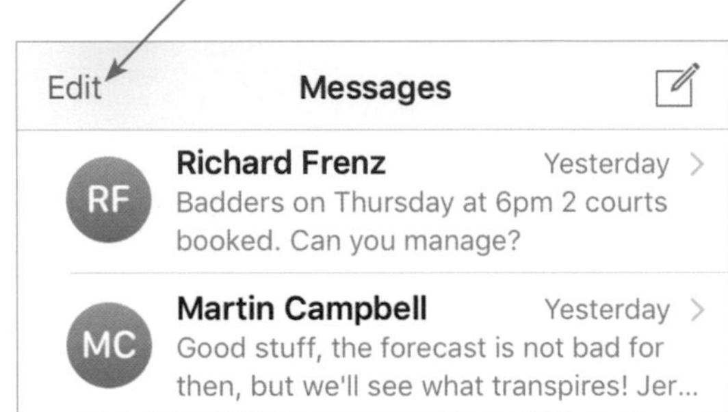

It is good housekeeping to delete conversations that have finished, otherwise you may end up with a long list of different ones.

3. Tap once next to any whole conversation(s) that you want to delete

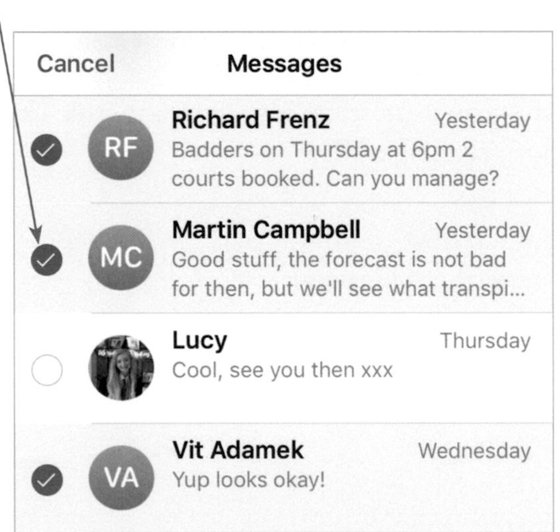

4. Tap once on the **Delete** button at the bottom right-hand corner of the screen to remove the selected conversation(s)

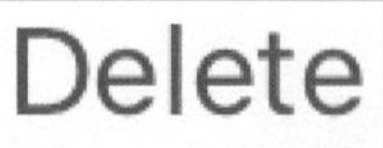

6 Camera and Photos

The iPhone has a high-quality camera, and the Photos app for viewing your photos.

The iPhone Camera

The cameras on the iPhone 12 range have the highest specifications to be included with any iPhone, and they take the art of digital photography on a smartphone to a new level. The iPhone 12 Pro and Pro Max are particularly effective for iPhones as they include three separate lenses, to enable a far greater area to be included in photos.

To take a quick photo, open the **Camera** app and press on either of the Volume buttons on the side of the iPhone.

iPhone 12 camera

The main iPhone 12 and iPhone 12 mini cameras consist of two lenses:

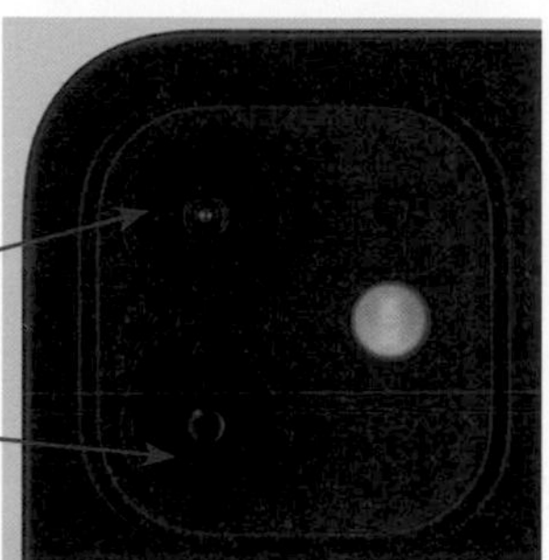

Tap on these buttons to switch between the two lenses.

Whenever you access your iPhone's camera, a small green dot appears at the top of the screen to indicate that the camera is in operation. This is a security feature so that you can see if anything has accessed your camera when you do not expect it. This is a new feature in iOS 14.

iPhone 12 Pro and Pro Max camera

The camera on the iPhone 12 Pro and Pro Max consists of three lenses:

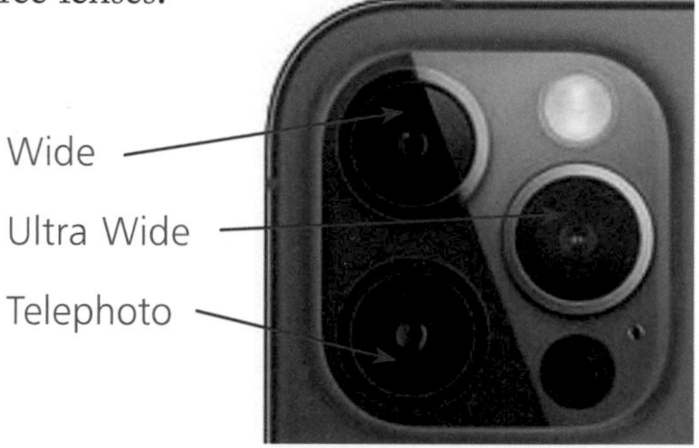

Tap on the same buttons as above for the iPhone 12 (the Pro and Pro Max both have an extra button that corresponds with the additional lens) to switch between the three lenses, or drag on the dial to change the angle of view.

Camera functionality

The general functionality of the iPhone 12 cameras can be accessed within the Camera app:

1. Tap once on the **Camera** app

2. Swipe here and select the **Photo** option. Tap once on this button to capture a photo

3. Tap once on this button to swap between the front or back cameras on the iPhone

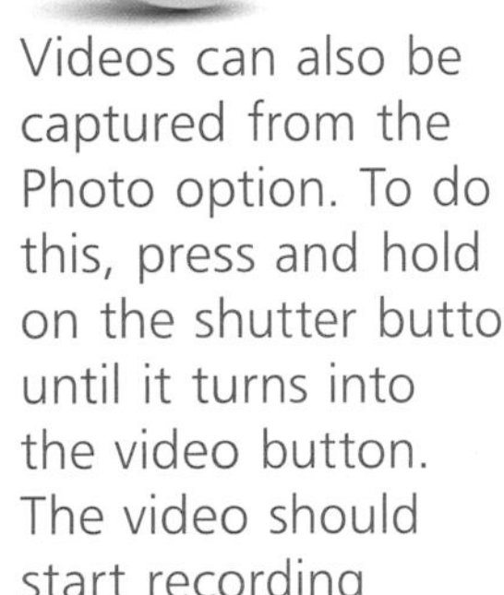

Videos can also be captured from the Photo option. To do this, press and hold on the shutter button until it turns into the video button. The video should start recording automatically. Release the button to end a video capture. When any video is captured it is stored within the **Photos** app.

Swipe left or right just above the shutter button, to access the different shooting options:

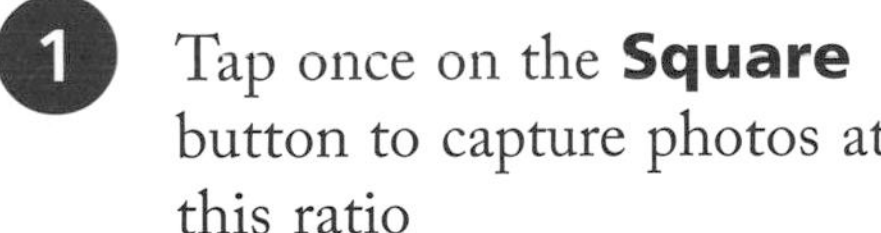

1. Tap once on the **Square** button to capture photos at this ratio

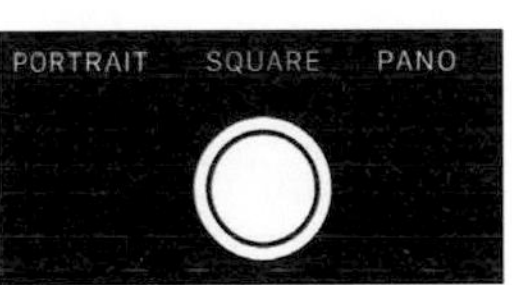

2. Tap once on the **Video** button and press the red shutter button to take a video

3. Tap once on the **Time-Lapse** button and press the shutter button (which appears in red with a ring around it) to create a time-lapse image: the camera keeps taking photos periodically until you press the shutter button again

Use the front-facing TrueDepth camera to take selfies (self-portraits of yourself, or a group of people). Use the video button to take a slow-motion video selfie, which Apple has decided to call a "slowfie".

...cont'd

Tap once on this button on either camera toolbar to turn it yellow, to take a Live Photo. This is a short animated image that can be viewed and edited in the Photos app.

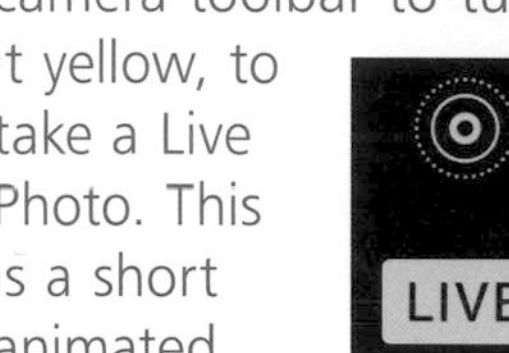

Tap once on this button on the bottom toolbar to apply a filter effect. When a filter effect has been selected, this button is displayed in the top right-hand corner of the camera window. It remains active until it is turned Off. To do this, tap once on the button to access the filters, and tap once on **Original**.

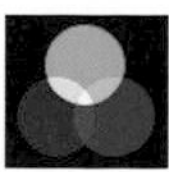

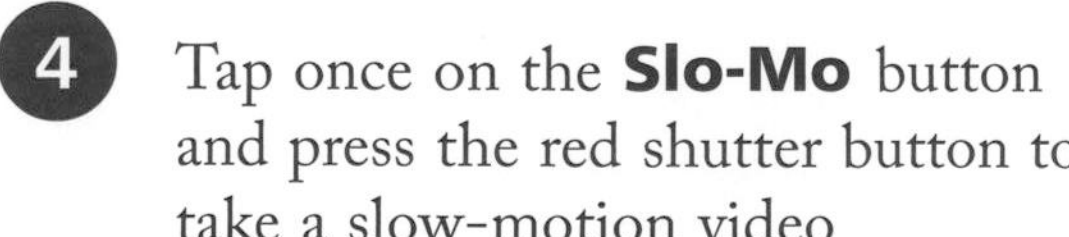

4. Tap once on the **Slo-Mo** button and press the red shutter button to take a slow-motion video

5. Tap once on the **Pano** button to create a panoramic image

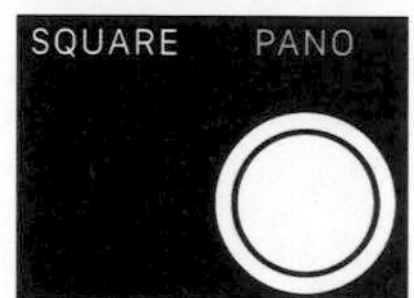

6. Move the iPhone slowly to the right to create the panorama. Each photo will be taken automatically when the camera is in the correct position

Camera functions

There are several options in the main camera window:

1. Tap once on the **Flash** button to set it for **Auto**, **On** or **Off.** Tap once on the **HDR** button, so it does not have a line through it, to take a composite photo of three separate images, to achieve the best exposure

2. Tap once on this button to expand the toolbar (which then appears at the bottom of the Camera window). Select the options for, from left to right: the **Flash**; **Live Photos** (see top tip); the **Aspect** (shape) of the photo; the **Self-timer** option; **Filters** (see bottom tip); and **HDR**

Portrait mode

Taking photos of people is one of the most common uses for the iPhone's camera. Using the iPhone camera in Portrait mode, it is possible to change the lighting of the photo. To do this:

1. Swipe here and tap once on the **Portrait** button to access options for portrait shots

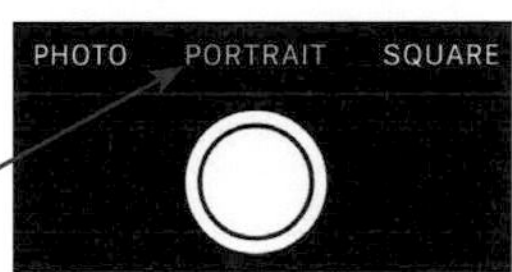

2. The lighting options are shown above the **Portrait** button. Tap once on each option to select the required lighting mode

Adding depth of field

Portrait photos can be enhanced by blurring the background behind the subject, so that they are more prominent. This is known as "depth of field". To do this:

1. Open the **Photos** app and tap once on a photo taken in Portrait mode

2. Tap once on the **f** number icon in the top left-hand corner, and drag this slider to apply a blurred effect to the background of the photo. The main subject will remain unchanged

3. Tap once of the **Done** button to apply the depth-of-field effect to the photo

When creating a depth-of-field effect, ensure the **Portrait** button at the top of the screen is On; e.g. yellow. Tap on it once to turn it Off and edit the whole photo, not just the background.

PORTRAIT

Photo Settings

iCloud sharing

Certain photo options can be applied within Settings. Several of these are to do with storing and sharing your photos via iCloud. To access these:

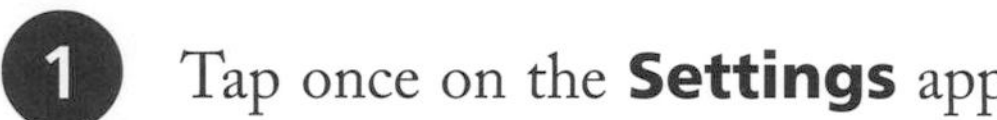

1. Tap once on the **Settings** app

2. Tap once on the **Photos** tab

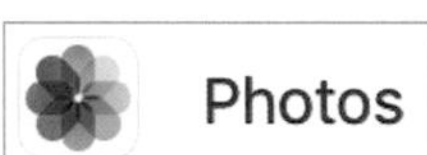

3. Drag the **iCloud Photos** button **On** to upload your whole iPhone photo library to the iCloud. You will then be able to access this from any other Apple devices that you have. Similarly, photos on your other Apple devices can also be uploaded to the iCloud, and these will be available on your iPhone

iCloud Photos 

4. Drag the **Upload to My Photo Stream** button **On** to enable all new photos and videos from your iPhone to be uploaded automatically to iCloud

Upload to My Photo Stream 

5. Drag the **Shared Albums** button **On** to allow you to create albums within the Photos app that can then be shared with other people via iCloud

Shared Albums 

Drag the **Grid** button in the **Camera** settings **On** to place a grid over the screen when you are taking photos with the camera, if required. This can be used to help compose photos by placing subjects using the grid.

Viewing Photos

Once photos have been captured, they can be viewed and organized in the Photos app. To do this:

1. Tap once on the **Photos** app

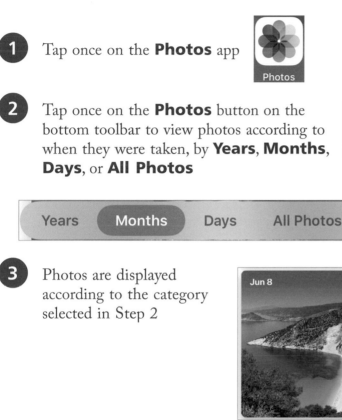

2. Tap once on the **Photos** button on the bottom toolbar to view photos according to when they were taken, by **Years**, **Months**, **Days**, or **All Photos**

Years Months Days All Photos

3. Photos are displayed according to the category selected in Step 2

4. If photos are displayed in **Days** or **All Photos** mode, tap once on the **Select** button to select specific photos by tapping on them, or by dragging over several photos

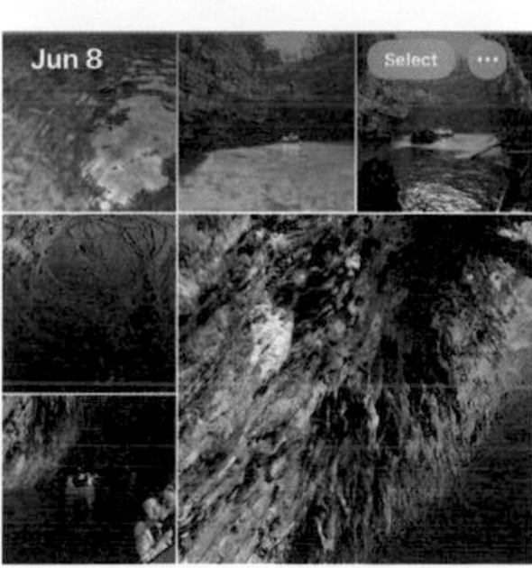

Select

5. Once photos have been selected, or if they are being viewed at full size, tap once on this button to **Share** them

Double-tap with one finger on a full-size photo to zoom in on it. Double-tap again to zoom back out. To zoom in to a greater degree, swipe outwards with thumb and forefinger. To zoom back out, pinch inwards with thumb and forefinger.

Tap once on the **Albums** button on the bottom toolbar to view available albums for storing photos. Tap once on this button to create a new album and select items to go in it.

For You Tab

In the Photos app, the For You section is where the best of your photos are selected and displayed automatically. To use this:

When a Memory is playing as shown in Step 3, tap once on an image on the screen and tap once on the **Edit** button in the top right-hand corner to access the editing options for the Memory. These include editing the music, title, duration, and the items in the Memory. Tap once on the **Done** button in the bottom right-hand corner to exit the editing mode.

1. Tap once on the **For You** button on the bottom toolbar of the Photos app

2. Memories are displayed in the **For You** section. These are collections of photos created by the Photos app, using what it determines are the best shots for a related series of photos

3. Tap once on a Memory to view its details. Tap once on the **Play** button to view a full-screen slideshow of all of the images, including music

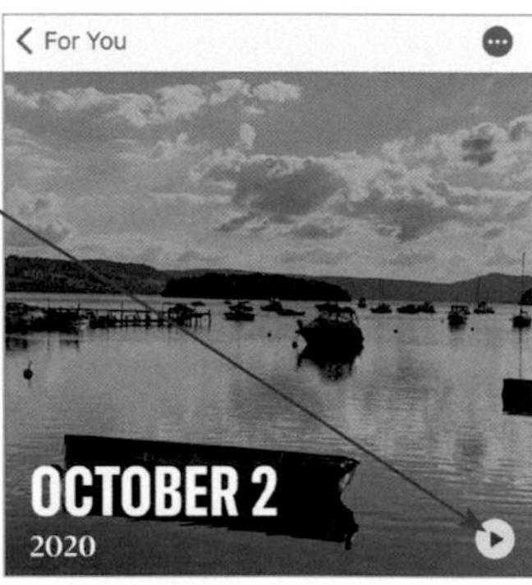

4. Swipe down the For You page to access more options for how photos are grouped and organized

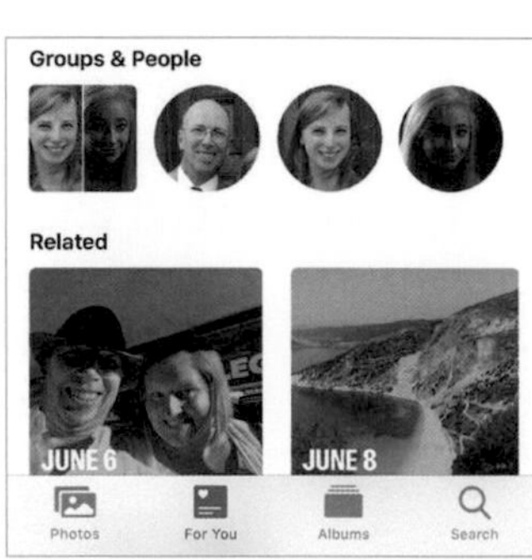

Editing Photos

The Photos app has options to perform a range of photo-editing operations. To use these:

1 Open a photo at full-screen size and tap once on the **Edit** button to access the editing tools, on the bottom toolbar

2 Tap once on the **Adjust** button to access color-editing options

3 Tap once on the **Auto** button to have auto-coloring editing applied to the photo

4 Swipe from right to left to access the full range of the Adjust options

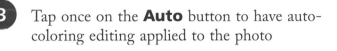

5 For each option, drag the slider to apply the required level of the effect

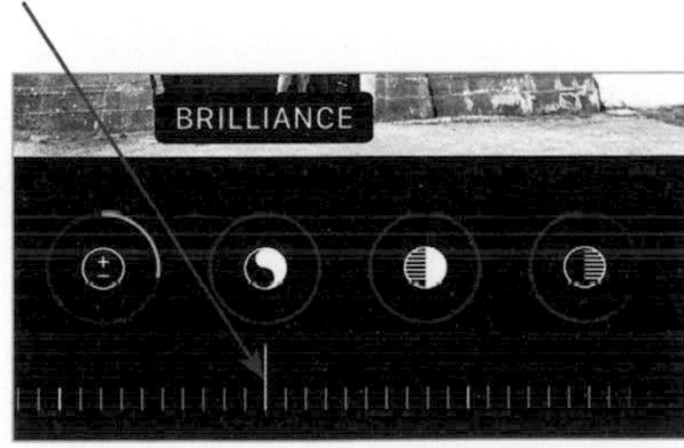

Editing changes are made to the original photo once the changes have been saved. These will also apply to any albums into which the photo has been placed.

The Adjust color-editing options include: Exposure; Brilliance; Highlights; Shadows; Contrast; Brightness; Saturation; and Vibrance.

Videos can now also have the same range of editing effects applied to them as still photos.

...cont'd

6. Tap once on the **Filters** button in Step 1 on page 119 to select special effects to be applied to the photo. Swipe left and right here to view the available filters. Tap once on one to apply it

If you reopen a photo that has been edited and closed, you have an option to **Revert** to its original state, before it was edited.

7. Tap once on this button in Step 1 on page 119 to access options for rotating the photo and cropping it, by dragging the resizing handles around the border of the photo. Use these options to, from left to right: straighten the photo by dragging the slider; flip it vertically; and flip it horizontally

Check out **Smartphone Photography in easy steps** at **www.ineasysteps.com** for more on using your iPhone to create stunning photographs.

8. For each function, tap once on the **Done** button to save the photo with the selected changes

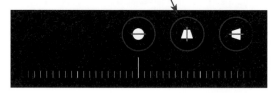

9. Tap once on the **Cancel** button to quit the editing process

7 The Online World

This chapter shows how to use your iPhone to keep ahead in the fast-moving world of online communications, using the web, email, social media, and video calls.

Getting Online

Connecting to Wi-Fi is one of the main ways that the iPhone can get online access. You will need to have an Internet Service Provider and a Wi-Fi router to connect to the internet. Once this is in place, you will be able to connect to a Wi-Fi network:

Don't forget

You can also get online access through your cellular network, which is provided by your phone network supplier. However, data charges may apply for this.

1. Tap once on the **Settings** app

2. Tap once on the **Wi-Fi** tab

3. Ensure the **Wi-Fi** button is in the **On** position

4. Available networks are shown here. Tap once on one to select it

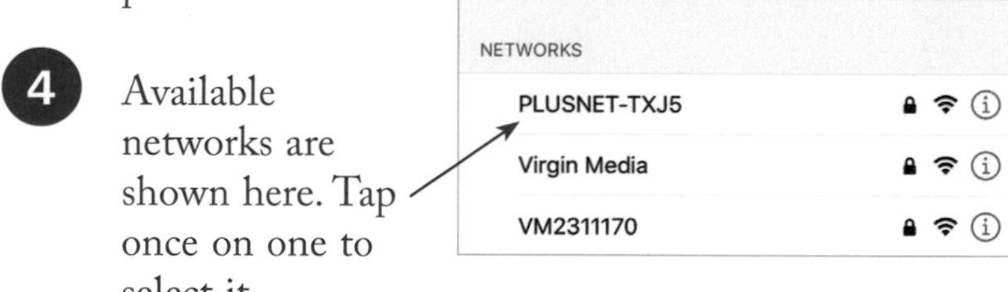

If you are connecting to your home Wi-Fi network, the iPhone should connect automatically each time, after it has been set up. If you are connecting in a public Wi-Fi area, you will be asked which network you would like to join.

5. Enter a password for your Wi-Fi router

6. Tap once on the **Join** button

7. Once a network has been joined, a tick appears next to it. This now provides access to the internet

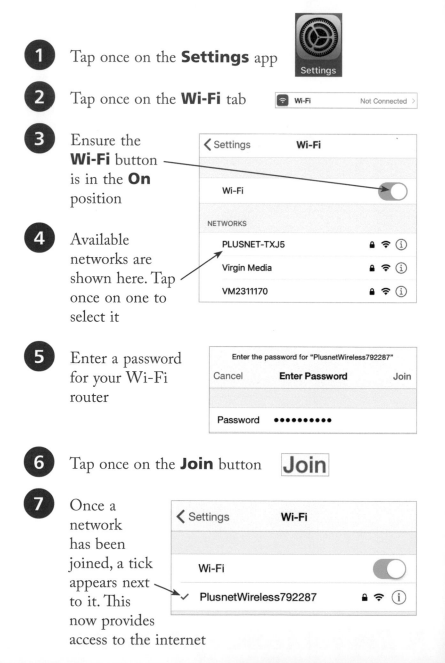

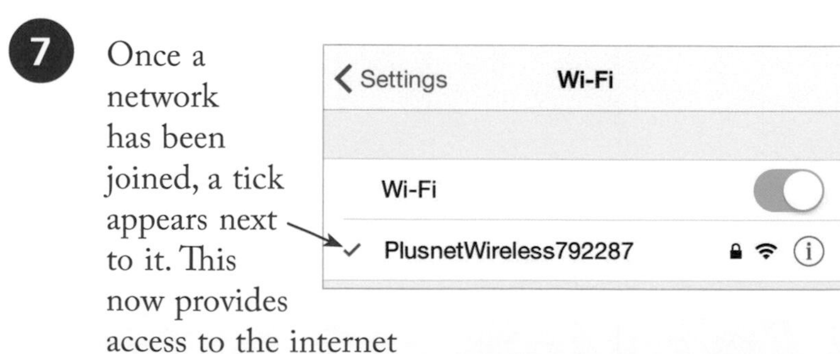

Safari Settings

Safari is the default web browser on the iPhone, and it can be used to bring the web to your iPhone. Before you start using Safari, there are a range of settings that can be applied:

1. Tap once on the **Settings** app

2. Tap once on the **Safari** tab

3. Make selections under the **Search** section for the default search engine, options for suggestions appearing as you type search words and phrases, and preloading the top-rating page in a search

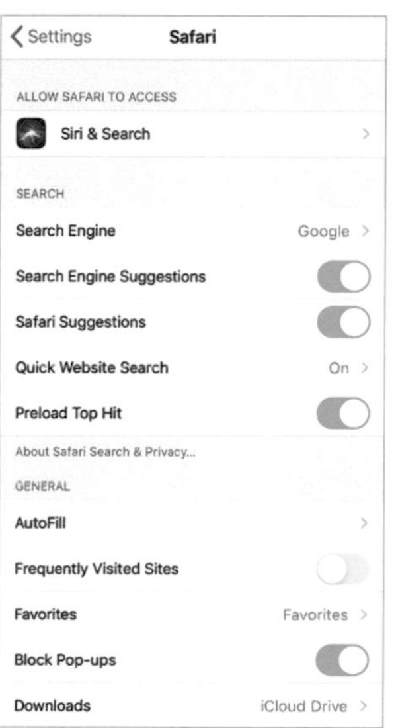

4. Make selections under the **General** section for entering passwords, specifying the items for the Favorites window, and blocking pop-ups

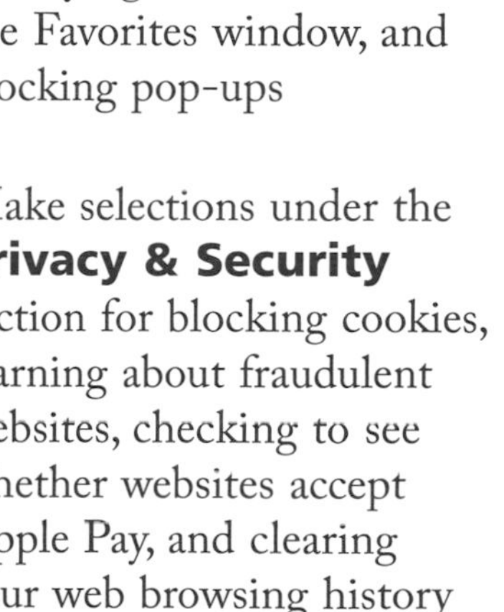

5. Make selections under the **Privacy & Security** section for blocking cookies, warning about fraudulent websites, checking to see whether websites accept Apple Pay, and clearing your web browsing history and web data

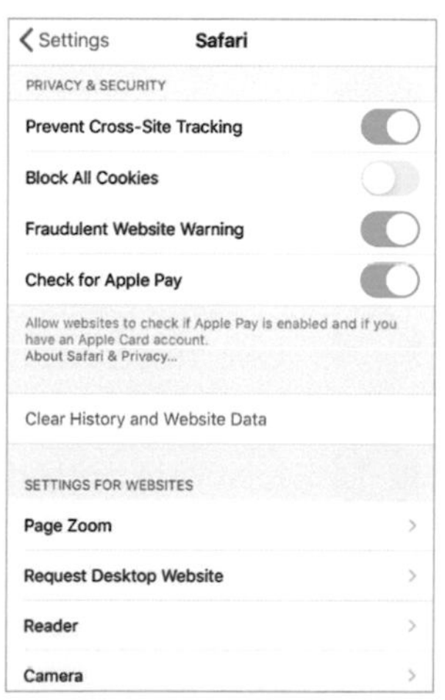

Because of the proliferation of apps available for the iPhone, you may find that you use Safari less than on a desktop or laptop computer. For example, most major news outlets have their own apps that can be used as stand-alone items, rather than having to use Safari to access the site. Look for apps for your favorite websites in the App Store, as a shortcut for accessing them quickly.

The iPhone 12 range has a setting for **Show Tab Bar**, which displays the open tabs along the top of the Safari window, if the iPhone is being used in Landscape mode.

Web Browsing with Safari

Hot tip

Tap once on this button in the Address Bar to access the web page options, including: **Show Reader View**, for viewing page without additional content; **Hide Toolbar**; **Request Desktop Website**; **Website Settings**; and a **Privacy Report** (see next tip).

AA

A	100%	A
Show Reader View		
Hide Toolbar		
Request Desktop Website		
Website Settings		
Privacy Report No Trackers Contacted		

The final option for the web page options is **Privacy Report**, which can show any websites that are tracking your online activity. This is a new feature in iOS 14.

To start browsing the web with Safari and enjoy the variety of the information within it:

1. Tap once on the **Safari** app

2. Enter a website address here in the Address Bar, or tap once on one of the items in the Start page – e.g. one of the Favorites, or one of the Siri suggestions

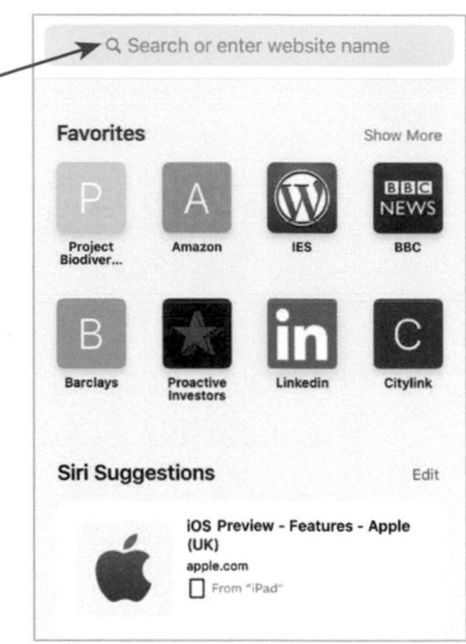

3. As you type in the Address Bar, website suggestions appear, and also search suggestions from Google

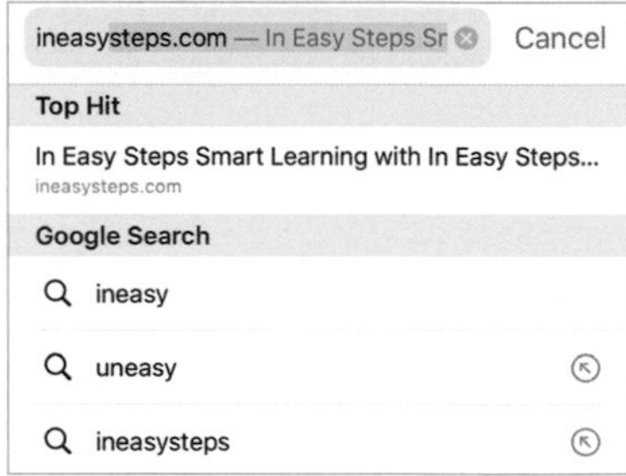

4. When you access a web page, use these buttons to visit the next and previous pages

5. Use this button to share a web page

6. Use this button to view bookmarks

7. Use this button to view, add and delete tabs (see pages 126-127)

Adding bookmarks

Everyone has favorite websites that they visit, and in Safari it is possible to mark these with bookmarks so that they can be accessed quickly. To do this:

1. Tap once on this button on the bottom toolbar

2. Tap once on the **Add Bookmark** button

Add Bookmark

3. Select a name and location for the bookmark, and tap once on the **Save** button

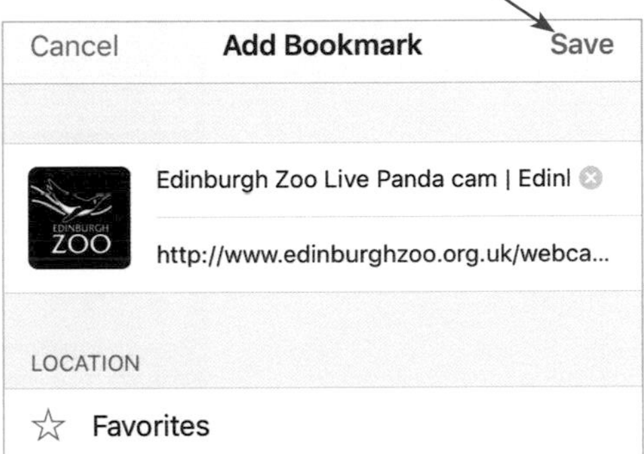

4. Tap once on the **Bookmarks** button, and tap once here to view your bookmarks

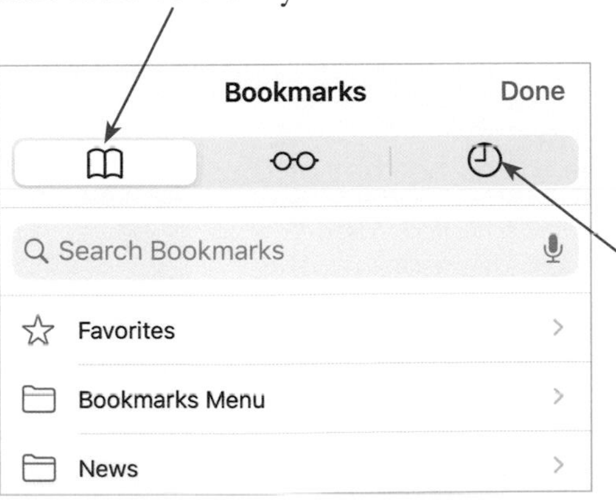

The **Share** button can be used to share a web page via Message, Mail, or social media sites such as Facebook or Twitter. It can also be used to add a web page link to a Note (see pages 152-153).

If the bottom toolbar is not visible on a web page, swipe downwards on the page to view it.

The **Bookmarks** button in Step 4 can also be used to access Reading List items. These are added from the **Share** button in Step 1, and enable items to be saved and read later, even if you are not connected to the internet. (The third button in Step 4 is for accessing your web browsing history.)

Using Tabs in Safari

In keeping with most modern web browsers, Safari uses tabs so that you can have several websites open at the same time. However, due to the fact that a smartphone's screen is smaller than those on a desktop or laptop computer, tabs operate in a specific way on the iPhone. To use tabs:

Press and hold on a tab to drag it into a different position in Tab View.

Press and hold the Tab button to get the option to close all open tabs in one action.

Tap once on the **Done** button at the bottom of the Tab View window to exit this and return to the web page that was being viewed when Tab View was activated.

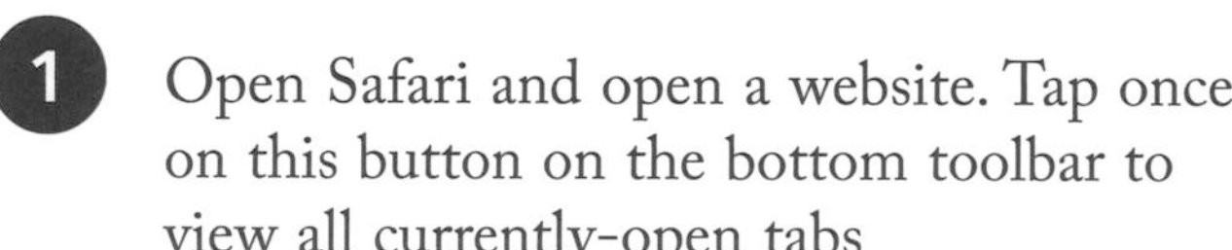

1. Open Safari and open a website. Tap once on this button on the bottom toolbar to view all currently-open tabs

2. Swipe up and down in Tab View to view all of the open tabs. Tap once on one to view that web page at full size

3. Swipe to the bottom of the page to view any tabs that you have open on another compatible Apple devices, such as an iPad, providing both devices share the same Apple ID

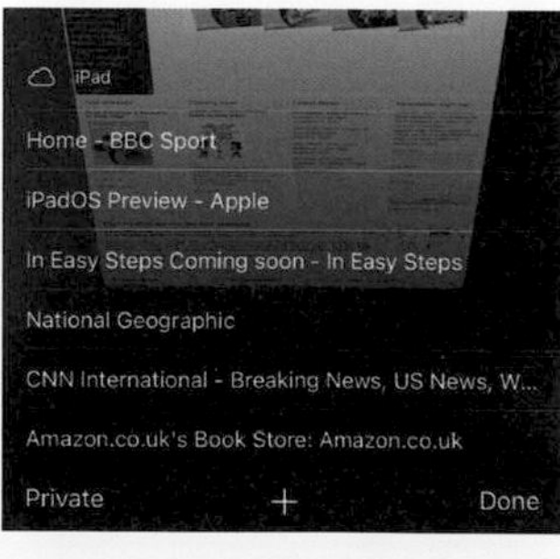

Opening tabs

To open more tabs in Safari on your iPhone:

1. Open the Tab View window as shown opposite, and tap once on this button 

2. Open the new tab by entering a web address in the Address Bar, or by tapping once on one of the items in the Favorites window

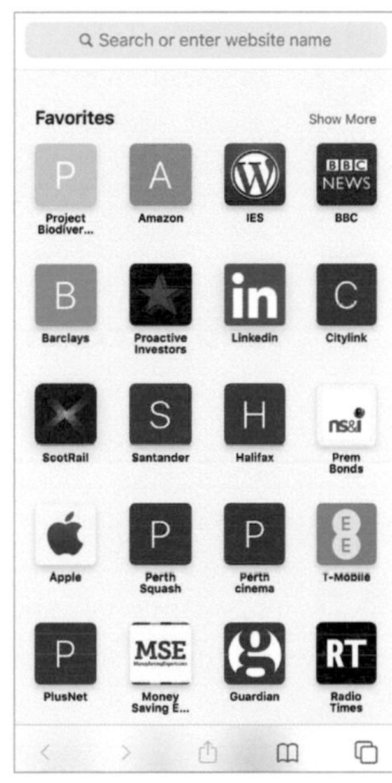

3. Tap once on the **Private** button in Tab View to open a new tab that is not recorded in your web history

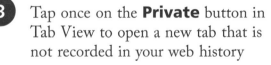

4. Open the private tab in the same way as a regular one. This is indicated by a dark bar at the top of the window

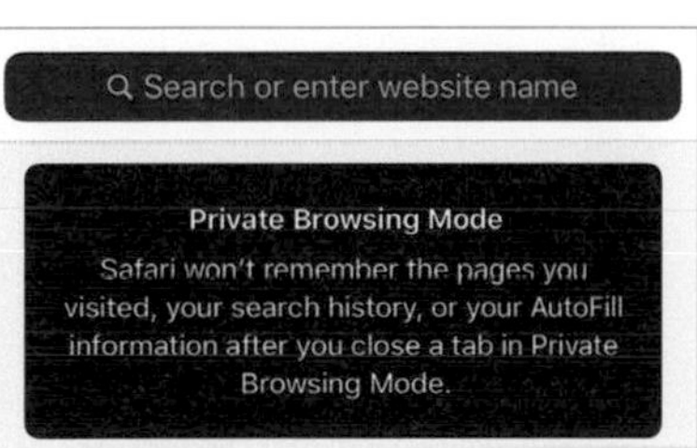

5. Tap once on this button to close any tab in Tab View 

The items that appear in the Favorites window can be specified with the Safari settings: **Settings** > **Safari** > **Favorites** and by then selecting a category. This page will appear when a new tab is opened, and also when you tap in the Address Bar to enter a web address.

Setting Up an Email Account

Email accounts

Email settings can be specified within the Settings app. Different email accounts can also be added there.

1. 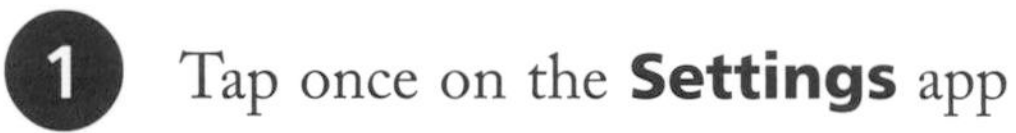Tap once on the **Settings** app

2. Tap once on the **Mail** tab

3. Tap once on the **Accounts** button

4. Tap once on the **Add Account** button to add a new account

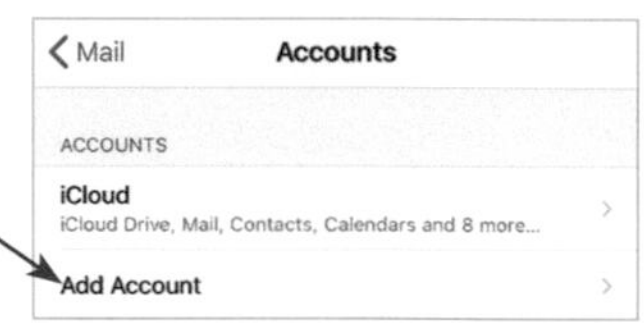

5. Tap once on the type of email account you want to add

6. Enter the details for the account, and tap on the **Next** button to move through the wizard

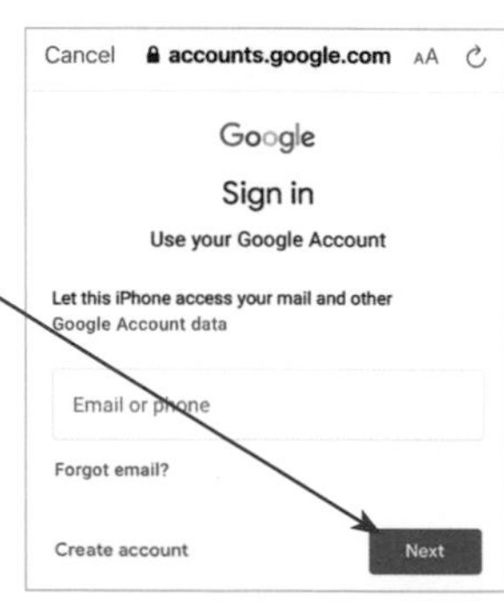

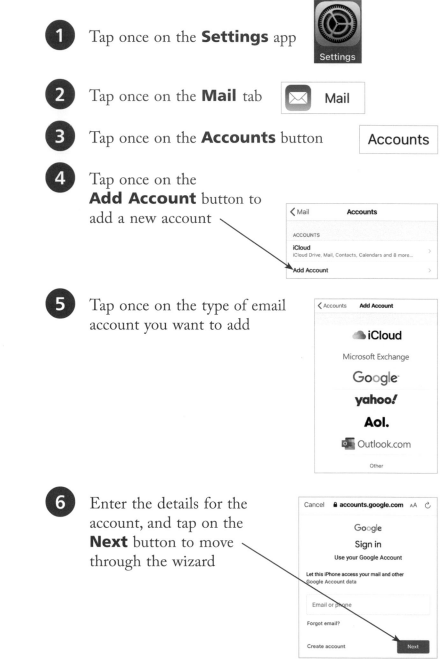

If your email provider is not on the **Add Account** list, tap once on **Other** at the bottom of the list and complete the account details using the information from your email provider.

7. Drag these buttons **On** or **Off** to specify which functions are to be available for the required account. Tap once on the **Save** button

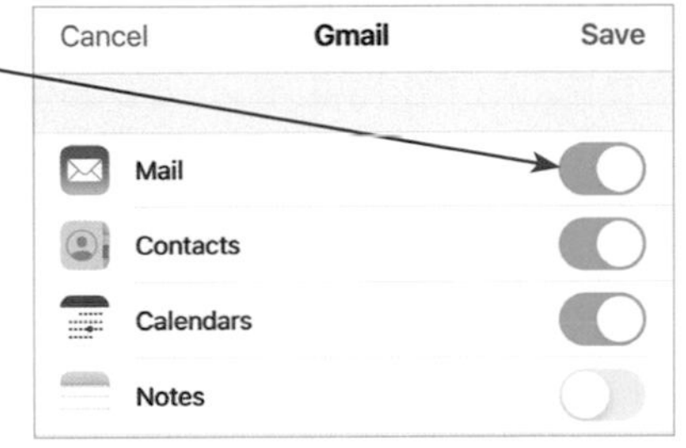

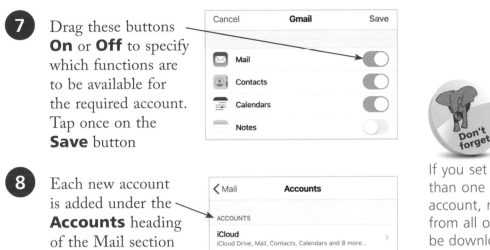

8. Each new account is added under the **Accounts** heading of the Mail section

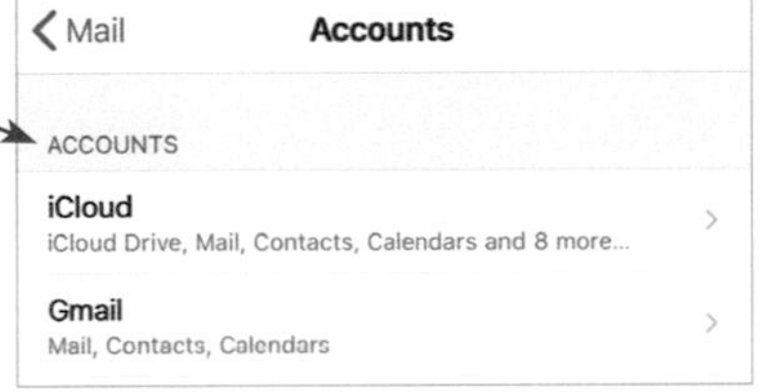

If you set up more than one email account, messages from all of them can be downloaded and displayed by **Mail**.

Email settings

Email settings can be specified within the Settings app:

1. Under the **Mail** section there are several options for how Mail operates and looks. These include how much of an email will be previewed in your Inbox, and options for accessing actions by swiping on an email

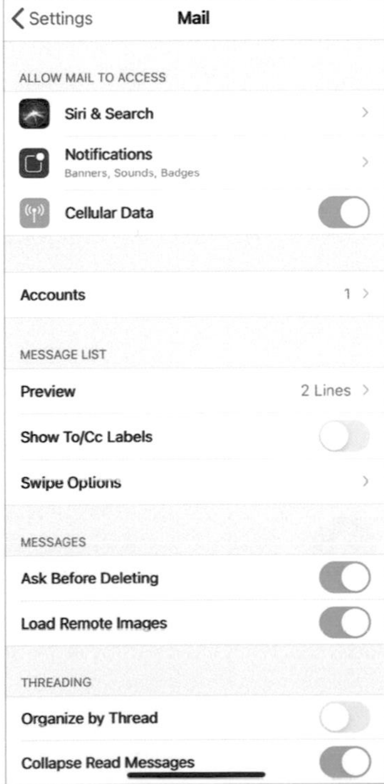

The **Organize by Thread** option can be turned **On** to show connected email conversations within your Inbox. If there is a thread of emails, this is indicated by this symbol:

Monday >

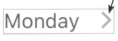

Tap on it once to view the thread.

Emailing

Use these buttons at the top of the window when you are reading an email to view the next and previous messages.

To delete an email from your Inbox, swipe on it from right to left, and tap once on the **Trash/Delete** button.

If the **Fetch New Data** option in **Settings** > **Mail** > **Accounts** is set to **Push**, new emails will be downloaded automatically from your mail server. To check manually, swipe down from the top of the mailbox pane. The Push option uses up more battery power.

Email on the iPhone is created, sent and received using the Mail app (although other email apps can be downloaded from the App Store). This provides a range of functionality for managing emails and responding to them.

Accessing Mail

To access Mail and start sending and receiving emails:

1. Tap once on the **Mail** app (the red icon in the corner displays the number of unread emails in your Inbox)

2. Tap once on a message to display it in the main panel

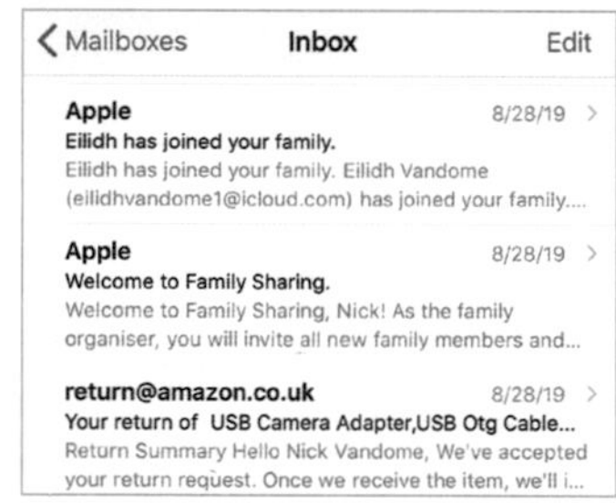

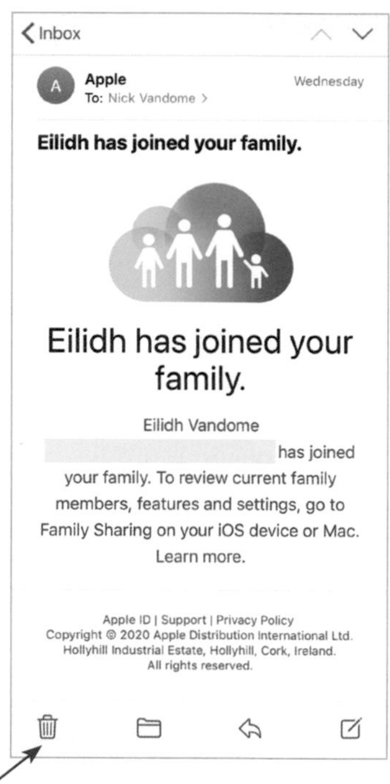

3. Use these buttons to, from left to right: delete a message; move a message to a different folder; or respond to a message (see next page)

4. Tap once on this button to reply to a message, reply to everyone in a conversation, forward it to a new recipient, delete it, flag it, mark it as unread, or move it to a folder

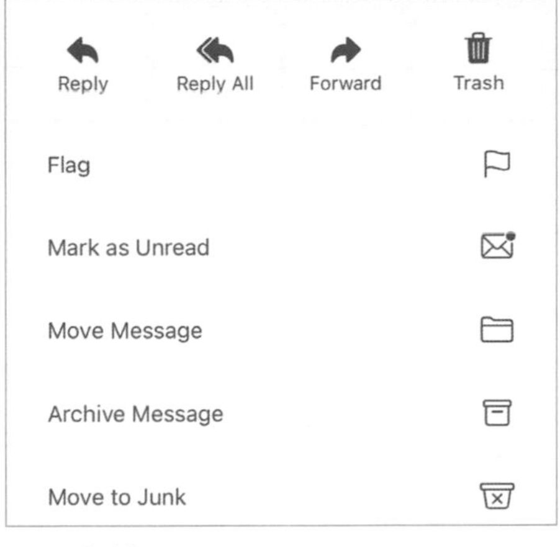

If the recipient is included in your Contacts app, their details will appear as you type in Step 2. Tap once on a name to add it in the To: box.

Creating email

To create and send an email:

1. Tap once on this button to create a new message
2. Enter a recipient name in the **To:** box

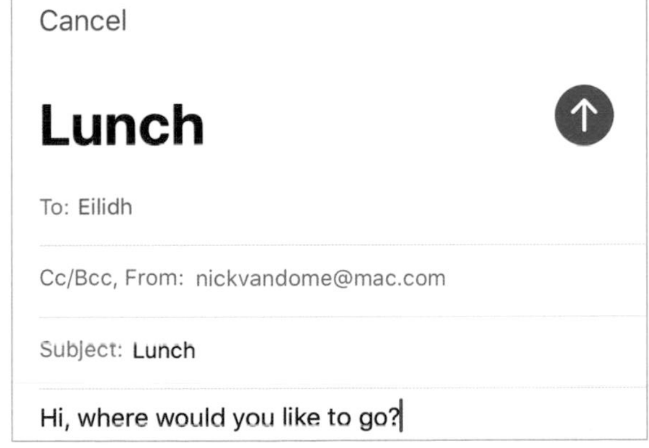

3. Enter a subject and body text
4. Tap once on the **Send** button to send the email to the recipient

When writing an email, these buttons above the keyboard can be used to, from left to right: change the text size; add a photo; take a photo; add a document; scan a document; or add a freehand sketch.

Having a Video Chat

Video chatting is a very personal and interactive way to keep in touch with family and friends around the world. The FaceTime app provides this facility with other iPhone, iPad, iPod Touch, and Mac computer users with FaceTime. To use FaceTime for video chatting:

1. Tap once on the **FaceTime** app

2. Tap once on this button to start a new video chat and tap once here to select a contact

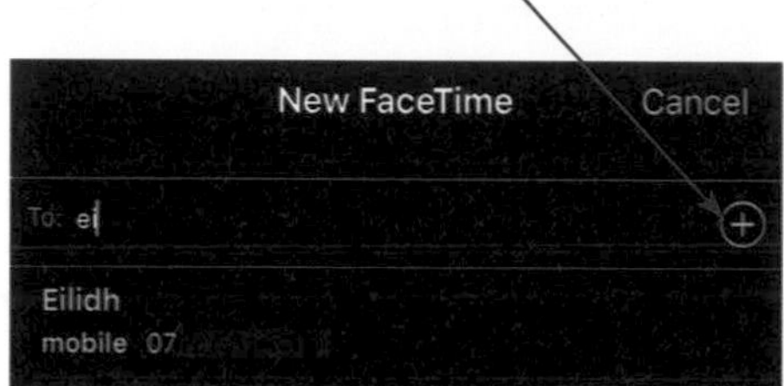

3. Tap once on a contact to access their details for making a FaceTime call

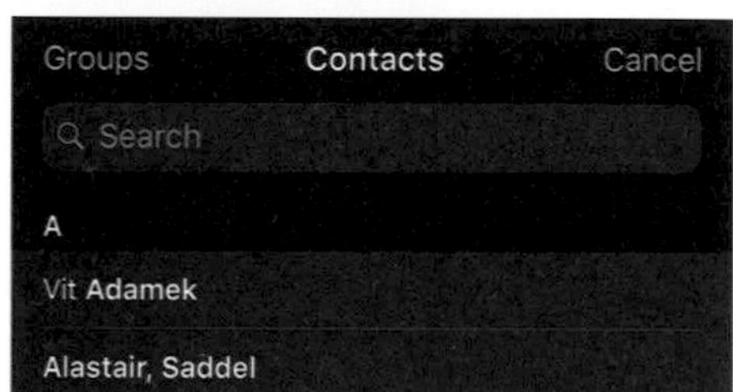

4. Tap once on their phone number or email address to make a FaceTime call. The recipient must have FaceTime on their iPhone, iPad, iPod Touch or Mac computer. Tap once on these buttons to make a video or audio call

Don't forget

To make video calls with FaceTime you need an active internet connection and to be signed in with your Apple ID.

The contacts for FaceTime calls are taken from the iPhone Contacts app. You can also add new contacts directly to the contacts list by tapping once on the **+** sign and adding the relevant details for the new contact.

Skype and Zoom are two more options for making free video calls. The apps can be downloaded from the App Store.

5. Once you have selected a contact, FaceTime starts connecting to them and displays this at the top of the screen

6. When you have connected, your contact appears in the main window and you appear in a picture-in-picture thumbnail in the corner

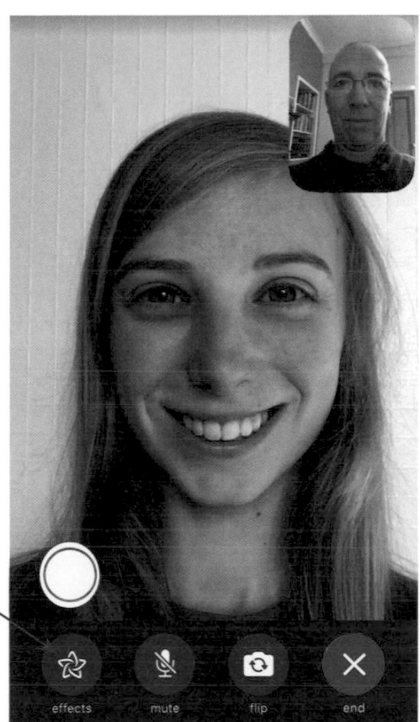

7. Tap once on this button to access effects options that can be added to your own video display, including filters and text

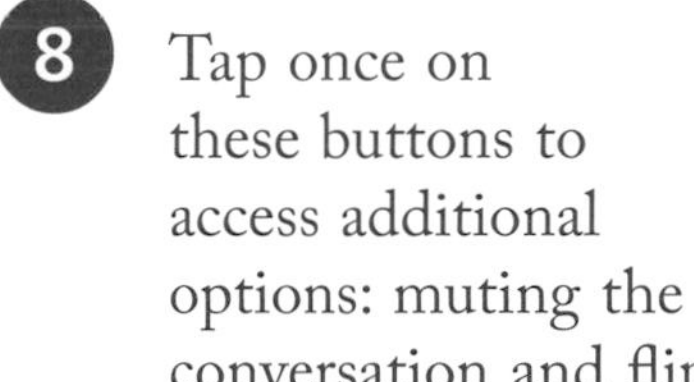

8. Tap once on these buttons to access additional options: muting the conversation and flipping the camera view

9. Tap once on this button to end a FaceTime call

Tap once on the **effects** button in Step 7 and tap once on this button to access any Animojis or Memojis that you have created (see page 105). Tap once on one to superimpose it over your own face in the FaceTime window.

Adding Social Media

Don't forget

Social media sites can be accessed from their own apps on the iPhone, and also from their respective websites, using Safari.

Check out **Facebook for Seniors in easy steps** for more help with using this app, at **www.ineasysteps.com**

Updates can be set to appear in your **Notification Center**. Open **Settings**, and tap once on the **Notifications** tab. Under the **Notification Style** heading, tap once on the social media site and select options for how you would like the notifications to appear.

Using social media sites such as Facebook, Twitter, Instagram, and Snapchat to keep in touch with family and friends has now become common across all generations. On the iPhone with iOS 14, it is possible to link to these accounts so that you can share content to them from your iPhone, and also view updates through the Notification Center. To add social media apps to your iPhone:

1. Open the App Store and navigate to the **Apps** > **Categories** > **Social Networking** section

   Social Networking

2. Tap once on the required apps to download them to your iPhone

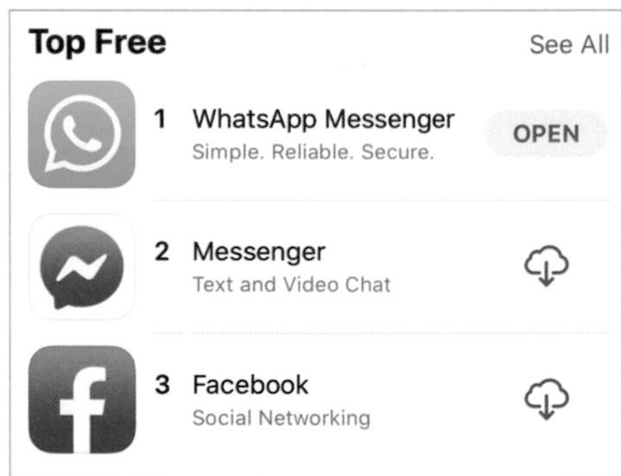

3. Tap once on an app to open it

4. If you already have an account with the social media service, enter your login details, or tap once on the **Create New Account** button to create a new account

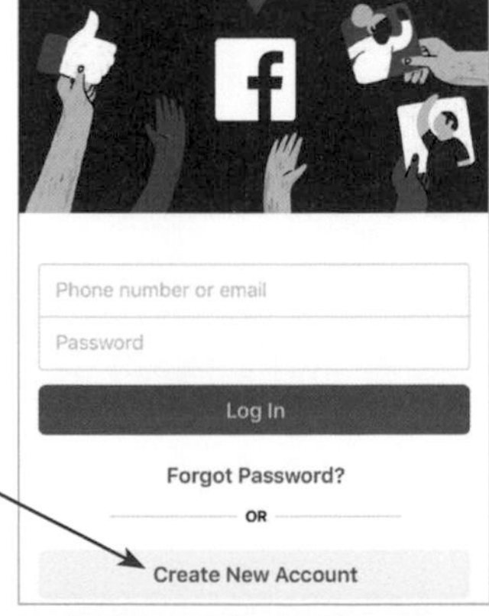

8 Hands on with Apps

Apps provide the iPhone with its functionality. This chapter details the built-in apps, and also shows how to access those in the App Store.

What is an App?

An app is just a more modern name for a computer program. Initially, it was used in relation to mobile devices such as the iPhone and the iPad, but it is now becoming more widely used with desktop and laptop computers, for both Mac and Windows operating systems.

You need an active internet connection to download apps from the App Store.

On the iPhone there are two types of apps:

- **Built-in apps**. These are the apps that come already installed on the iPhone.
- **App Store apps**. These are apps that can be downloaded from the online App Store. There is a huge range of apps available there, covering a variety of different categories. Some are free, while others have to be paid for. The apps in the App Store are updated and added to on a daily basis, so there are always new ones to explore.

Within a number of apps there is a **Share** button that can be used to share items through a variety of methods, including Messages, email, Facebook and Twitter.

There are also two important points about apps (both built-in and those from the App Store) to remember:

- Apart from some of the built-in apps, the majority of apps do not interact with each other. This means that there is less chance of viruses being transmitted from app to app on your iPhone, and they can operate without a reliance on other apps.
- Content created by apps is saved within the app itself, rather than within a file structure on your iPhone; e.g. if you create a note in the Notes app, it is saved there; if you take a photo, it is saved in the Photos app. Content is usually also saved automatically when it is created or edited, so you do not have to worry about saving it as you work on it.

Built-in Apps

The built-in iPhone apps are the ones that appear on the Home screen when you first get your iPhone:

- **App Store**. This can be used to access the online App Store, from where additional apps can be downloaded and updated.

- **Books**. This is an app for downloading electronic books, which can then be read on the iPhone.

- **Calculator**. This is a basic calculator, which can also be accessed from the Control Center.

- **Calendar**. An app for storing appointments, important dates, and other calendar information. It can be synced with iCloud.

- **Camera**. This gives direct access to the front-facing and rear-facing iPhone cameras.

- **Clock**. This displays the current time, and can be used to view the time in different countries. It also has an alarm clock and a stopwatch.

- **Compass**. This can be used to show you the direction of North. You can give the compass access to your location so that you can follow it from where you are.

- **Contacts**. An address book app. Once contacts are added here they can then also be accessed from other apps, such as Mail.

- **FaceTime**. This app uses the front-facing FaceTime camera to hold video or audio chats with compatible Apple devices.

- **Files**. This is used to back up items and make them available to other Apple devices.

When you first open some apps they will display options for location access; e.g. whether the app can access your current location. The options are for: allowing access while using the app; allowing access once; or not allowing access. If you select to allow access once, you will be prompted with the same query the next time you use the app. This is a feature designed to prevent apps from constantly having access to your location. Location settings can also be applied in **Settings** > **Privacy** > **Location Services** and then by tapping once on the app name.

If you don't want your contacts to be accessed by other apps, open **Settings** > **Privacy** > **Contacts** and drag the button for these apps **Off**.

Although iTunes has been removed from Mac computers with the macOS operating system, the iTunes Store is still a part of iOS 14 and can be used to download a range of content, including music and movies. These items are then displayed in their respective apps; i.e. the Music and TV apps, which can both access content too.

Check out **Smart Homes in easy steps** for more help with this app, at **www.ineasysteps.com**

You need an Apple ID to obtain content from the iTunes Store and the Book Store.

- **Find My**. This can be used to view the location of family and friends, based on their Apple mobile devices and Mac computers. See pages 184-185.

- **Health**. This stores and collates a range of health information. See pages 149-151.

- **Home**. This is a new app in iOS 14 that can be used to control certain compatible functions within the home, such as heating controls.

- **iTunes Store**. This app can be used to browse the iTunes Store, where content can be downloaded to your iPhone.

- **Mail**. This is the email app for sending and receiving email on your iPhone.

- **Maps**. Use this app to view maps from around the world, find specific locations, and get directions to destinations.

- **Measure**. This can be used to measure the length or perimeter of items.

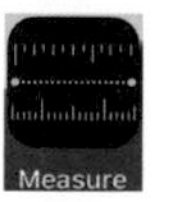

- **Messages**. This is the iPhone messaging service, which can be used for SMS text messages and iMessages between compatible Apple devices.

- **Music**. An app for playing music on your iPhone and also viewing cover artwork. You can also use it to create your own playlists.

- **News**. This collates news stories from numerous online publications and categories.

- **Notes**. If you need to jot down your thoughts or ideas, this app is just perfect for that.

- **Photos**. This is an app for viewing, editing and sharing your photos and videos.

- **Podcasts**. This can be used to download podcasts from within the App Store.

Podcasts are audio or video programs, and they cover an extensive range of subjects.

- **Reminders**. Use this app to help keep organized, when you want to create to-do lists and set reminders for events.

- **Safari**. The Apple web browser that has been developed for viewing the web on your iPhone.

- **Settings**. This contains a range of settings for the iPhone (see pages 20-21 for details).

- **Stocks**. Use this to display the latest stock market prices and add your own companies.

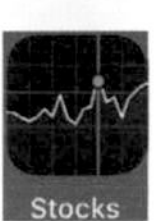

- **Tips**. This can be used to display tips and hints for items on your iPhone.

The Translate app is a new feature in iOS 14.

- **Translate**. This can be used for translations in real-time conversations, using 11 languages.

- **TV**. This is an app for viewing videos from the TV Store, and also streaming them to a larger HDTV monitor.

- **Voice Memos**. This can be used to record short audio reminders that can be stored and played on the iPhone.

The TV app can also be used to access the Apple TV+ service. This is a subscription service for streaming original TV shows and movies from Apple TV.

- **Wallet**. This can be used to store credit, debit, and storecard details, for making payments with Apple Pay (in some locations). It can also be used for storing coupons, boarding passes, event tickets and more.

- **Watch**. This can be used to pair an iPhone with the Apple Watch and apply a range of settings.

- **Weather**. Displays weather details for your location and destinations around the world.

About the App Store

While the built-in apps that come with the iPhone are flexible and versatile, apps really come into their own when you connect to the App Store. This is an online resource, and there are thousands of apps there that can be downloaded and then used on your iPhone, including categories from Lifestyle to Medical and Travel.

To use the App Store, you must first have an Apple ID. This can be obtained when you first connect to the App Store. Once you have an Apple ID, you can start exploring the App Store and the apps within it:

1. Tap once on the **App Store** app on the Home screen

2. The latest available apps are displayed on the Homepage of the App Store, including the featured and best new apps

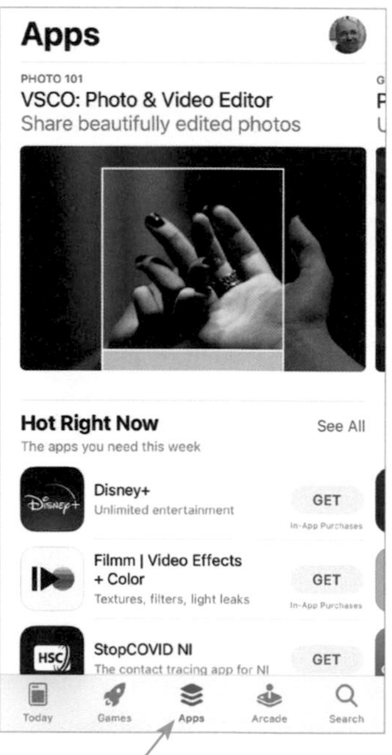

3. Tap on these buttons to view items according to **Today**, **Games**, **Apps**, **Arcade** and **Search**

The items within the Today section of the App Store change on a regular basis, so it is always worth looking at it from time to time.

Viewing apps

To view apps in the App Store and read about their content and functionality:

1. Tap once on an app

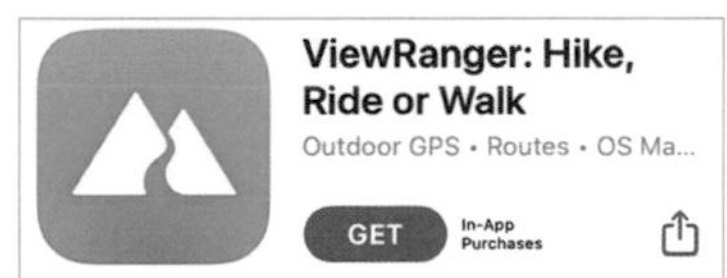

2. General details about the app are displayed

3. Swipe left or right here to view additional information about the app, and view details

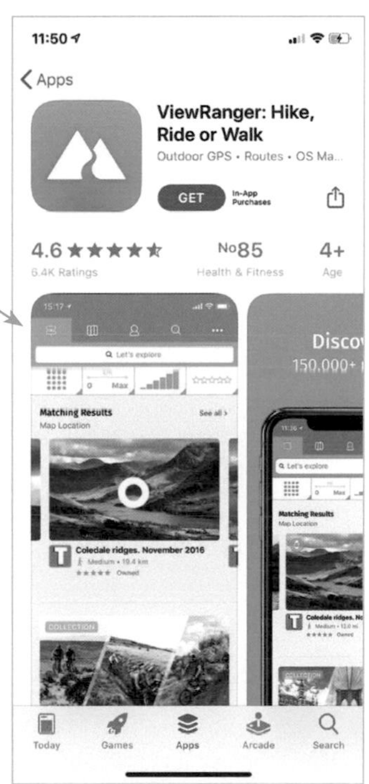

If it is an upgraded version of an app, this page will include details of any fixes and improvements that have been made.

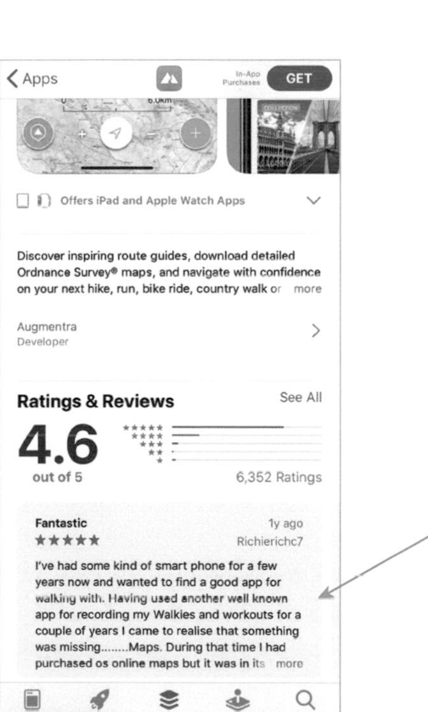

4. Scroll down the page to see additional information including reviews and new items in this version of the app

Finding Apps

Featured

Within the App Store, apps are separated into categories according to type. This enables you to find apps according to particular subjects. To do this:

Don't forget

Some apps will differ depending on the geographical location from which you are accessing the App Store.

1. Tap once on the **Apps** button on the toolbar at the bottom of the App Store

2. Scroll up and down to view all of the sections within the Apps Homepage, and scroll left and right to view items within each section heading

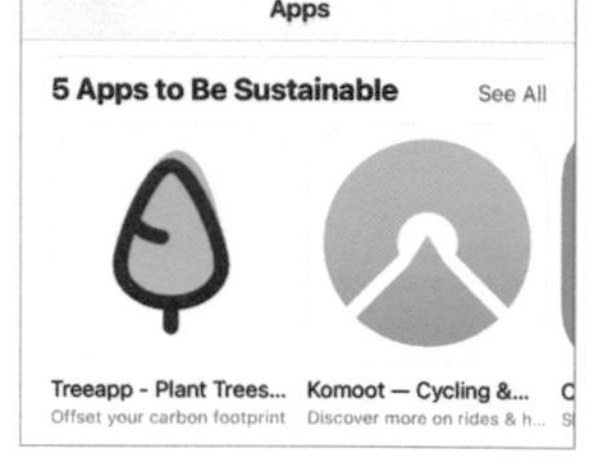

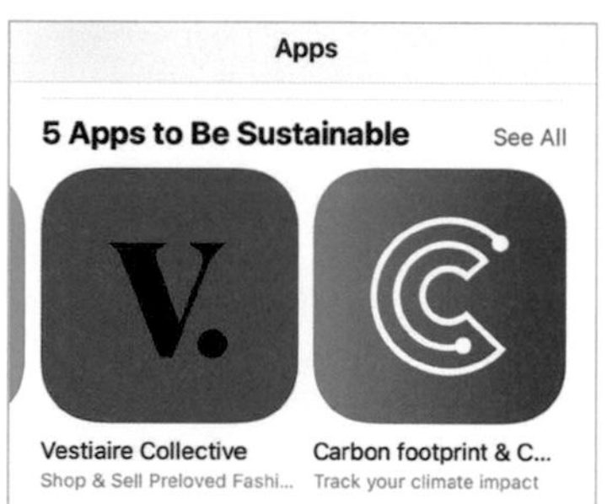

There are an increasing number of AR (Augmented Reality) apps in the App Store. These are apps that combine real-life images, either within the app or from the device's camera, that are used with graphical elements; e.g. constellations can be drawn over an image of the sky in an astronomy app.

3. Scroll down the page to the **Top Categories** section, and tap once on the **See All** button to view the full range of categories of apps

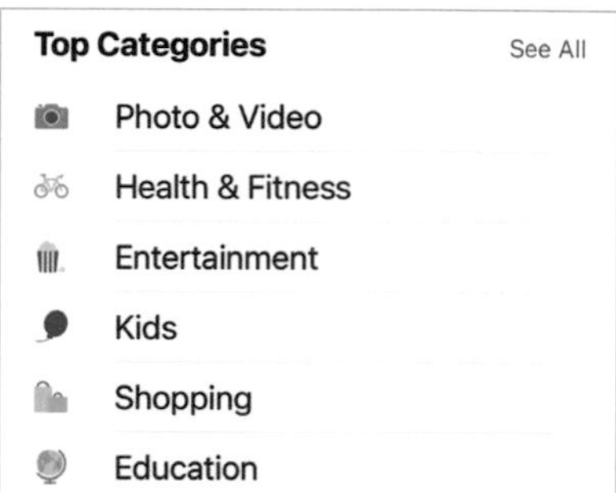

4. Tap once on a category to view the items within it. This can be navigated in the same way as the main Homepage in the App Store; e.g. swipe up and down to view sections, and left and right on each panel to view the available apps

Top Charts

To find the top-rated apps:

1. Tap once on the **Apps** button on the toolbar at the bottom of the App Store

2. Scroll down the page to view the **Top Free** and **Top Paid** apps

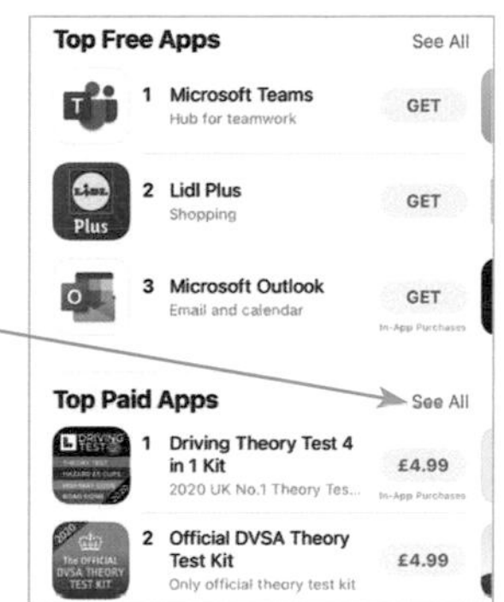

3. Tap once on the **See All** button to view all of the Top Paid or Top Charts apps

Do not limit yourself to just viewing the top apps. Although these are the most popular, there are also a lot of excellent apps within each category.

Searching for apps

Another way to find apps is with the App Store Search box, which appears at the top of the App Store window once it has been accessed. To use this to find apps:

1. Tap once on the **Search** button at the bottom of the window to access the Search box

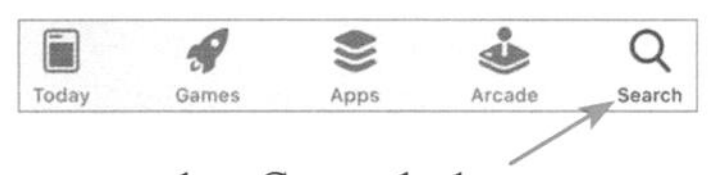

2. Tap in the Search box to activate the keyboard and enter a search keyword or phrase

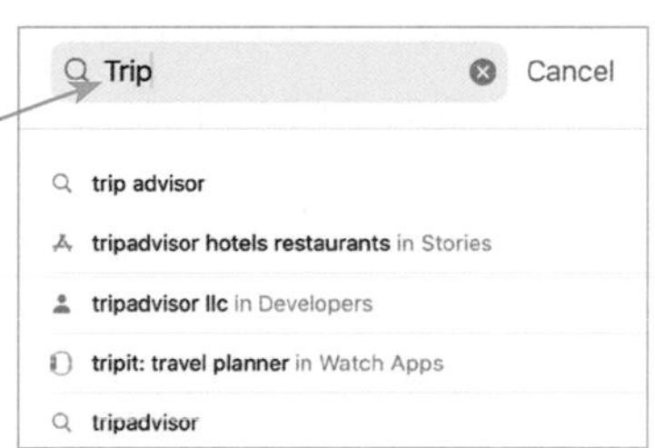

3. Suggested apps appear as you are typing

4. Tap on an app to view it

For more information about using the iPhone virtual keyboard, see pages 92-101.

Downloading Apps

When you identify an app that you would like to use, it can be downloaded to your iPhone. To do this:

Apps usually download in a few minutes or less, depending on the speed of your Wi-Fi connection.

Some apps have "in-app purchases". This is additional content that has to be paid for when it is downloaded.

1. Find the app you want, using the **App Store**

2. Tap once on the **Price** or **Get** button

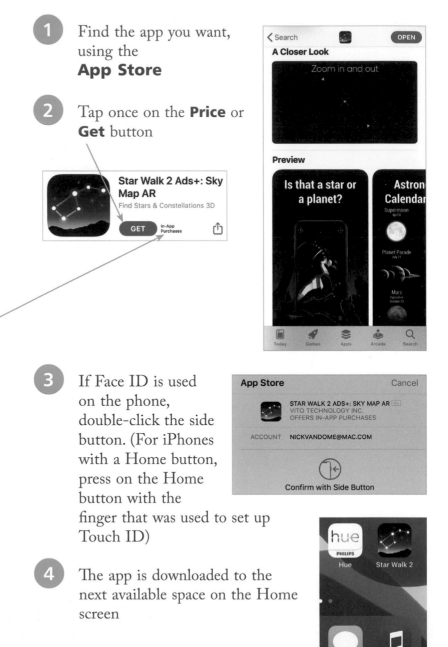

3. If Face ID is used on the phone, double-click the side button. (For iPhones with a Home button, press on the Home button with the finger that was used to set up Touch ID)

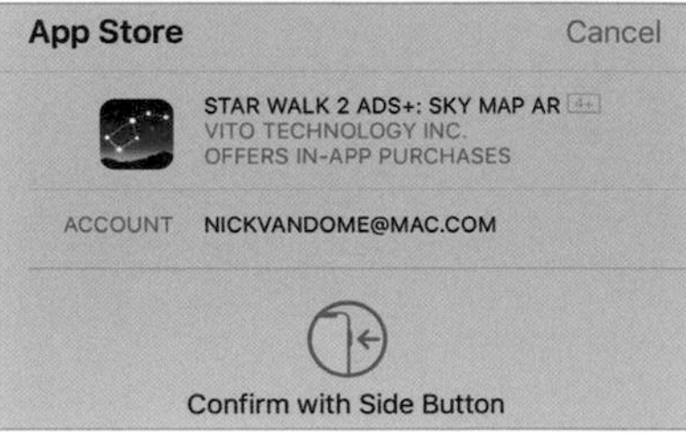

4. The app is downloaded to the next available space on the Home screen

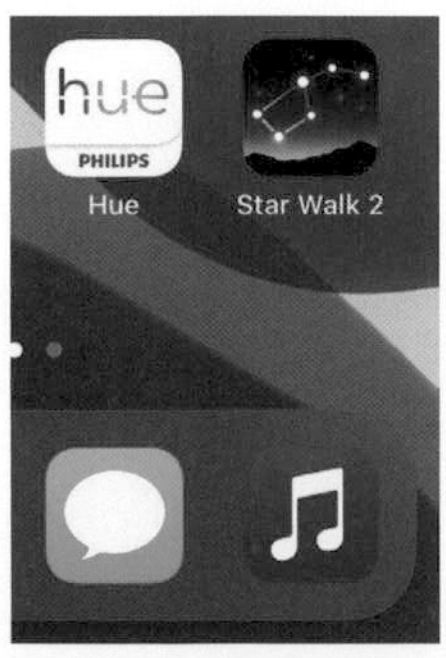

Updating Apps

The publishers of apps provide updates that bring new features and improvements. You do not have to check your apps to see if there are updates – you can set them to be updated automatically through the Settings app. To do this:

1. Open **Settings** and tap on the **App Store** tab

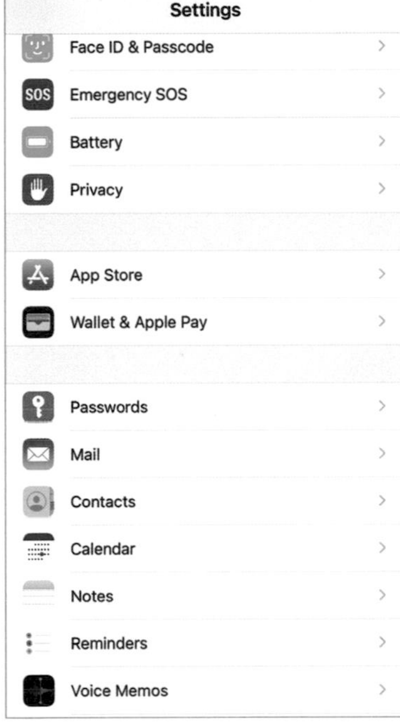

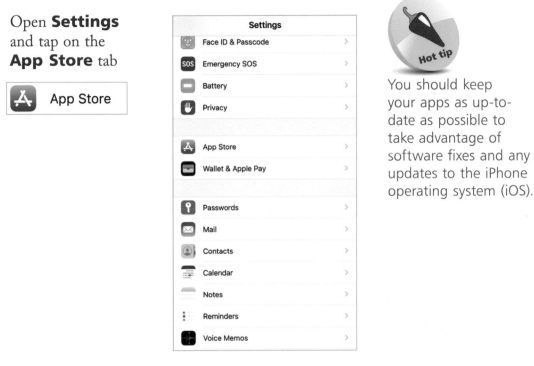

You should keep your apps as up-to-date as possible to take advantage of software fixes and any updates to the iPhone operating system (iOS).

2. Drag the **App Updates** button under **Automatic Downloads On** to enable automatic updates for apps

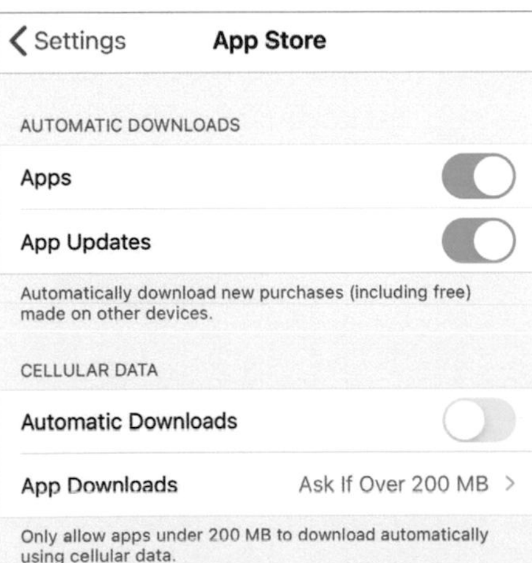

Managing your Apps

As more apps are added it can become hard to find the ones you want, particularly if you have to swipe between several screens. However, it is possible to organize apps into individual folders to make using them more manageable. To do this:

Apps can also be managed with the App Library, which is a new feature in iOS 14. See page 33 and pages 36-37 for more details.

1. Press on an app until it starts to jiggle and a cross appears at the top-left corner

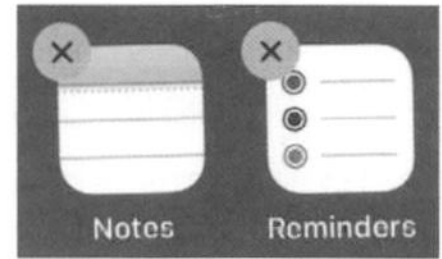

2. Drag the app over another one

3. A folder is created, containing the two apps. The folder is given a default name, usually based on the category of the first app

4. Tap once on the folder name and type a new name, if required

5. Tap on the **done** button on the keyboard to finish creating the folder

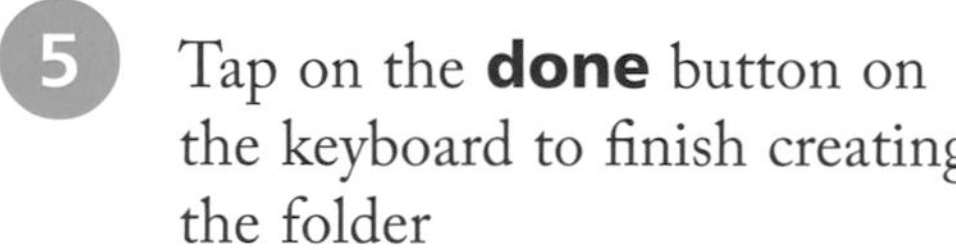

6. The folder is added on the Home screen. Tap on this to access the items within it (press and hold on it to move it)

Press on the cross that appears on an app in Step 1 to delete it. If you need it again, it can be reinstalled by downloading from the App Store, at no cost.

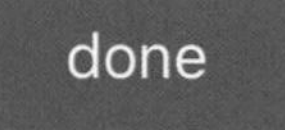

Folders can also be added to the Dock after you have created them, enabling several apps to be stored here.

9 Apps for Every Day

The iPhone has apps to make your daily life run more smoothly, from staying healthy to keeping notes.

Apple Watch with the iPhone

Don't forget

The Apple Watch has to be "paired" with an iPhone, using the Watch app.

The App Store has a **Health & Fitness** category and also a **Medical** category, to cover a wide range of health-related issues. Many of the apps can be used with the Apple Watch. There is also an **Apple Watch Apps** category.

If you have a pre-existing medical condition, or are on any medication, always consult your doctor before using a new health or fitness app that could have an impact on this.

The Apple Watch has now reached its sixth version: Apple Watch Series 6. This is much more than a watch, though; it is also a body monitoring device. It has a number of sensors on the back, which monitor information such as heart rate and body movement. There is also an activity app to measure your fitness activities. A lot of this data can be sent to the Health app on the iPhone, where it can be stored and analyzed in greater depth.

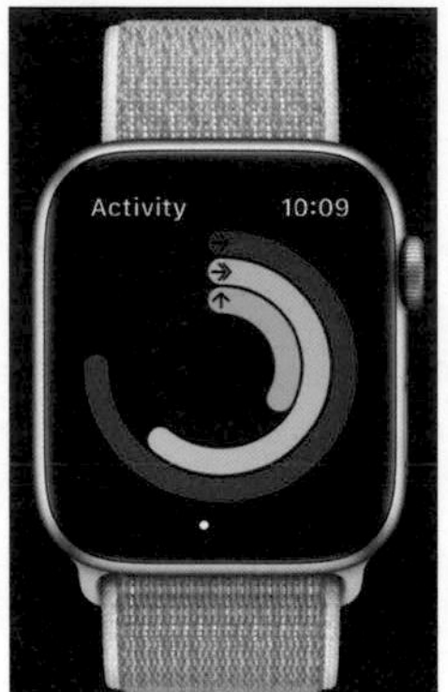

The Apple Watch Series 6 has an always-on display (the previous versions only showed the display when the watch on the wearer's wrist was moved towards their face), and battery life of up to 18 hours before a charge is required.

Some previous versions of the Apple Watch had to be paired (linked) with the iPhone to access certain functionality, such as making and receiving calls. However, the Apple Watch Series 6 has a cellular connectivity so that it can be used for phone calls, without the need to have an iPhone with you.

The Apple Watch Series 6 also has a host of useful apps and features, aimed at improving health and fitness: there is an Electrocardiogram (ECG) app that includes an electrical heart sensor that can show your heart rhythm; blood oxygen sensors for measuring your blood oxygen levels; built-in fall detection that can alert an emergency contact if you have a fall; a Noise app for measuring the sound level around you; a Sleep app for monitoring your sleep patterns; and the Activity app for measuring daily exercise tasks.

The Apple Watch Series 6 includes a Compass app, which, in conjunction with the Maps app, is ideal for displaying directions when you are out and about.

There is also a wide range of interchangeable bands that can be used with the Apple Watch, so that you can customize it just the way you want.

Using the Health App

The Health app is available in iOS 14, and it enables you to input and analyze a wide range of health and fitness information. There are two main areas within the app:

Summary

This displays an overview of items that have been specified to appear here. To use this:

1. Tap once on the **Summary** button on the bottom toolbar

2. The summary information is displayed for a range of health and fitness categories

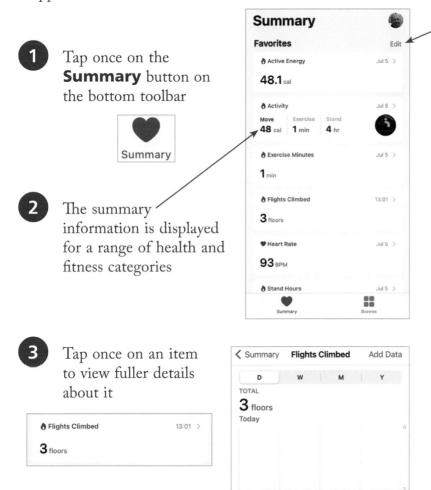

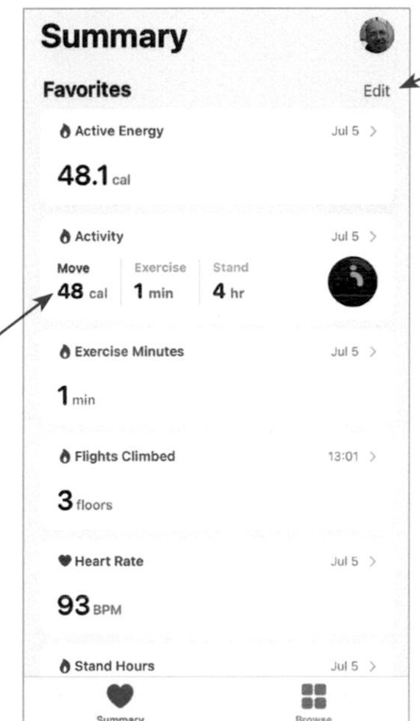

3. Tap once on an item to view fuller details about it

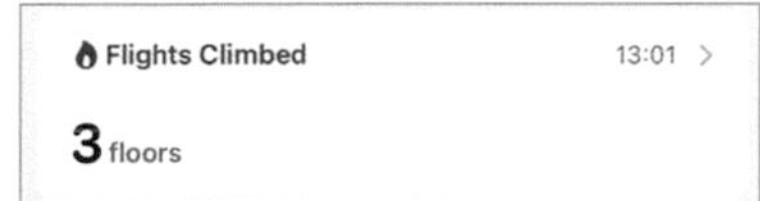

The items that appear on the Summary page can be edited, by tapping once on the **Edit** button in Step 1. On the Edit Favorites page, tap once next to the items that you want to appear, so that they have a solid star next to them.

...cont'd

Browse

This displays the available categories within the Health app, and shows any data that has been added for them.

Beware

When adding data, do so at regular intervals, to build up a comprehensive set of results for analysis by the Health app.

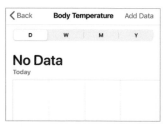

1. Tap once on the **Browse** button on the bottom toolbar

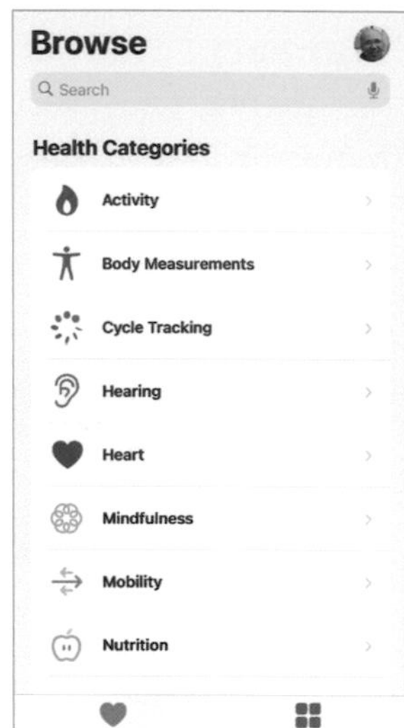

2. The range of health and fitness categories is displayed. Swipe down the page to view more items

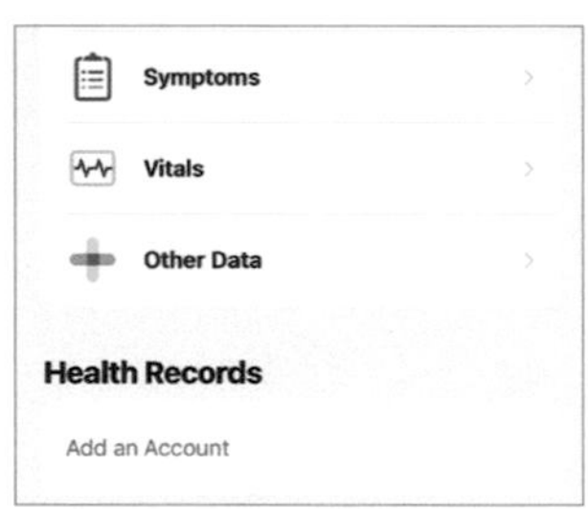

Hot tip

In addition to fitness categories, a range of medical information can also be entered and stored in the Health app, including specific medical conditions and immunizations.

3. Tap once on an item to view fuller details

4. For each item, health data can be entered manually (see next page)

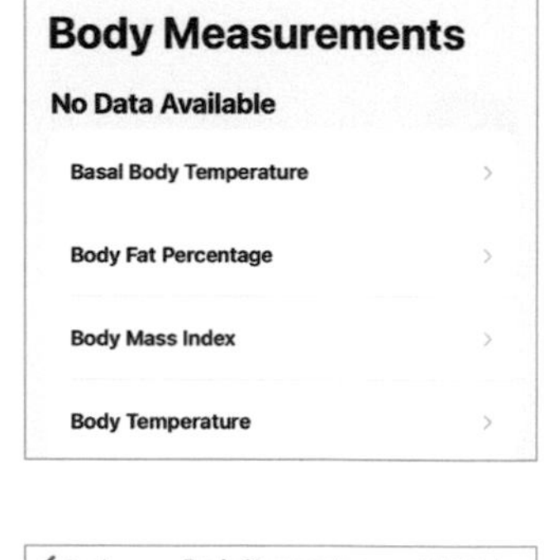

Adding health data

To enter data for the categories in the Health app:

1. Tap once on the **Summary** button

2. Tap once on one of the categories on the Summary page

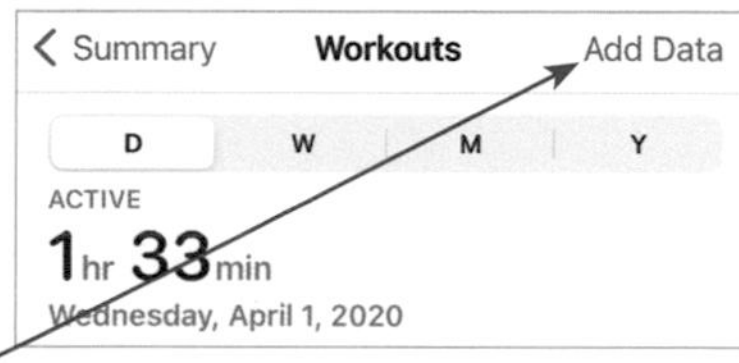

3. Tap once on the **Add Data** button

Add Data

4. Enter the details for the selected item; e.g. entering the type and duration of a specific workout. Tap once on the **Add** button

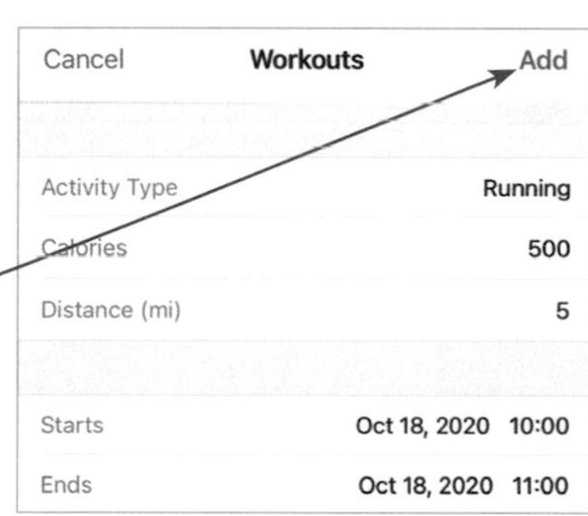

5. The data is added for the selected item and this will be collated and stored within the Health app. Tap on these buttons to view the data for **Day**, **Week**, **Month**, and **Year**. Tap once on the **Summary** button to return to the main Summary page

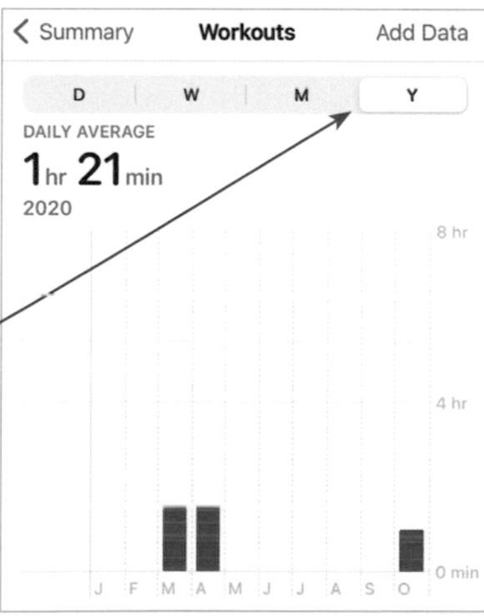

Summary

Health data can be added for the full range of categories in the **Browse** section by tapping once on the **Add Data** button in Step 4 on the previous page.

Some items in the Health app have data added automatically, such as Walking + Running, Steps, and Flights Climbed, in the Activity category.

See **iPhone & Apple Watch for Health & Fitness in easy steps** for more help on using these devices to achieve your health goals.

Jotting Down Notes

It is always useful to have a quick way of making notes of everyday things, such as shopping lists, recipes, or packing lists for traveling. On your iPhone, the Notes app is perfect for this function. To use it:

1. Tap once on the **Notes** app

2. Tap once on this button on the bottom toolbar to create a new note

3. Enter text for the note. The first line of a note becomes its title in the left-hand Notes panel

4. The toolbar above the keyboard can be used for adding content to the note. (Tap once on the cross to close the toolbar)

5. Double-tap on text to select it, and tap once on this button to access text formatting options

Aa

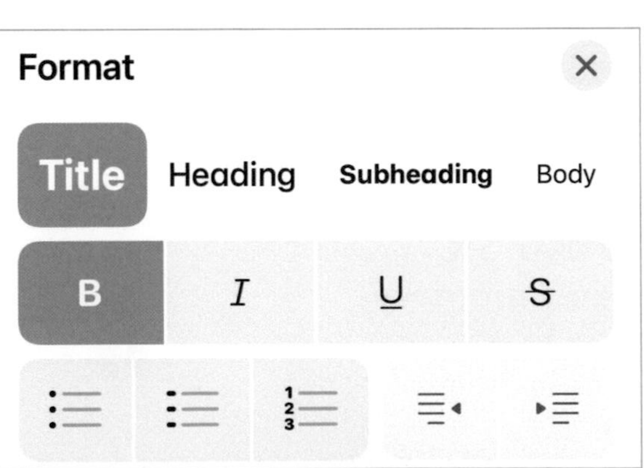

Don't forget

If iCloud is turned **On** for Notes (**Settings** > **Apple ID** > **iCloud** > **Notes**) then all of your notes will be stored here and will be available on any other iCloud-enabled devices that you have.

Tap once on this button on the top toolbar of a note to access a range of options for the note. These include options for: scanning items into a note; pinning a note; locking a note; or deleting it. There are also options for: sharing the current note; searching for items; moving a note to a folder within the Notes app; and applying lines and grids over a note.

6 Tap once on this button to create a checklist. Add items to the list. Tap once on a check button to add a tick and show it as completed

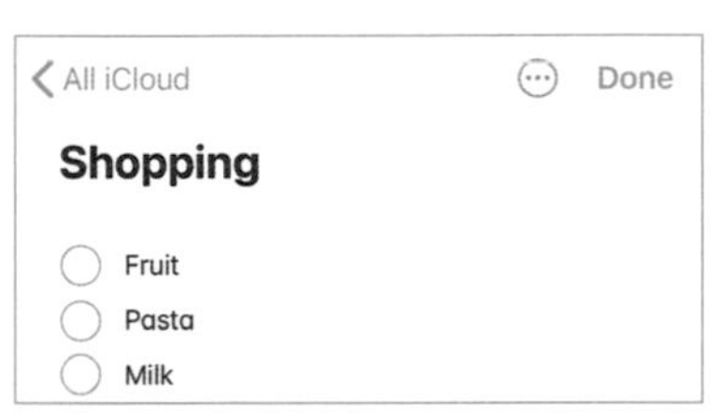

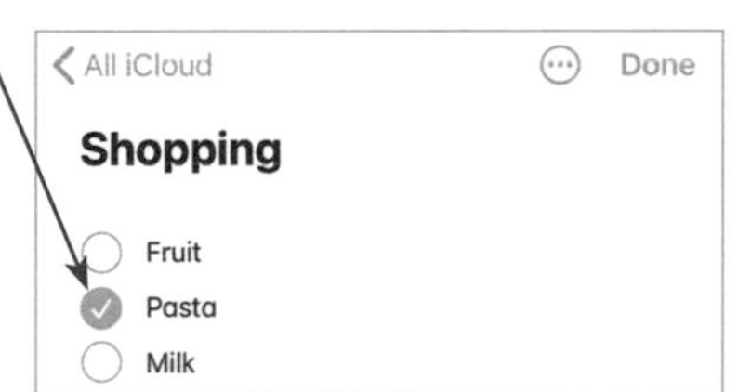

For more information about selecting text, see page 101.

7 Tap once on this button to add a handwritten item or drawing

8 Tap once on this button to add a photo or video to a note. Select a photo or video from your library, or take a new one

Choose Photo or Video

Take Photo or Video

Scan Documents

9 By default, the most recently-created or edited note appears at the top of the Notes panel. However, it is possible to pin your most frequently-used notes to the top of this panel. To do this press and hold on the note to be pinned and tap once on the **Pin Note** button. The note is pinned at the top of the Notes panel

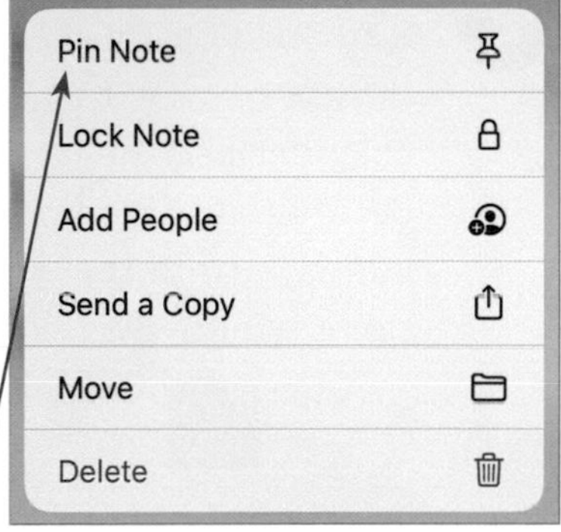

Pinning notes in the Notes panel is a new feature in iOS 14.

Keeping Up-to-Date

The Calendar app can be used to add events and appointments and keep yourself up-to-date with your daily, weekly, monthly, and annual activities.

1. Tap once on the **Calendar** app

2. If **Month** view is displayed, tap once here to access **Year** view. In Year view, tap once on a month to view it

3. Tap once on a day to view it (the current day is highlighted red)

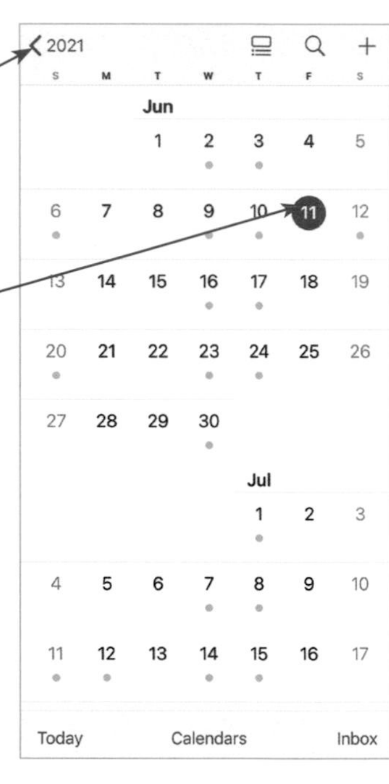

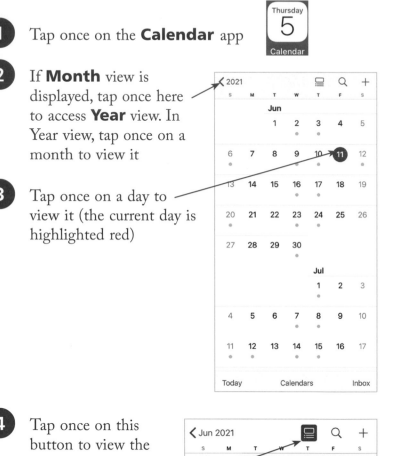

4. Tap once on this button to view the calendar and any events that have been added, within the same window

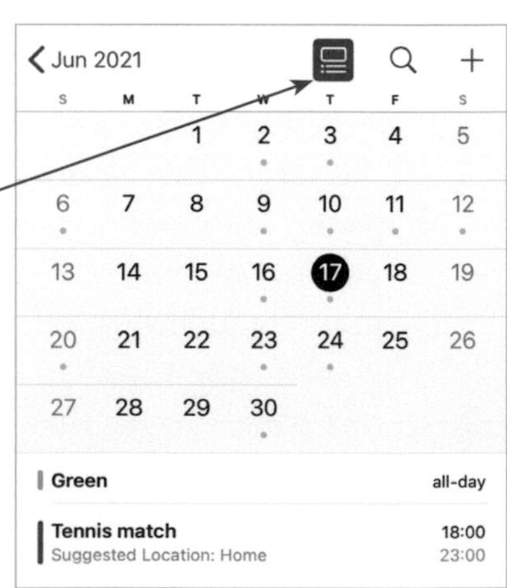

Tap once on the **Today** button from any date to view the current date, in whichever view you are currently in.

Today

Adding events

To add new events to the calendar:

1. Press and hold on a time slot within Day view, or tap once on this button

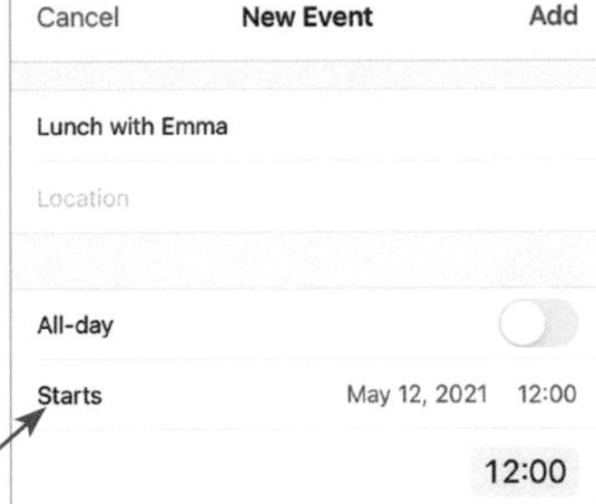

2. Enter a title for the event, and tap once on the **Starts** button to add a start time. Tap once on the time and enter a new time, as required

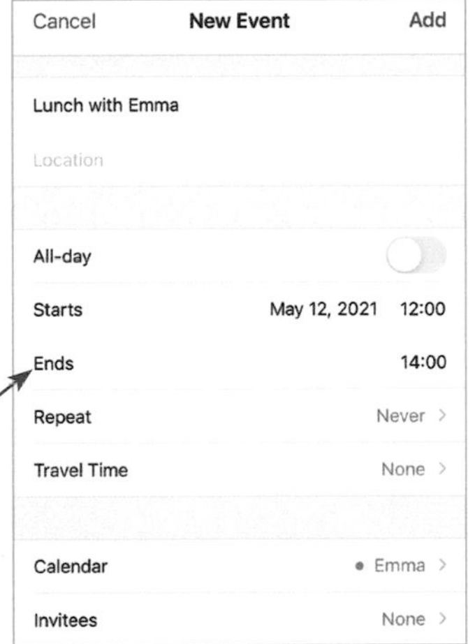

3. Add an end time, by tapping on the **Ends** button, and also a repeat frequency (for recurring events such as birthdays). Select a specific calendar for the event and add an alert, if required. Tap once on the **Add** button to create the event

4. Tap once on this button to view a list of your current events and appointments

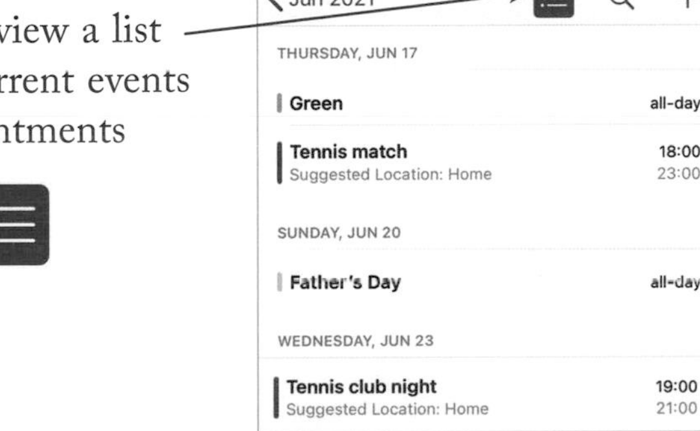

Drag the **All-day** button **On** to set an event for the whole day, rather than adding specific start and end times.

The repeat frequency for an event can be set to every day, every week, every 2 weeks, every month, or every year. There is also a **Custom** option for specific time periods.

Setting Reminders

Another useful organization app is Reminders. This enables you to create lists for different topics and then set reminders for specific items. A date and time can be set for each reminder, and when this is reached, the reminder appears on your iPhone screen. To use Reminders:

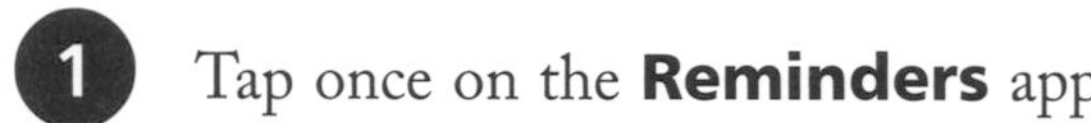

1. Tap once on the **Reminders** app

2. The items that have been created are listed under smart lists at the top of the window (collated according to the type of list) and also beneath the **My Lists** headings. This includes reminders and lists. Tap once on the **Edit** button to reorder or delete any of the My Lists items

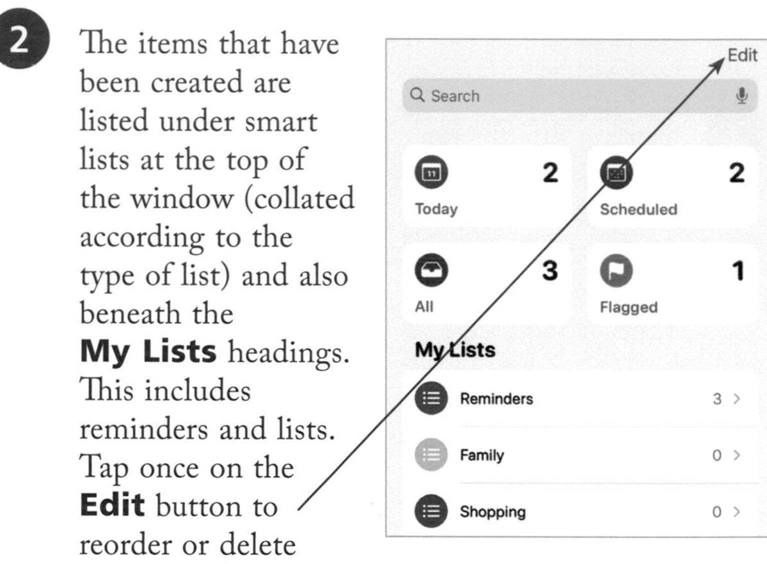

3. Tap once on one of the smart lists to view the items that have been created within it

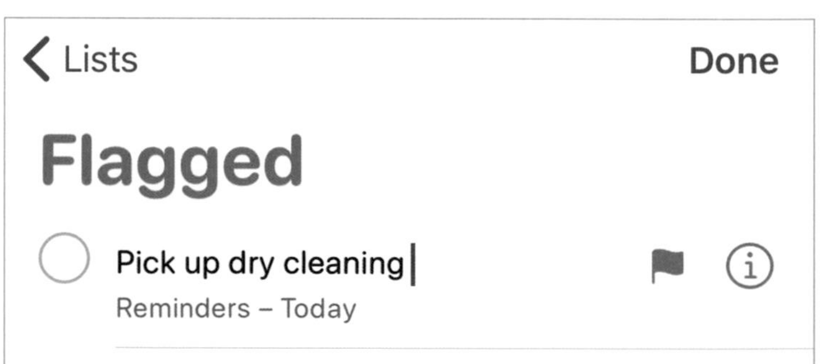

Don't forget

The items created under the **My Lists** heading are collated into the smart lists at the top of the window, according to items that have been added to them. For instance, if a reminder has had a flag added to it, it will appear in the **Reminders** list and also under the **Flagged** smart list. Any subsequent flagged lists will also appear here.

Creating reminders

To create new reminders and lists:

1. Tap once on one of the options (e.g. Reminders), and tap once on the **New Reminder** button

2. Enter the title of the reminder and tap once on the **i** button to access the **Details** window

3. Enter the details of the item, including a day and time for a reminder alert, a repeat schedule for the reminder, and a flag or priority tag for the reminder. Tap once on the **Done** button when the details for the reminder have been added

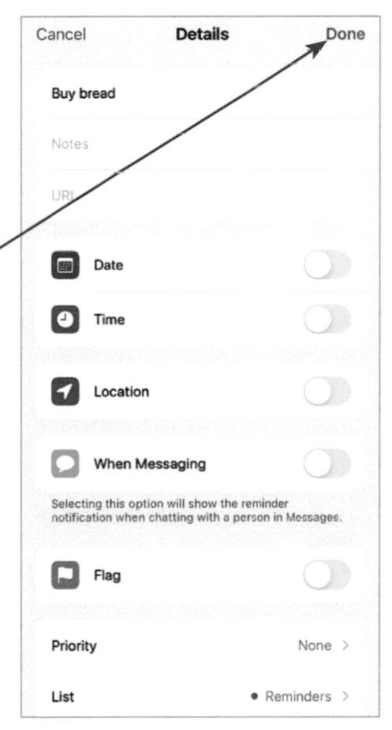

4. When creating an entry for the Reminders app, use the Quick Toolbar above the keyboard to, from left to right: add the date and time for the item; add a location for it; add a flag; or add a photo to the item

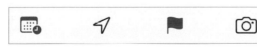

Once a reminder item has been created, it is displayed with any details next to it; e.g. time, location, flag or priority tag.

Getting the News

The iPhone with iOS 14 is ideal for keeping up with the news, whether you are on the move or at home. This is made even easier with the News app, which can be used to collate news stories from numerous online media outlets, covering hundreds of subjects. To use it:

1. Tap once on the **News** app

2. Tap once on the **Today** button on the bottom toolbar to view the latest stories in your news feed

3. The latest news stories are displayed. Swipe down the page to view specific categories such as Trending Stories

4. Tap once on the **Following** button on the bottom toolbar to view subjects or publications that you are following; i.e. they are used to populate your news feed

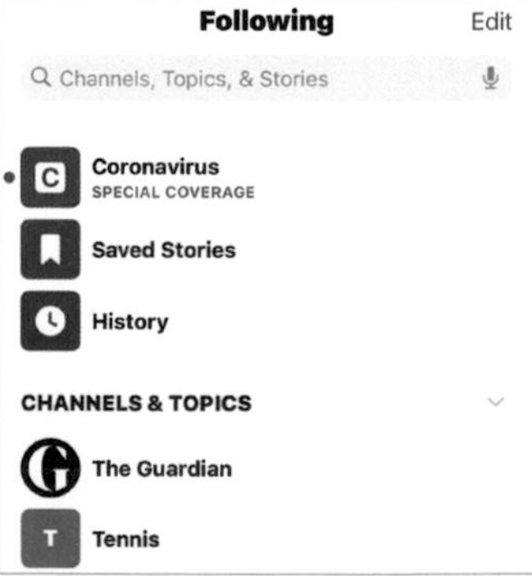

Tap once on the **News+** button on the bottom toolbar to access Apple's subscription service for the News app.

To delete an item from the Following section on the Channels page, tap once on the **Edit** button in the top right-hand corner, and tap once on the red circle next to the item you want to delete. This will remove its related content from your news feed.

10 Relaxing with your iPhone

This chapter shows how to relax with your iPhone by playing music and reading.

Around the iTunes Store

Don't forget

Although iTunes has been removed from Mac computers with the macOS operating system, the iTunes Store is still a part of iOS 14 and can be used to download a range of content, including music and movies. These items are then displayed in their respective apps; i.e. the Music and TV apps.

Tap once on the **Genres** button at the top of the Music Homepage to view items for different musical genres and styles.

Genres

Downloaded movies and TV shows take up a lot of storage space on the iPhone.

The iPhone performs an excellent role as a mobile entertainment center: its versatility means that you can carry your music, videos, and books in your pocket. Much of this content comes from the online iTunes Store. To access this and start adding content to your iPhone:

1. Tap once on the **iTunes Store** app

2. The iTunes Store interface is similar to the App Store. Tap once on the **Featured** or **Charts** tabs at the top of the window to view these headings

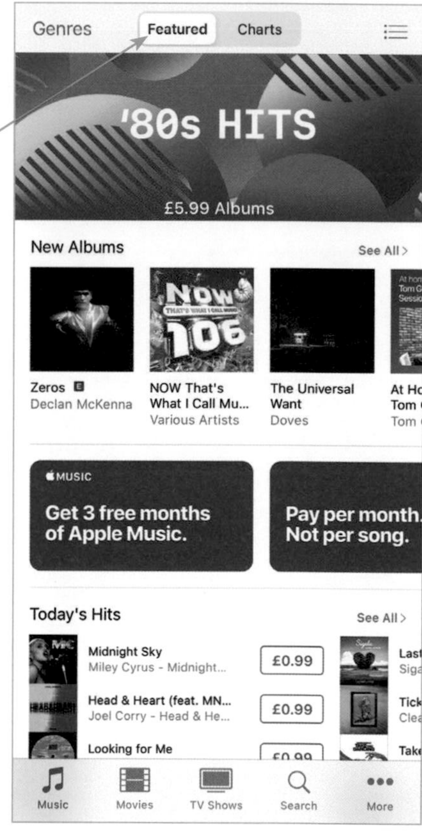

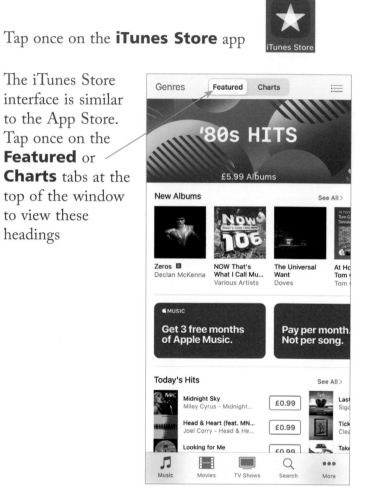

3. Use the buttons on the bottom toolbar to access content for **Music**, **Movies** and **TV Shows**

4 Swipe to the left and right on each panel to view items within it

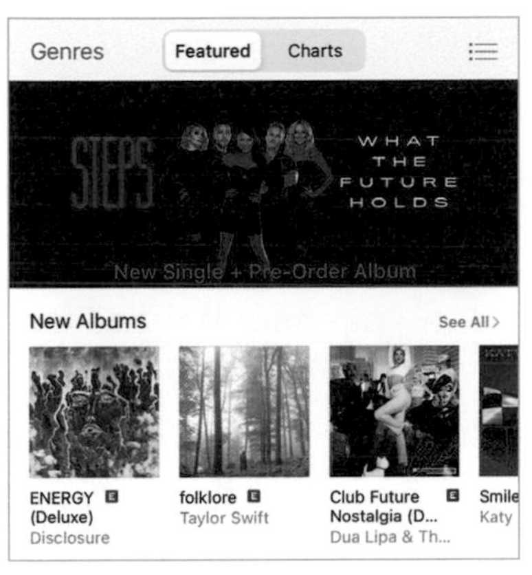

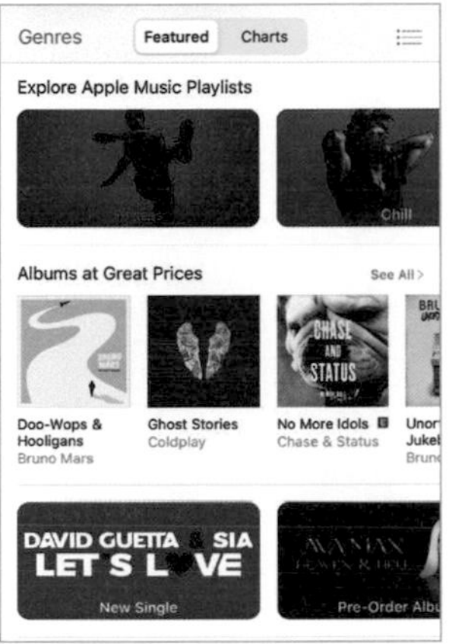

5 Swipe up and down to view more headings

Tap once on the **Charts** tab at the top of the iTunes Store window to view the top-ranking items for the category that is being viewed.

6 Tap once on the **Movies** button to view the movies in the iTunes Store. These can be bought or rented

7 Tap once on the **TV Shows** button to view the TV shows in the iTunes Store. These can be bought or rented

8 Tap once on the **More** button to access additional content

9 Tap once on the **Genius** button to view suggested content, based on what you have already bought from the iTunes Store

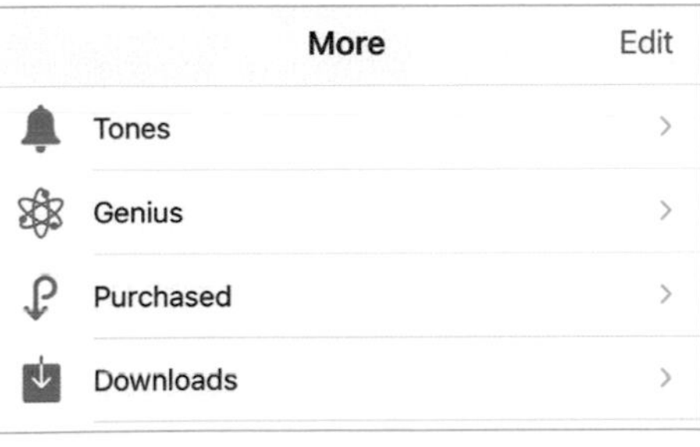

Don't forget

To view all of your iTunes purchases, tap once on the **More** button on the bottom toolbar and tap once on the **Purchased** button. View your purchases by category (Music, Films/Movies or TV Programmes/ Shows), and tap once on the cloud symbol next to a purchased item to download it to your iPhone.

Buying Items

Once you have found the content you want in the iTunes Store, you can then buy it and download it to your iPhone.

If you have set up Apple Pay (see pages 66-67) you will be able to use this to buy items in the iTunes Store. Use the Face ID function (see page 24) to authorize the payment using Apple Pay.

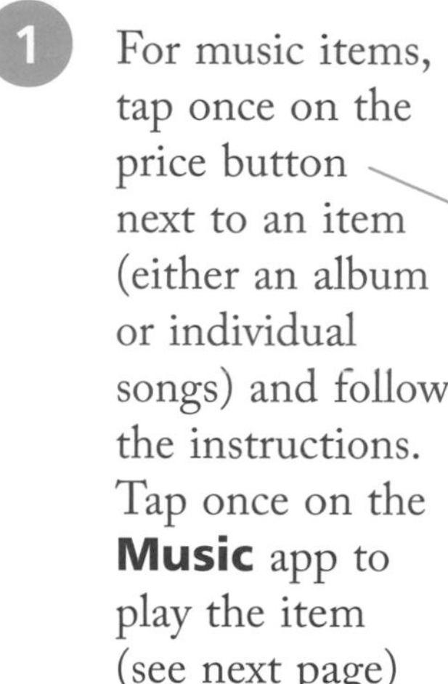

1. For music items, tap once on the price button next to an item (either an album or individual songs) and follow the instructions. Tap once on the **Music** app to play the item (see next page)

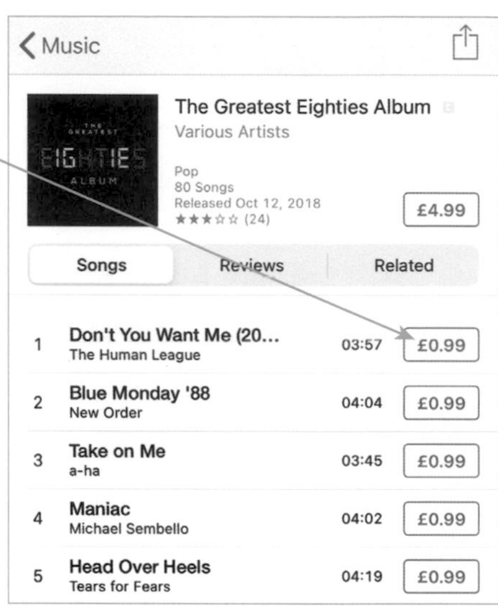

2. For movies and TV shows, tap once on the **Buy** or **Rent** button next to the title. Tap once on the **TV** app to play the item

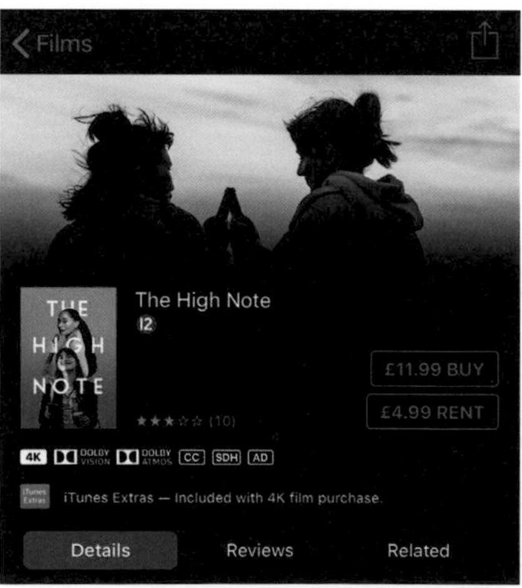

For rented movies and TV shows, you have 30 days to watch an item after you have downloaded it. After you have started watching, you have 48 hours until it expires.

Music on the iPhone

Once music has been bought from the iTunes Store, it can be played on your iPhone using the Music app. To do this:

1. Tap once on the **Music** app

2. Tap once on the **Library** button on the bottom toolbar

3. Select one of the options for viewing items in the Library. These include **Playlists**, **Artists**, **Albums**, **Songs**, and **Downloaded**

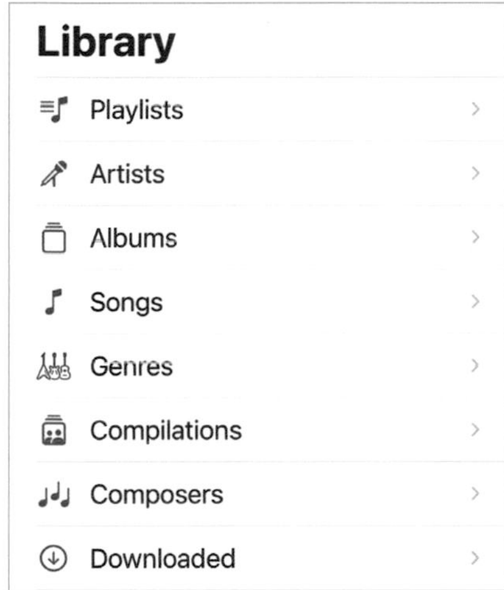

4. For the **Artists** section, tap once on an artist to view details of their songs on your iPhone

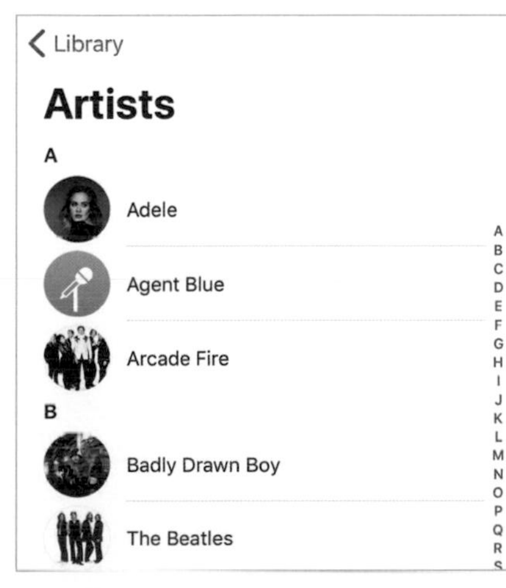

To create a playlist of songs, tap once on the **Playlists** button in Step 3, then tap once on the **New Playlist** button. Give it a name and then add songs from your Library, using the **Add Music** button.

...cont'd

Tap once on this button in Step 5 to access a menu for the current track. This includes options to download the track, delete it from the Music app Library, add it to a playlist, or share it.

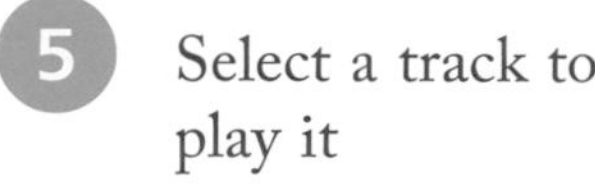

5. Select a track to play it

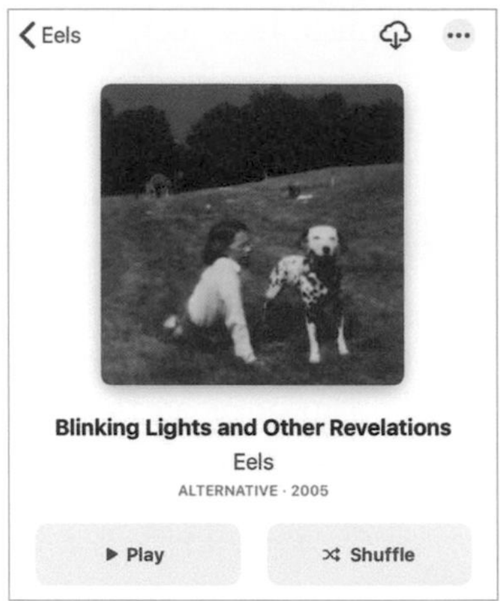

6. A limited version of the music controls appears at the bottom of the window

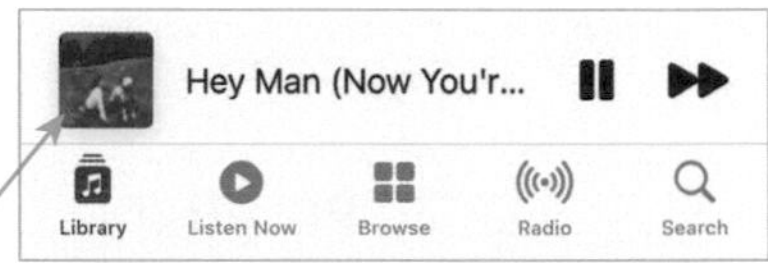

7. Tap once here to view the full version of the music controls. Use these buttons to return to the start of a track, play/pause a track, fast-forward, and adjust the volume

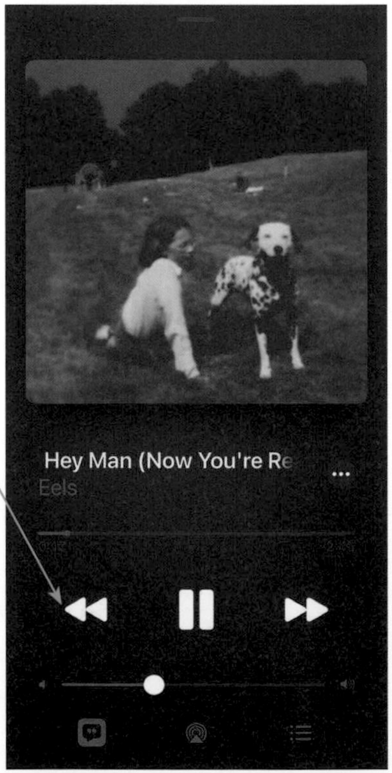

By default, music that has been bought from the iTunes Store is kept online and can be played on your iPhone by streaming it over Wi-Fi. However, it is also possible to download tracks to your iPhone so that you can play them without being online. Tap once on this button to download a specific track.

Using Apple Music

Apple Music is a service that makes the entire Apple iTunes Library of music available to users. It is a subscription service, but there is a three-month free trial. Music can be streamed over the internet or downloaded so you can listen to it when you are offline. To start with Apple Music:

1. Tap once on the **Music** app

2. Tap once on the **Listen Now** button

3. Tap once on the **Try It Free** button to activate a three-month free trial of Apple Music

4. After the three-month free trial there will be an option to **Choose Your Plan** if you want to continue with Apple Music, and pay a subscription. The options are for **Individual**, **Student** or **Family**. Select one of the options and tap once on the **Join Apple Music** button. Once you have joined Apple Music, you will be able to listen to the entire Apple Music Library

To end your Apple Music subscription at any point (and to ensure you do not subscribe at the end of the free trial), open the **Settings** app. Tap once on the **Apple ID** button, and tap once on the **Subscriptions** button. Under **Subscriptions**, tap once on the Apple Music subscription and tap once on the **Cancel Subscription** button. By default, subscriptions renew automatically if they are not canceled.

Reading

In addition to audio and visual content from the iTunes Store, it is also possible to read books on your iPhone using the Books app. To do this:

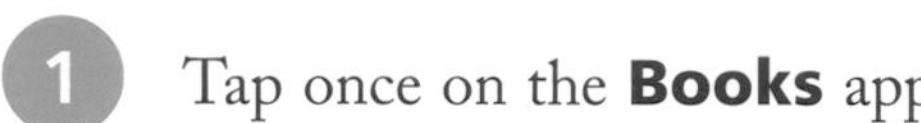

1. Tap once on the **Books** app

2. Tap once on the **Reading Now** button on the bottom toolbar to view any items you have in your Library

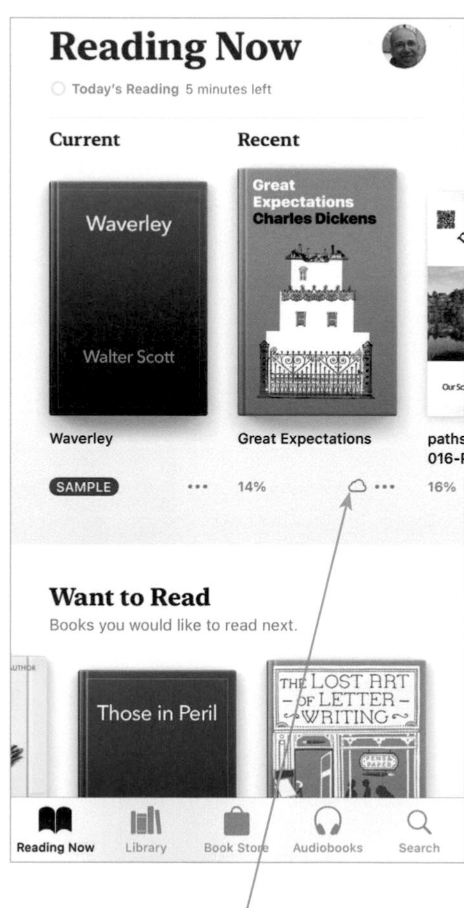

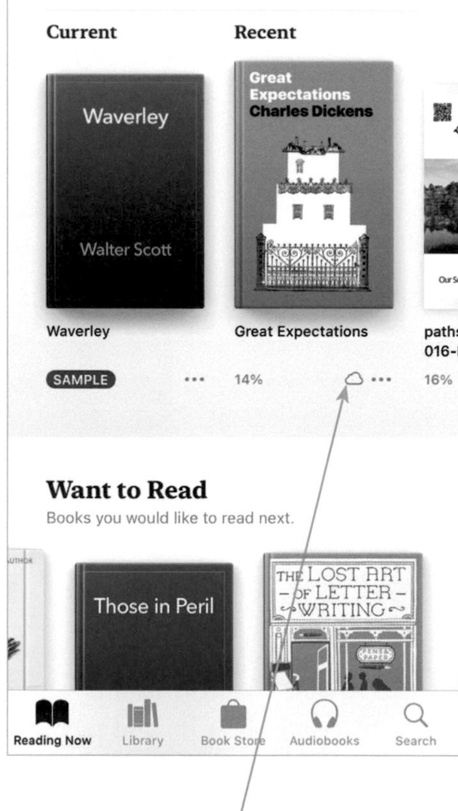

3. If a title has a cloud icon next to it, tap once on this to download the book to your iPhone

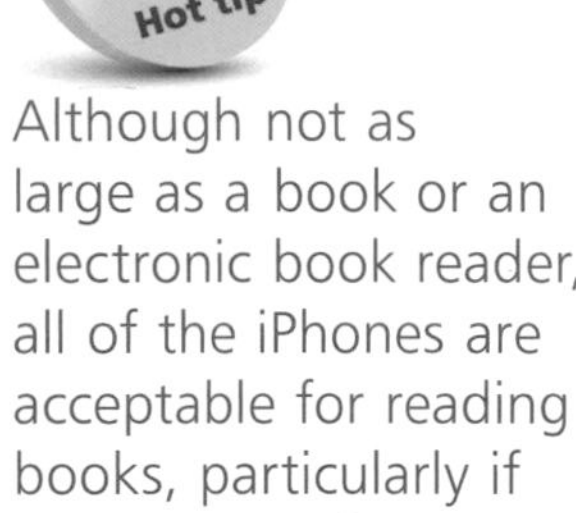

Although not as large as a book or an electronic book reader, all of the iPhones are acceptable for reading books, particularly if you are traveling.

4. Tap once on the **Library** button on the bottom toolbar to view books that have been downloaded and added to the Library section

5. Tap once on a title to open it for reading. Tap once here to access options for browsing collections within the Library; e.g. looking for books in certain categories such as Crime and Romance

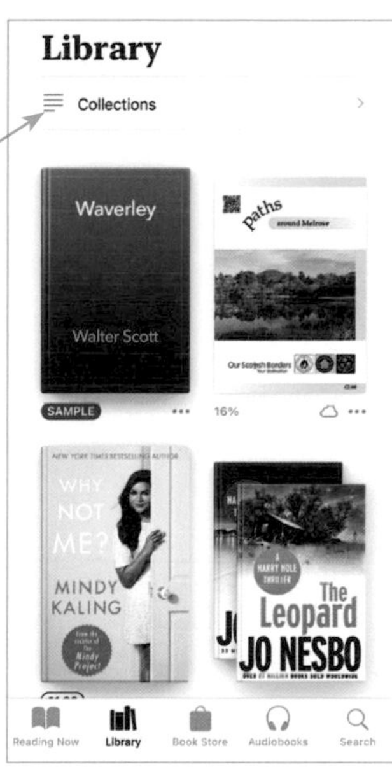

6. Tap once on the **Book Store** button on the bottom toolbar to view books in the Book Store

If you have a Kindle account, you can download the Kindle app from the App Store and use this to connect to your account and all of the books within it.

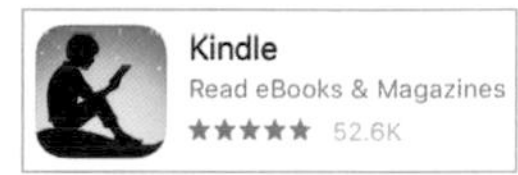

Once books have been downloaded to your iPhone, tap once on a title in the **Library** section to read it. Tap on the left or right of the screen to move between pages, or swipe from the left or right edges. Tap in the middle of a page to activate the reading controls at the top of the screen, including Table of Contents, text size, and color options.

Researching

With your iPhone in your hand, you literally have a world of information at your fingertips. Whatever your hobby or interest, you will be able to find out a lot more about it using several different options:

By default, the search engine used by Safari is Google. However, this can be changed in **Settings** > **Safari** > **Search Engine**.

1. Press and hold the **On/Off** button (or the **Home** button for older iPhones) to access **Siri** and make an enquiry this way

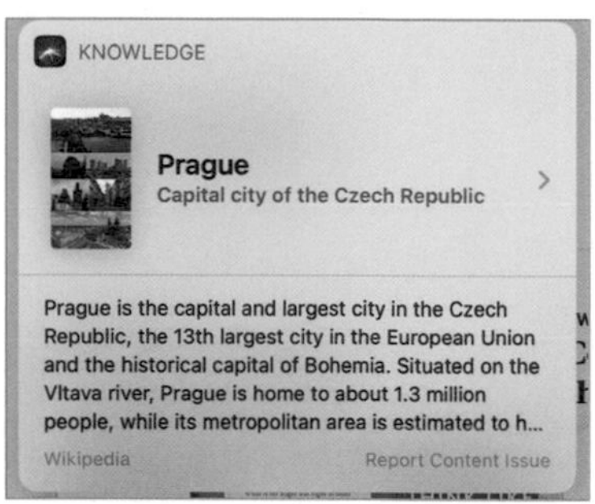

Online shopping is another excellent option on your iPhone. This can be done by looking up online stores using the Safari web browser, or by downloading specific apps such as the Amazon or eBay apps. Online price comparison sites or apps can also be used to find the best prices on the web.

2. Use the **App Store** to search for apps for your chosen subject

3. Use **Safari** to find related websites and also general information about a specific topic

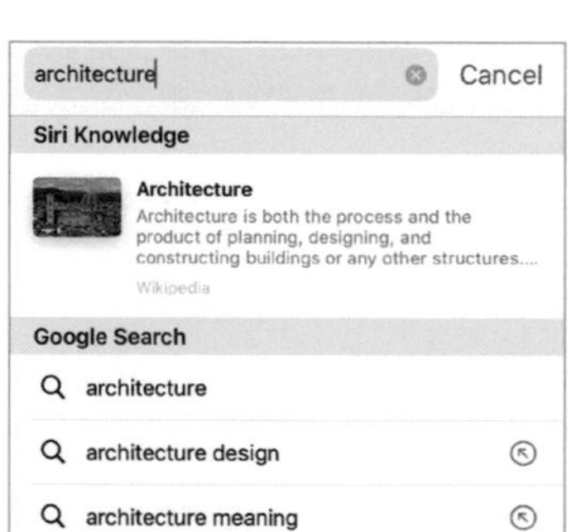

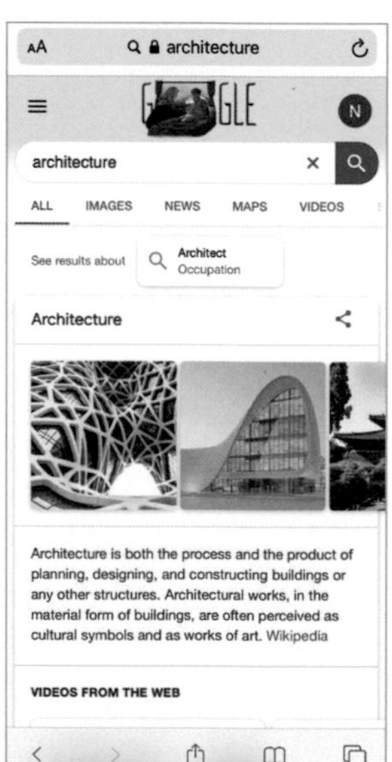

11 On the Go

The iPhone is a great companion whenever you are out and about anywhere, whether at home or abroad.

Finding Locations

Finding locations around the world is only ever a couple of taps away when you have your iPhone and the Maps app.

Hot tip

The Maps app works best if you have Location Services turned On, so that it can show your current location and give directions in relation to this. To turn on Location Services, go to **Settings** > **Privacy** > **Location Services** > **Maps** and tap once on **While Using the App**.

When you tap in the Maps Search box it expands towards the top of the screen. Below the Search box are options for adding favorite locations. Tap once on a location to add its details or tap once on the **Add** button to include a new location.

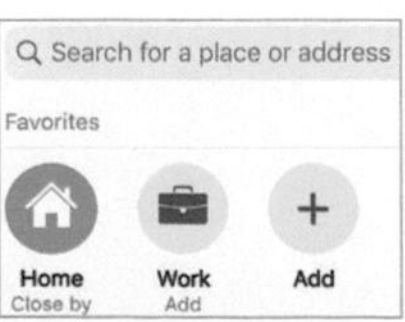

1. Tap once on the **Maps** app

2. The Search box is at the bottom of the window

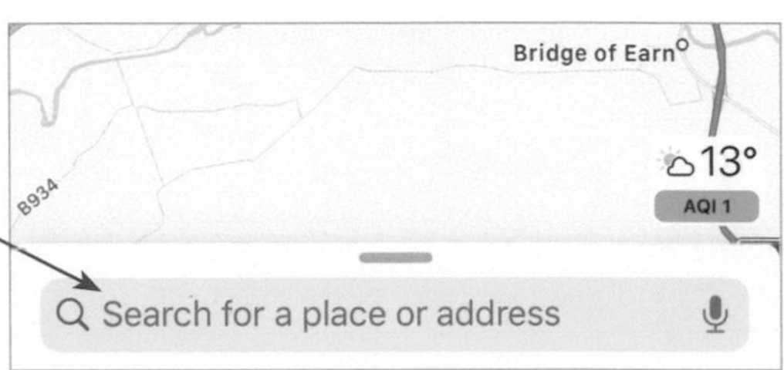

3. Enter an item into the Search box. As you type, suggestions appear underneath. Tap on one to go to that location

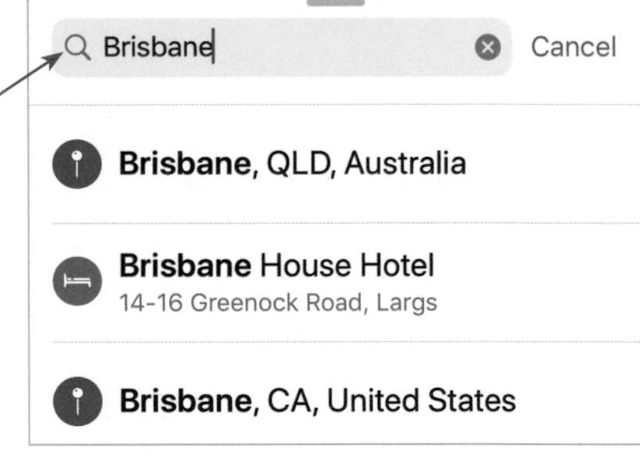

4. For the current location, options for searching over items such as food outlets, shops, and entertainment are available. Tap on one of these to see results for these categories in the current location

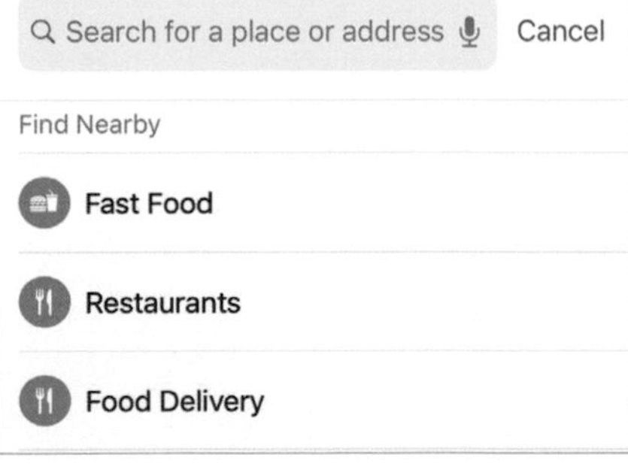

5. The location selected in Step 3 is displayed, with information about it at the bottom of the window

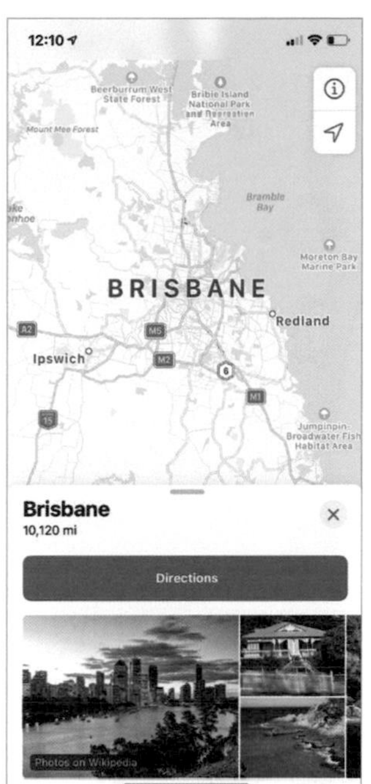

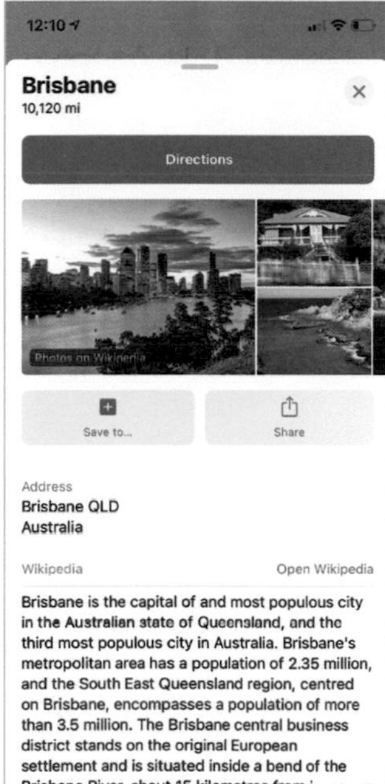

6. Swipe up from the bottom of the window to view full details about the location, including photos, address, phone number, and website address, if available

7. At the top of the Maps app window, tap once on this icon for map style options 

8. Select either **Standard (Map)**, **Transit** or **Satellite** to view the map in that style

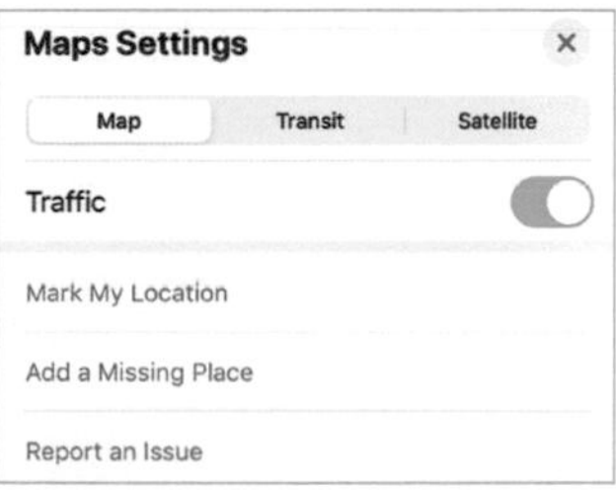

If a specific street is being viewed, tap once on this icon to view the location in street view, which provides a photographic interface, from where you can explore the location.

Some locations have a 3D Flyover Tour feature. This is an automated tour of a location, featuring its most notable sites. It covers major cities around the world, and the list is regularly being added to. If it is available for a location, tap once on the **Flyover** button at the bottom of the window, below the **Directions** button. Tap once on the **Start City Tour** button to start the Flyover Tour. Try it with a location such as New York, London or Paris.

Getting Directions

Wherever you are in the world, you can get directions between two locations. To do this:

You can enter the Start point as your current location. Tap once on this button to view your current location.

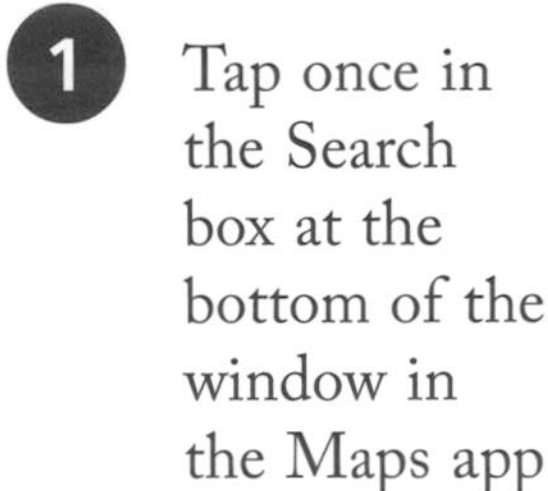

1. Tap once in the Search box at the bottom of the window in the Maps app

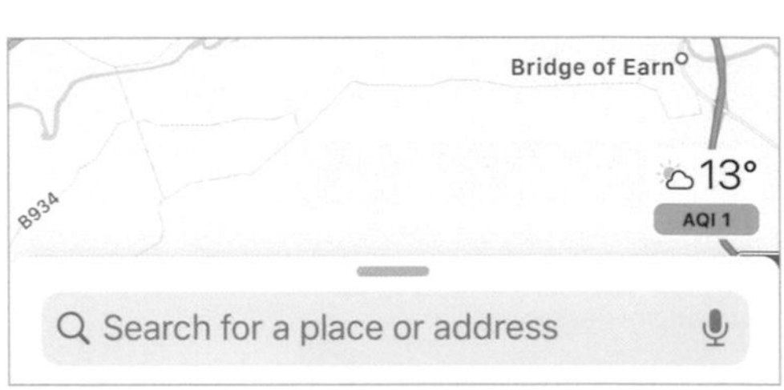

2. Enter the destination (by default, this is from your current location)
3. Tap once on the **Directions** button. The route is shown on the map

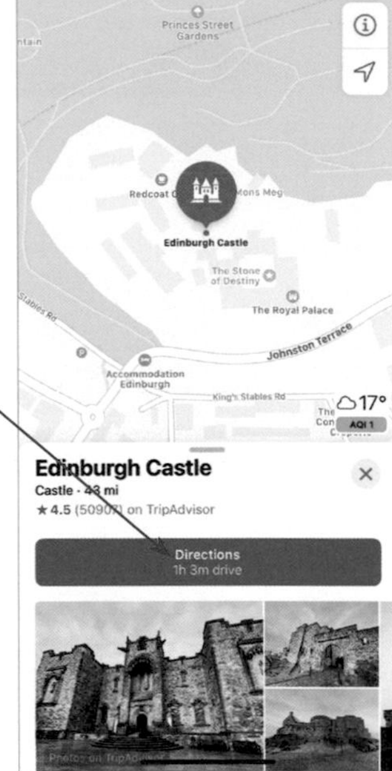

If you enter the name of a landmark you may also be shown other items that have the same name, such as businesses.

Directions for cycling is a new feature in iOS 14, but it is not currently available for all locations.

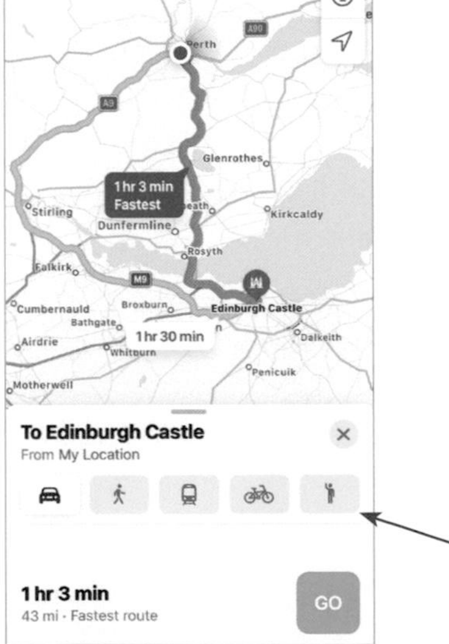

4. Tap once on these buttons at the bottom of the window to view the route for **Drive**, **Walk**, **Transit, Cycle**, or a taxi **Ride** using an appropriate app

5 Tap once on the **Go** button to view step-by-step instructions on the map

6 The route is displayed, from your starting location. Audio instructions tell you the directions to be followed. You can use the Volume buttons (on the side of the iPhone) to increase or decrease the sound. As you follow the route, the map and instructions are updated

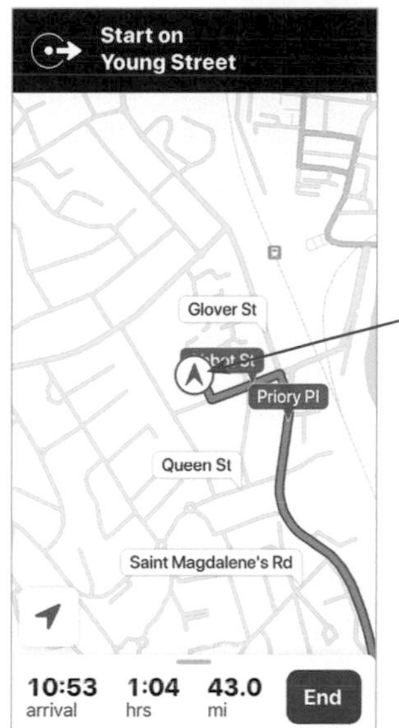

7 Swipe up from the bottom of the screen to access options for viewing items such as gas stations and food outlets on the route. These are displayed on the map, in relation to the current route being followed

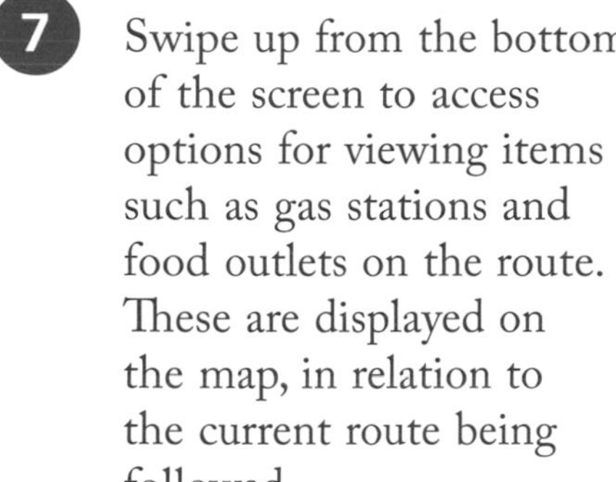

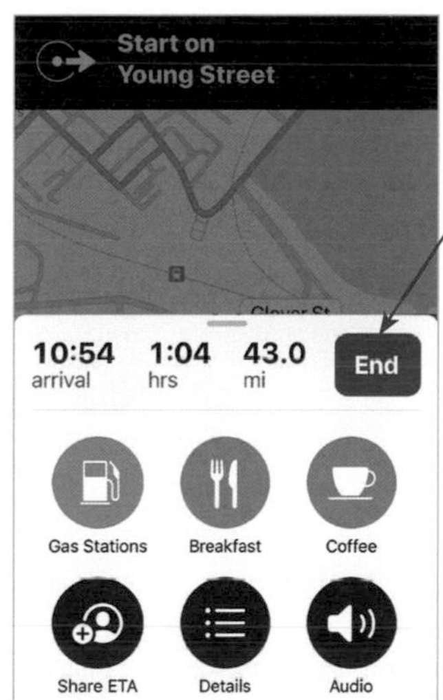

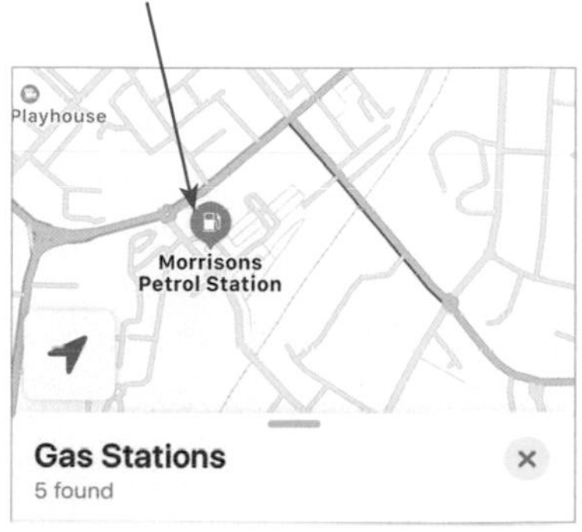

The arrow in Step 6 points in the current direction of travel; i.e. the direction in which the iPhone is pointing.

Tap once on the **End** button and then the **End Route** button to stop following the current route.

For some destinations, alternative routes will be displayed, depending on distance and traffic conditions. Tap once on the alternative route to select it. Directions for each route can be selected at the bottom of the window.

Booking a Trip

Most major travel retailers have had their own websites for a number of years. They have now moved into the world of apps, and these can be used on your iPhone to book almost any type of vacation, from cruises to city breaks.

It is always worth searching different apps to get the best possible price. In some cases, it is cheapest to buy different elements of a vacation from different retailers; e.g. flights from one seller and accommodation from another.

Several apps for the iPhone (and their associated websites) offer full travel services where they can deal with flights, hotels, insurance, car hire, and excursions. These include:

- **Expedia**
- **KAYAK**
- **Orbitz**
- **Travelocity**

These apps usually list special offers and last-minute deals on their Homepages, and they offer options for booking flights, hotels, car hire, and activities separately.

Most travel apps have specific versions based on your geographical location. You will be directed to these by default.

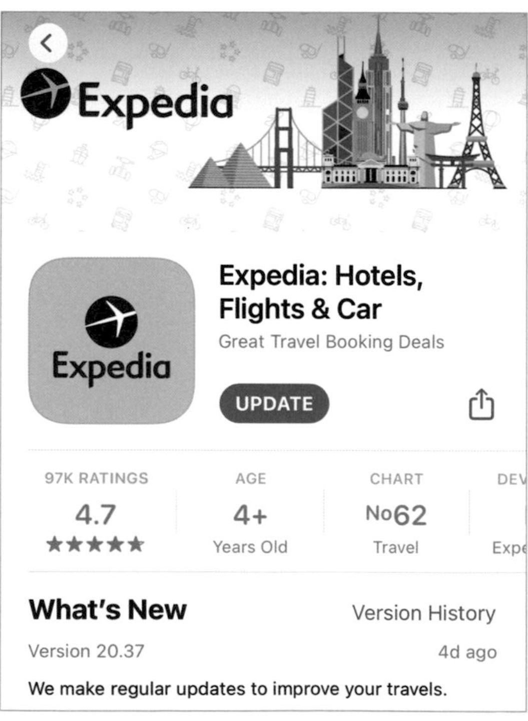

Tripadvisor

One of the best resources for travelers is Tripadvisor. Not only does the app provide a full range of opportunities for booking flights and hotels, it also has an extensive network of reviews from people who have visited the countries, hotels, and restaurants on the site. These are independent, and usually very fair and honest. In a lot of cases, if there are issues with a hotel or restaurant, the proprietor posts a reply to explain what is being done to address any problems.

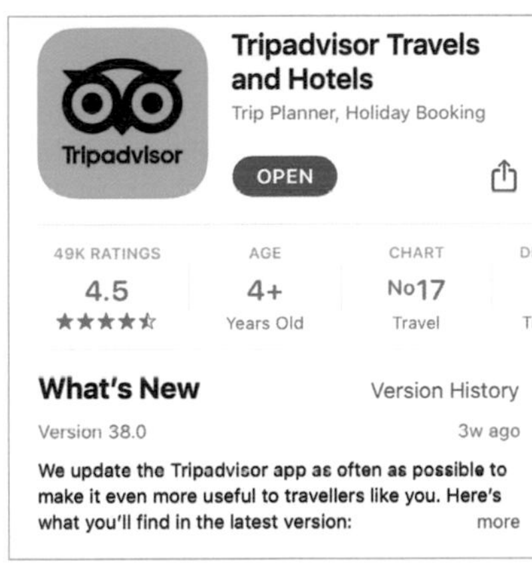

Tripadvisor has a certain sense of community, so post your own reviews once you have been places, to let others know about your experience.

Cruises

There are also apps dedicated specifically to cruises. One to look at is iCruise, which searches over a range of companies for your perfect cruise vacation.

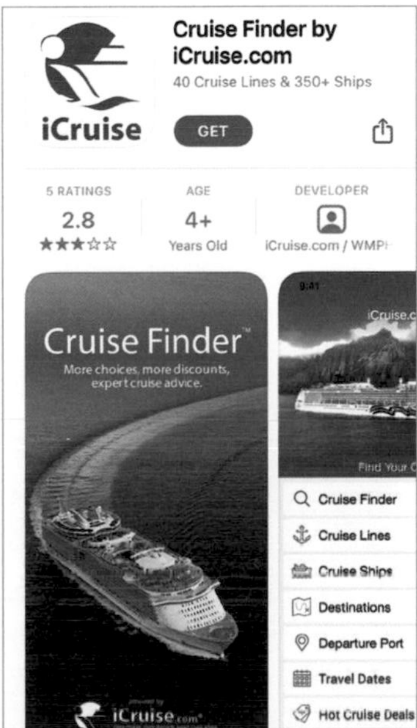

Booking Hotels

The internet is a perfect vehicle for finding good-value hotel rooms around the world. When hotels have spare capacity, this can quickly be relayed to associated websites and apps, where users can often benefit from cheap prices and special offers. There are plenty of apps that have details of thousands of hotels around the world, such as:

Hot tip

Most hotel apps have reviews of all of the listed establishments. It is always worth reading these, as it gives you a view from the people who have actually been there.

Trivago

An app that searches over one million hotels on more than 250 sites, to ensure you get the right hotel for the best price.

Hotels.com

A stylish app that enables you to enter search keywords into a Search box on the Home screen to find hotels based on destination, name, or local landmarks.

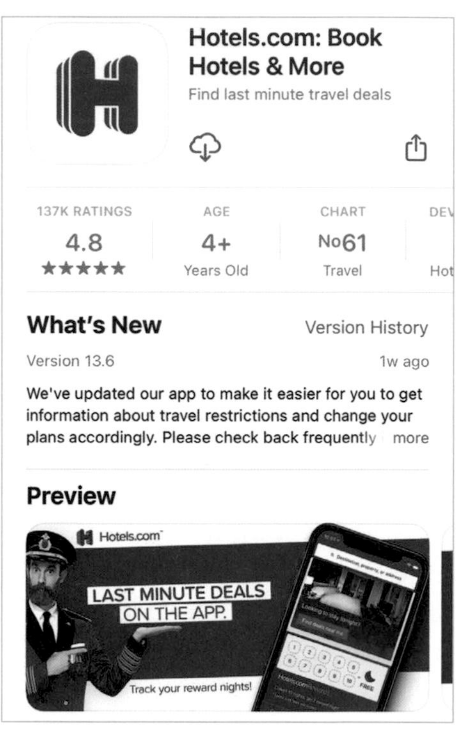

Currency converters can also be downloaded from the App Store so that you can see how much your money is worth in different countries.

Booking.com

Another good, fully-featured hotel app that provides a comprehensive service and excellent prices.

HotelTonight

An app that specializes in getting the best deals for hotels around the world. Some genuine bargains can be found here, for hotels of all categories.

Finding Flights

Flying is a common part of modern life and although you do not have to book separate flights for a vacation (if it is part of a package), there are a number of apps for booking flights and also for following the progress of those in the air:

Skyscanner – travel deals

This app can be used to find flights at airports around the world. Enter your details such as leaving airport, destination and dates of travel. The results show a range of available options, covering different price ranges and airlines.

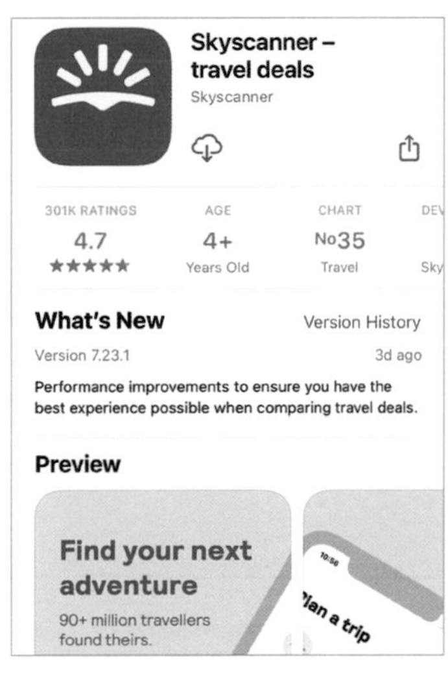

Flight apps need to have an internet connection in order to show real-time flight information.

Flightradar24

If you like viewing the path of flights that are in the air, or need to check if flights are going to be delayed, this app provides this inflight information. Flights are shown according to flight number and airline.

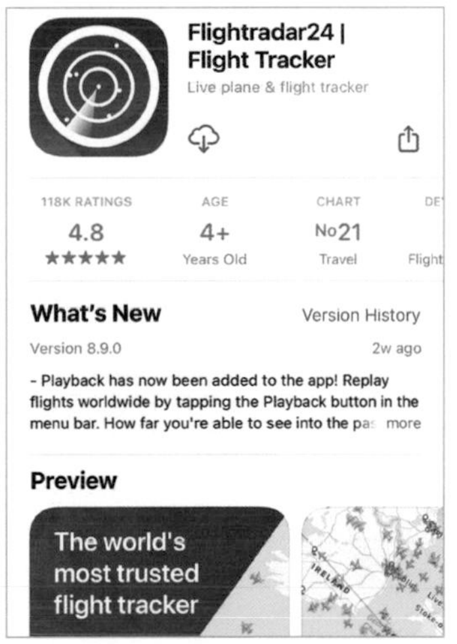

FlightAware Flight Tracker

Another app for tracking flights, showing arrivals and departures and also information about delays. It can track commercial flights worldwide.

Speaking their Language

When you are traveling abroad, it is always beneficial to learn some of the language of the country you are visiting. With your iPhone at hand, this has become a whole lot easier, and there are a number of options:

1 Translation apps that can be used to translate words, phrases and sentences in every language you probably need

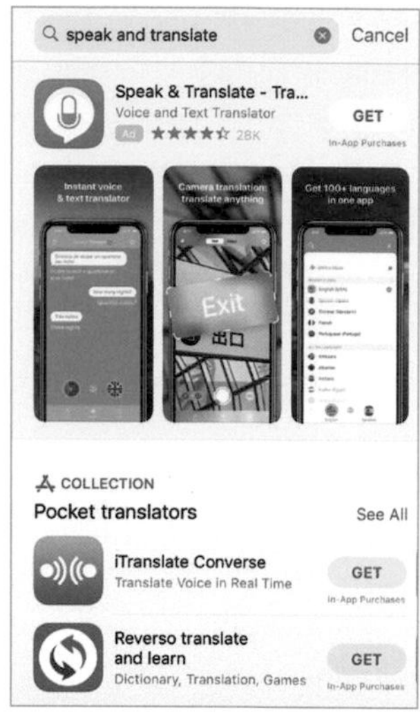

Some language apps are free, but they then charge for additional content, known as "in-app purchases".

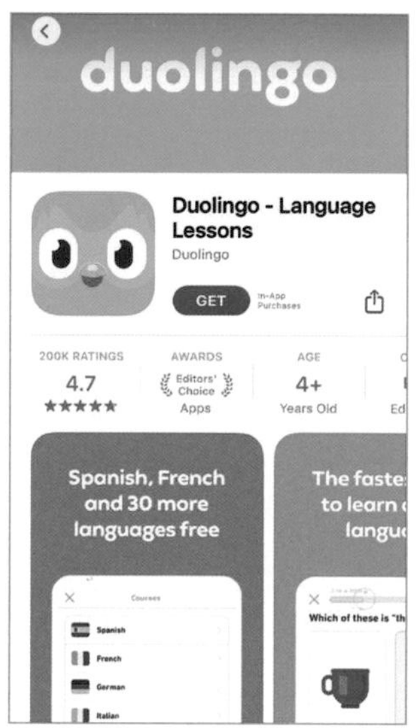

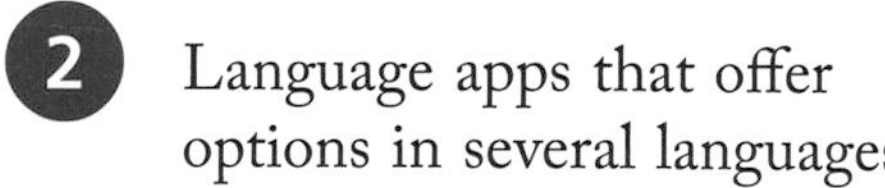

2 Language apps that offer options in several languages

3 Specific language apps, where you can fully get to grips with a new language

12 Practical Matters

This chapter looks at accessibility and security.

Accessibility Issues

The iPhone tries to cater to as wide a range of users as possible, including those who have difficulty with visual, hearing, or physical and motor issues. There are a number of settings that can help with these areas. To access the range of Accessibility settings:

You will have to scroll down the page to view the full range of Accessibility options.

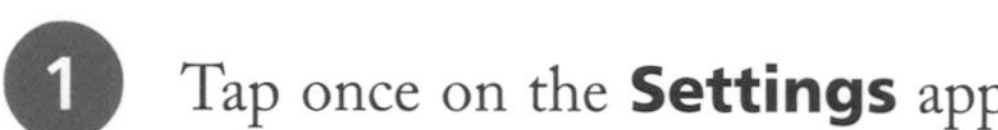

1. Tap once on the **Settings** app

2. Tap once on the **Accessibility** tab

3. The settings for **Vision**, **Physical and Motor**, **Hearing**, and **General** are displayed here

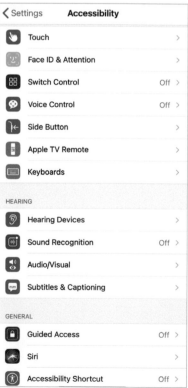

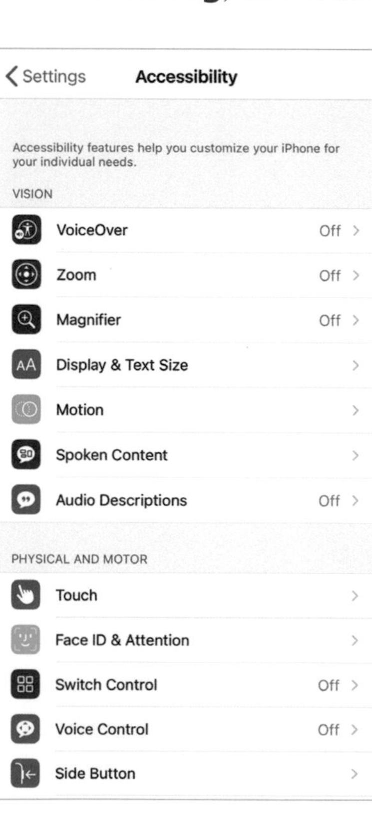

Tap once on **Vision** > **Display & Text Size** and drag the **On/Off Labels** button **On** to show the relevant icons on the On/Off buttons.

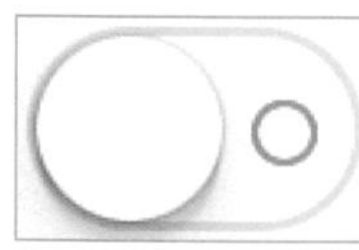

Vision settings

These can help anyone with impaired vision. There are options to hear items on the screen and also for making text easier to read:

1. Tap once on the **VoiceOver** link

VoiceOver
Off

2. Drag this button **On** to activate the VoiceOver function. This then enables items to be spoken when you tap on them

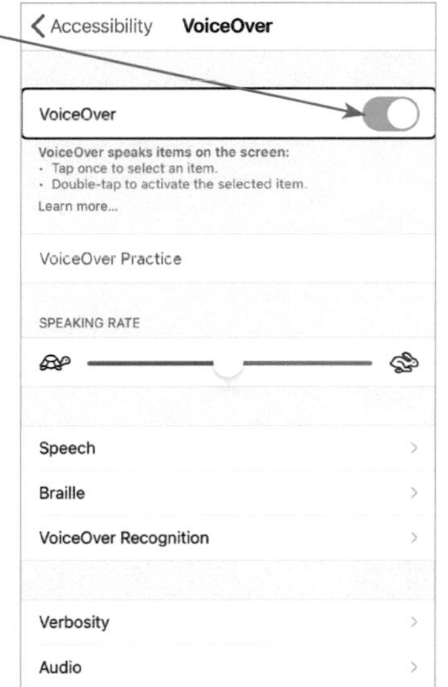
Accessibility
VoiceOver
VoiceOver
VoiceOver speaks items on the screen:
• Tap once to select an item.
• Double-tap to activate the selected item.
Learn more...
VoiceOver Practice
SPEAKING RATE
Speech
Braille
VoiceOver Recognition
Verbosity
Audio

3. Select options for VoiceOver as required, such as speaking rate and pitch

4. Tap once on an item to select it (indicated by the black outline) and have it read out. Double-tap to activate a selected item or perform an action

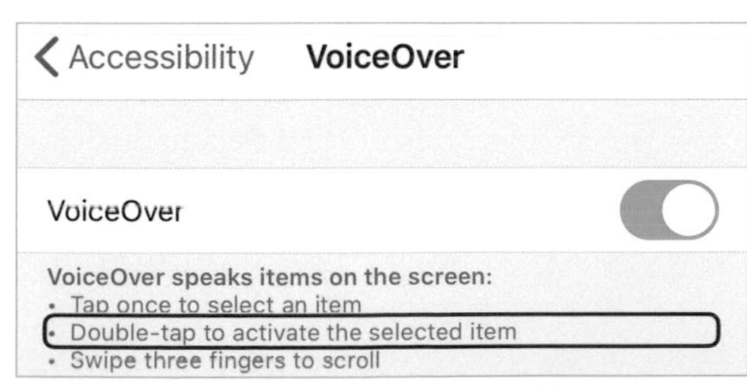
Accessibility
VoiceOver
VoiceOver
VoiceOver speaks items on the screen:
• Tap once to select an item
• Double-tap to activate the selected item
• Swipe three fingers to scroll

Beware

VoiceOver works with the built-in iPhone apps and some apps from the App Store, but not all of them.

Don't forget

Another useful Accessibility function is **AssistiveTouch**, within the **Physical and Motor** > **Touch** section. This offers a range of options for accessing items via tapping on the screen, rather than having to swipe with two or more fingers. Tap once on this icon to access the items within AssistiveTouch after it has been turned **On**.

...cont'd

Zoom settings

Although the iPhone screens are among the largest in the smartphone market, there are times when it can be beneficial to increase the size of the items that are being viewed. This can be done with the Zoom feature. To use this:

1. Access the Accessibility section as shown on page 180, and tap once on the **Zoom** link

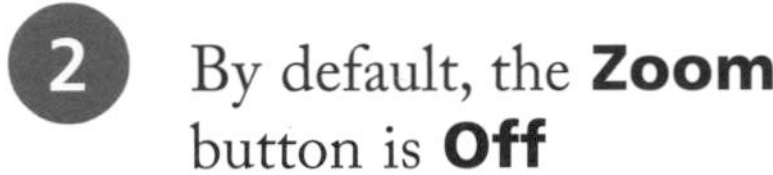
Zoom
Off

2. By default, the **Zoom** button is **Off**

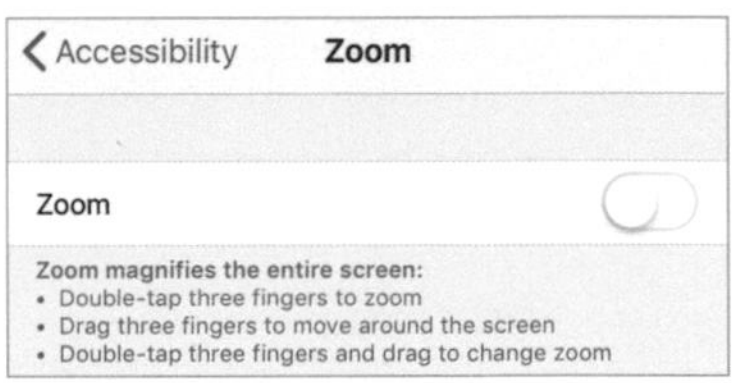
Accessibility
Zoom
Zoom
Zoom magnifies the entire screen:
• Double-tap three fingers to zoom
• Drag three fingers to move around the screen
• Double-tap three fingers and drag to change zoom

3. Drag the **Zoom** button **On** to activate the Zoom window

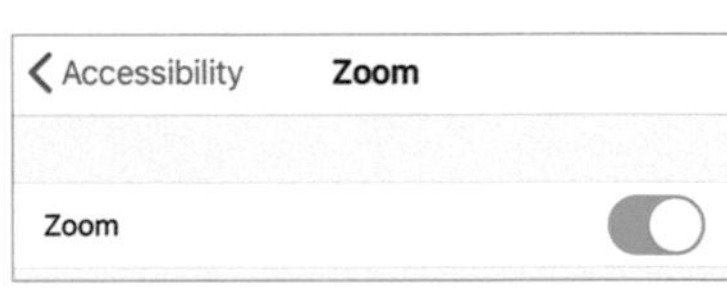
Accessibility
Zoom
Zoom

4. Drag on this button to move the Zoom window around the current screen. Drag with three fingers within the Zoom window to move the screen area within it

• Drag three fingers to move around the
• Double-tap three fingers and drag to c
Follow Focus
Show Controller
The Zoom Controller allows quick access to zoom controls:
• Tap once to show the Zoom menu
• Double-tap to zoom in and out
• When zoomed in, drag to pan zoom content
• 3D Touch to Peek Zoom
Zoom Region Window Zoom
Zoom Filter None
MAXIMUM ZOOM LEVEL
5.0x

Hot tip

Drag the **Show Controller** button in Step 4 **On** in the Zoom settings to display a control button for the Zoom window. Tap once on the control button to view its menu of additional features, such as zooming in for greater or lesser amounts.

5 The Zoom window can also be used on the keyboard to increase the size of the keys. As in Step 4, drag with three fingers to move to other parts of the keyboard

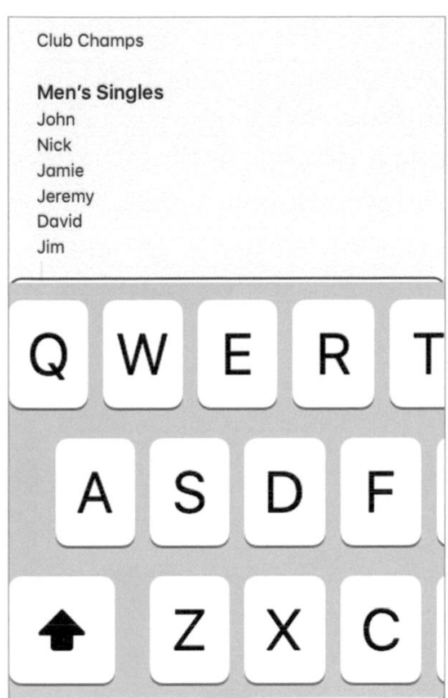

The Accessibility settings can also be used to add functionality to the back of the iPhone, by tapping on it. To do this, access **Accessibility** > **Touch**. Swipe up the page and tap once on the **Back Tap** button. Tap once on the **Double Tap** or **Triple Tap** buttons to select options for these actions on the back of the iPhone. Tap once on one of the options to be performed for the double-tap or triple-tap action. This is a new feature in iOS 14.

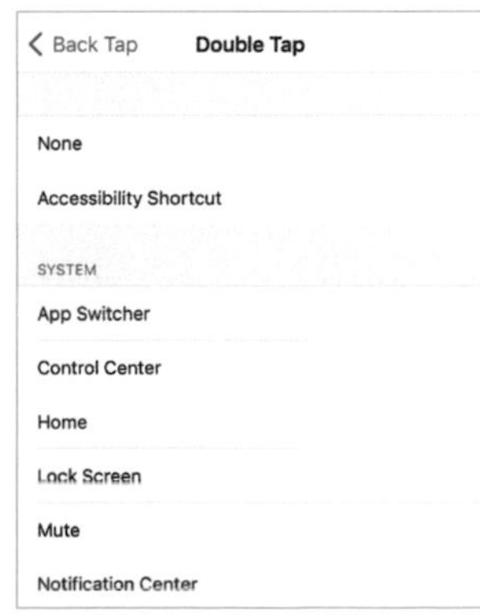

Text size can also be increased within the Accessibility settings. To do this:

1 Under the **Vision** section, tap once on the **Display & Text Size** link

2 Tap once on the **Larger Text** button

3 Drag the **Larger Accessibility Sizes** button **On** to enable compatible apps to show larger text sizes

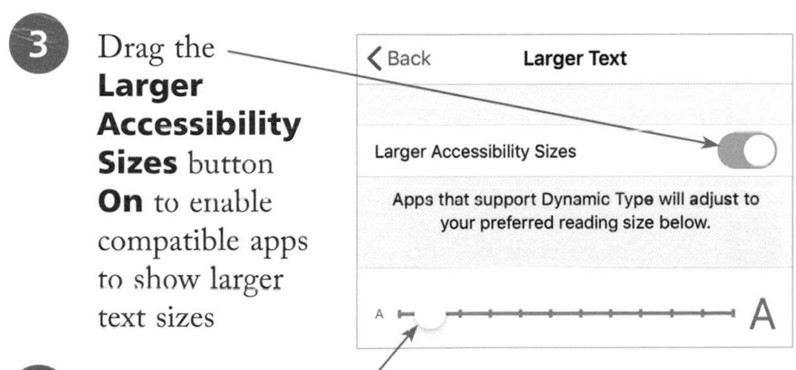

4 Drag this slider to set the text size

Finding your iPhone

No-one likes to think the worst, but if your iPhone is lost or stolen, help is at hand. The Find My iPhone function (operated through the iCloud service) allows you to locate a lost iPhone, and send a message and an alert to it. You can also remotely lock it, or even wipe its contents. This gives added peace of mind, knowing that even if your iPhone is lost or stolen, its contents will not necessarily be compromised. To set up Find My iPhone:

Location Services has to be turned **On** to enable the Find My iPhone service. This can be done in the Settings app (**Settings** > **Privacy** > **Location Services** and drag the **Location Services** button **On**).

1. Tap once on the **Settings** app and tap once on the Apple Account ID button

Settings
Search
Nick Vandome
Apple ID, iCloud, Media & Purchases

2. Tap once on the **Find My** button

Find My

3. Tap once on the **Find My iPhone** link (if it is showing **Off**. If it is **On** then Find My iPhone is already activated)

Find My iPhone Off

4. Drag the **Find My iPhone** button **On** to be able to find your iPhone on a map

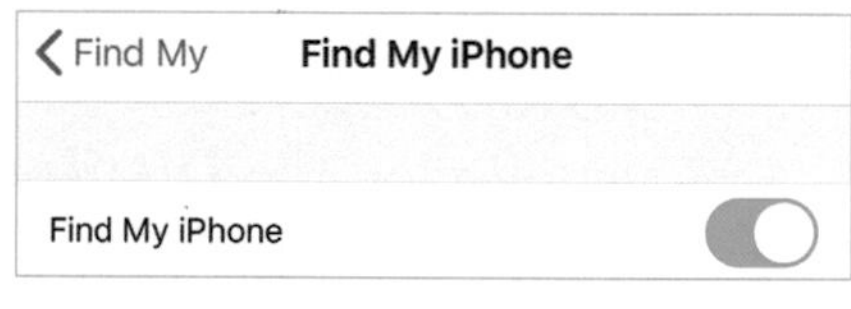

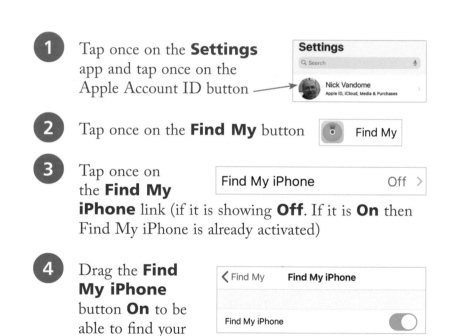

If you are using Family Sharing (see pages 74-77), you can use the Find My app to locate the devices of other Family Sharing members. This can be done from your online iCloud account, or with the Find My app.

Finding a lost iPhone

Once you have set up Find My iPhone, you can search for it through the iCloud service. To do this:

1. Log in to your iCloud account at **www.icloud.com** and tap once on the **Find iPhone** button (you also have to sign in again with your Apple ID)

2. Tap once on the **All Devices** button and select your iPhone. It is identified, and its current location is displayed on the map

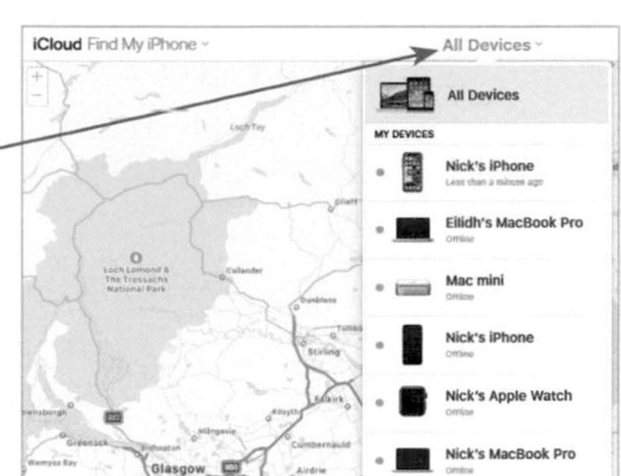

3. Tap once on the green circle to view details about when your iPhone was located

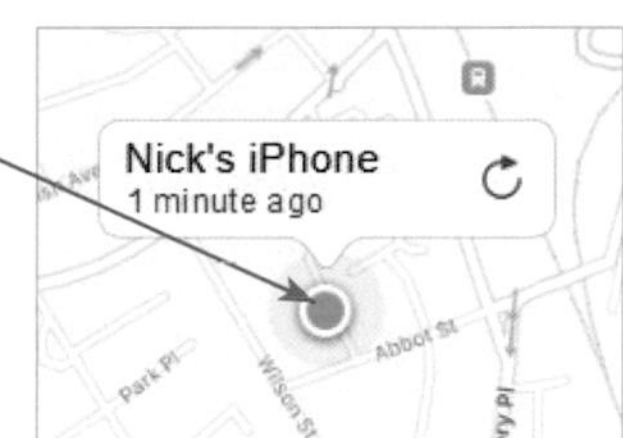

4. Tap once on the **Play Sound** button to send a sound alert to your iPhone

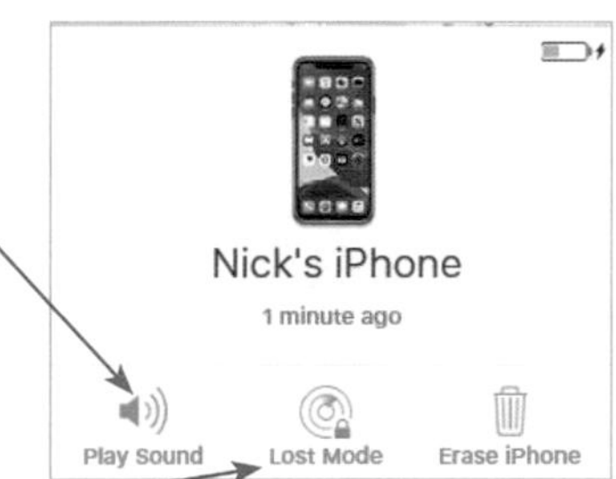

5. Tap once on the **Lost Mode** button to lock your iPhone

6. Enter a phone number where you can be contacted (optional) and tap once on the **Next** button

7. A message can also be added to be displayed on the lost iPhone. Tap once on the **Done** button to lock the iPhone. It is locked using its existing passcode, which is required to unlock it

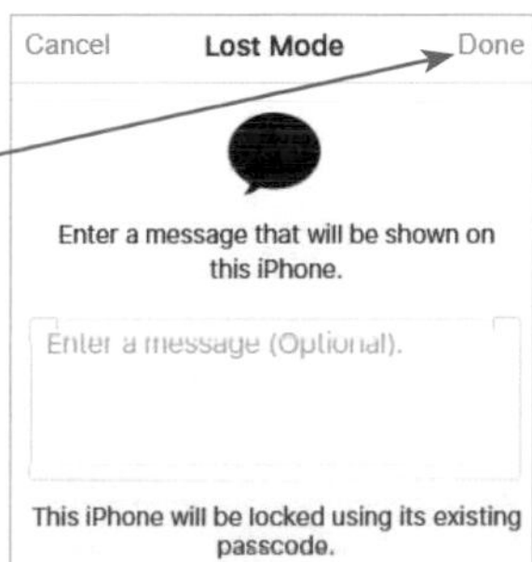

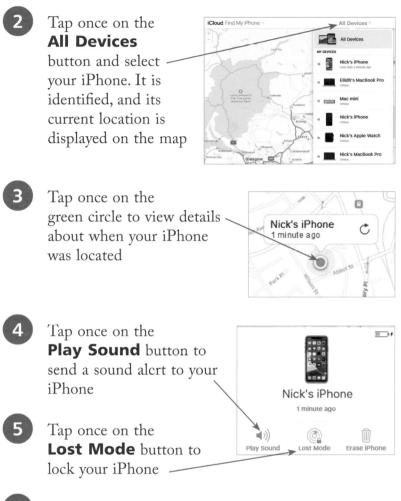

Click once on the **Erase iPhone** button in Step 4 to delete the iPhone's contents. This should be done as a last resort if you think the contents may be compromised. It is important to back up your iPhone to iCloud in case you do ever have to erase its contents. This can be done in **Settings** > **Apple ID** > **iCloud** > **iCloud Backup** by dragging the **iCloud Backup** button **On**. Backups are done automatically when the iPhone is connected to Wi-Fi (see page 73).

If you have Apple Pay set up on your iPhone, this will be suspended if Lost Mode is enabled. It will be reactivated when the passcode is entered to unlock it and your Apple ID entered within Settings.

Avoiding Viruses

As far as security from viruses on the iPhone is concerned, there is good news and bad news:

- The good news is that, due to its architecture, most apps on the iPhone do not communicate with each other unless specifically required to, such as the Mail and the Contacts apps. So, even if there were a virus, it would be difficult for it to infect the whole iPhone. Also, Apple performs rigorous tests on apps that are submitted to the App Store (although even this is not foolproof; see next bullet point).
- The bad news is that no computer system is immune from viruses and malware, and complacency is one of the biggest enemies of computer security. The iPhone's popularity means it is an attractive target for hackers and virus writers. There have been instances of photos in iCloud being accessed and hacked, but this was more to do with password security, or lack of, than viruses. There have also been some rare, malicious attacks centered on the code used to create apps for the App Store. In some cases, certain apps were affected before the virus was located and remedial action taken. This is a reminder of the need for extreme vigilance against viruses, and for users to check in the media for information about any new attacks. Search the web for "latest viruses" to find websites that specialize in identifying the latest software viruses and threats.

Don't forget

Malware is short for malicious software, designed to harm your iPhone or access and distribute information from it.

Apple also checks apps that are provided through the App Store, and this process is very robust. This does not mean that it is impossible for a virus to infect the iPhone, so keep an eye on the Apple website to see if there are any details about iPhone viruses.

Antivirus options

There are a few apps in the App Store that deal with antivirus issues, although not actually removing viruses. Two options to look at are:

- **McAfee** apps. The online security firm has a number of apps that cover issues such as privacy and passwords.
- **Norton** apps. Similar to McAfee, Norton offers a range of security apps for the iPhone.

A

B

C

D

E

F

G

H

I

K

Q

R

S

T

U

V

W

Z